Copyright 2020 by Willard Thomas -All rights reserved.

No part of this book may be reproduced or transmitted in any form or by any means, electronic or mechanical, including photocopying and recording, or by any information storage and retrieval system, without permission in writing from the publisher. This is a work of fiction. Names, places, characters and incidents are either the product of the author's imagination or are used fictitiously, and any resemblance to any actual persons, living or dead, organizations, events or locales is entirely coincidental. The unauthorized reproduction or distribution of this copyrighted work is illegal .

Disclaimer Notice:

Please note the information contained within this document is for educational and entertainment purposes only. All effort has been executed to present accurate, up to date, reliable, complete information. No warranties of any kind are declared or implied. Readers acknowledge that the author is not engaged in the rendering of legal, financial, medical, or professional advice. The content within this book has been derived from various sources. Please consult a licensed professional before attempting any techniques outlined in this book.

CONTENTS

Introduction 7
Breakfast 8
    Cheesy Egg and Bacon 8
    Coconut Sausage Mix 8
    Tomato Frittata 8
    Cauliflower Frittata 8
    Parsley Eggs 9
    Mushroom Eggs 9
    Peppers and Eggs Mix 9
    Parmesan Eggs 9
    Pork Casserole 9
    Coconut Avocado and Chicken Mix 10
    Ricotta Eggs 10
    Spinach Casserole 10
    Lemon Pancake 10
    Cinnamon Eggs 11
    Dill and Avocado Frittata 11
    Ham and Kale Bake 11
    Chili Bake 11
    Cheesy Bacon Casserole 12
    Creamy Asparagus Bake 12
    Cauliflower Rice and Turkey Casserole 12
    Sausage and Spinach 12
    Creamy Eggs 12
    Zucchini Casserole 13
    Avocado and Zucchini Bake 13
    Almond Avocado Mix 13
    Beef Casserole 13
    Shrimp Casserole 14
    Chili Eggplant Eggs 14
    Coconut Muffins 14
    Lime Nutmeg Roll 14
    Creamy Eggs and Broccoli 15
    Chili Tomatoes Bowls 15
    Stuffed Peppers 15
    Veggie Casserole 15
    Chicken Meatballs 16
    Kale Muffins 16
    Almond Buns 16
    Chives and Sprouts Casserole 17
    Coconut Sausages 17
    Feta Eggs 17
    Creamy Green Tea 17
    Zucchini Bread 17
    Sausages and Peppers Hash 18
    Mixed Veggies Burrito 18
    Zucchini Quiche 18
    Green Beans Casserole 18
    Cheddar Beef and Sprouts Casserole ... 19
    Chili Frittata 19
    Basil Sprouts and Eggs 19
    Cilantro Pork Meatballs 19
    Shrimp Omelet 20
    Chia Bowls 20
    Coconut Porridge 20
    Berry Pudding 20
    Artichoke and Asparagus Mix 20
    Cayenne Sprouts Hash 21
    Walnuts Yogurt 21
    Ham and Tomato Bake 21
    Beef Meatloaf 21
    Paprika and Shallots Omelet 22
Lunch 23
    Beef and Mushrooms 23
    Cauliflower Bowls 23
    Broccoli Soup 23
    Chicken Soup 23
    Creamy Beef Mix 23
    Chili Soup 24
    Sausage Soup 24
    Chicken Stew 24
    Shrimp Soup 24
    Chicken and Olives Stew 25
    Lemon Lamb and Cauliflower 25
    Steak and Tomato Salad 25
    Okra Stew 25
    Green Beans Stew 26
    Lamb and Coconut Stew 26
    Chicken and Okra Stew 26
    Calamari Stew 26
    Lemon Pork Stew 26
    Spinach and Tomato Soup 27
    French Onion Soup 27
    Spicy Chicken Soup 27
    Cabbage Stew 27
    Turkey Soup 28
    Ground Beef Soup 28
    Coconut Mushroom Mix 28
    Salmon Stew 28
    Walnut Beef Mix 29
    Tomato Chili 29
    Eggplant Stew 29
    Ginger and Broccoli Soup 29
    Salmon Skewers 29
    Coconut Halibut 30
    Zucchini and Shrimp 30
    Zucchini Stew 30
    Ground Beef and Leeks 30
    Lemongrass Short Ribs 31
    Cinnamon Beef 31
    Leeks Soup 31
    Pork Stew 31

Cauliflower Rice and Tomatoes............31	Green Beans and Radishes......................43
Roast and Peppers 32	Swiss Chard Saute 43
Kale and Shrimp.....................................32	Glazed Leeks 43
Bacon and Zucchinis...............................32	Oregano Beans and Cucumber............... 43
Sausage Stew...32	Chard and Radishes 44
Garlic Chicken Mix..................................33	Bok Choy and Radishes 44
Shrimp and Tomatoes 33	Mushroom Stew 44
Spiced Chicken.......................................33	Herbed Mushrooms 44
Sugar Snap Peas Soup............................33	Leeks and Cauliflower Mash 44
Ginger Lamb...33	Cherry Tomatoes Sauté.......................... 45
Balsamic Beef 34	Ginger Peppers 45
Side Dishes 35	Mozzarella Zucchinis and Leeks............. 45
Spinach Mix..35	Hot Tomatoes 45
Tomato and Spaghetti Squash 35	Smashed Cauliflower 46
Hot Green Beans 35	Tomato and Eggplant Salad................... 46
Butter Zucchini.......................................35	Garlic Eggplant Mix................................ 46
Dill Broccoli..35	Radish and Tomato Salad....................... 46
Tomato and Radish 36	Paprika Spaghetti Squash 46
Balsamic Leeks 36	Rhubarb and Zucchini Mix..................... 47
Rosemary Cauliflower 36	Snacks and Appetizers................................ 48
Butter Mushrooms 36	Chicken Bites 48
Paprika Green Beans..............................36	Paprika Almonds.................................... 48
Spicy Kale...37	Mixed Nuts... 48
Mushroom and Kale 37	Beef and Zucchini Wraps 48
Creamy Green Beans..............................37	Cauliflower Bites.................................... 48
Artichoke and Broccoli Mix.....................37	Cheese Sticks 49
Collard Greens and Mushrooms.............37	Eggplant Bread 49
Lime Zucchini Noodles 38	Almond Granola..................................... 49
Swiss Chard Mix.....................................38	Chili Walnuts.. 49
Green Beans and Tomato Casserole......38	Pork Bites... 50
Parsley and Tomato Green Beans...........38	Turkey Meatballs 50
Paprika Peppers.....................................38	Tomato Salmon Meatballs 50
Cabbage and Tomatoes 39	Pecans Bowls... 50
Zucchini and Cabbage 39	Sausage Dip... 50
Zucchini and Radish Mix........................39	Butter Pork Ribs..................................... 51
Thyme Mushrooms 39	Chicken Dip 51
Mint Peppers 39	Chia Chicken Bites 51
Garlic Green Beans 40	Cocktail Shrimp...................................... 51
Asparagus and Onion Mix 40	Coconut Mushrooms Caps 51
Tofu and Green Beans............................40	Mozzarella Broccoli Bites....................... 52
Lime Cauliflower.....................................40	Bacon Dip... 52
Oregano Green Beans 40	Chili Dip 52
Masala Broccoli 41	Shrimp Tortillas 52
Curry Mushrooms 41	Smoked Hazelnuts................................. 52
Celery Puree..41	Tomato Chicken Wings 53
Coconut Celery......................................41	Worcestershire Chicken 53
Rosemary Bok Choy 41	Almond Bars 53
Coconut Radish Mix...............................42	Paprika Dip... 53
Okra and Artichokes...............................42	Turkey Bites and Sauce 53
Red Cabbage Sauté................................42	Masala Hazelnuts................................... 54
Broccoli and Cauliflower Bake................42	Pizza Dip 54
Nutmeg Artichokes.................................42	Salmon Spread 54
Eggplants and Olives..............................43	Balsamic Beef Meatballs 54

Hot Ham	55
Sausage Bites and Sauce	55
Cheddar Dip	55
Shrimp Skewers	55
Chives Wings	55
Creamy Dip	56
Tofu Bites	56
Fish Bites	56
Cauliflower Popcorn	56
Cayenne Chorizo	56
Milky Chicken Sticks	56
Oregano Dip	57
Cayenne Shrimps	57
Masala Green Beans Bowl	57
Shrimp Meatballs	57
Garlic Pork Slices	58
Zucchini Bites	58

Fish and Seafood 59

Poached Trout	59
Seafood Bowls	59
Salmon Soup	59
Shrimp Bake	59
Shrimp and Salmon Skewers	60
Shrimp Salad	60
Shrimp and Fennel Soup	60
Italian Shrimp Tortillas	60
Creamy Tuna	61
Salmon and Radish Soup	61
Cajun Shrimp	61
Balsamic Salmon	61
Tomato Shrimps	61
Oregano Salmon	62
Crab Dip	62
Ginger Mackerel	62
Creamy Sea Bass	62
Oregano Crab	62
Parmesan Salmon	63
Balsamic Mussels	63
Spicy Tuna	63
Turmeric Calamari	63
Thyme Sea bass	64
Shrimp and Zucchini	64
Lemon Cod	64
Cinnamon Mackerel	64
Parsley Salmon	64
Cheesy Tuna	65
Spiced Shrimp	65
Seafood Stew	65
Shrimp and Green Beans	65
Salmon and Spinach Bake	66
Chili Squid	66
Calamari Rings and Broccoli	66
Tilapia and Tomatoes	66
Tuna and Cabbage Mix	66
Mozzarella Fish	67
Marinara Shrimp	67
Butter Salmon and Avocado	67
Mustard Shrimp	67
Salmon and Asparagus	67
Avocado and Shrimp	68
Tilapia and Radish Bites	68
Balsamic Scallops	68
Lemon Crab Legs	68
Cod Patties	68
Cod Soup	69
Salmon and Cauliflower Chowder	69
Coconut Catfish	69
Saffron Tilapia	69
Caraway Cod	70
Chili Shrimp and Okra	70
Nutmeg Halibut	70
Lime Cod and Shrimps	70
Fish and Salsa Bowl	71
Shrimp Curry	71
Sage Halibut	71
Sea Bass and Celery	71
Herbed Shrimp	71
Stevia Salmon	72

Poultry 73

Nutmeg Chicken	73
Chili Chicken	73
Mozzarella Chicken	73
Garlic Chicken	73
Chicken and Tomatoes	74
Fennel Chicken Mix	74
Chicken and Scallions Mix	74
Basil Chicken	74
Chicken and Tahini Sauce	74
Paprika Chicken and Sauce	75
Cheddar Chicken	75
Chicken Salad	75
Chicken and Eggplant	75
Chicken and Onions Mix	76
Creamy Chicken	76
Turkey and Peppers	76
Dill Turkey	76
Chicken with Cheese	76
Chicken and Zucchinis	77
Ground Chicken Mix	77
Lime Chicken Drumsticks	77
Chicken with Spinach	77
Rosemary Turkey	78
Chicken Breast with Capers	78
Duck and Berries	78
Chicken and Okra	78
Chicken and Cucumber	78

- Shredded Chicken ... 79
- Almond Chicken ... 79
- Chicken and Mushrooms ... 79
- Salsa Chicken ... 79
- Chicken and Kale ... 79
- Cumin Chicken ... 80
- Cilantro Chicken ... 80
- Turkey with Tomatoes and Eggplants . 80
- Chicken and Sour Cream Sauce ... 80
- Chicken Cubes and Pesto ... 81
- Chicken and Celery ... 81
- Marjoram Chicken ... 81
- Chicken and Cabbage ... 81
- Chicken and Walnuts ... 81
- Chicken, Tomatoes and Olives ... 82
- Ground Chicken and Green Beans ... 82
- Chicken and Tomato Sauce ... 82
- Lemon Turkey ... 82
- Chicken and Coconut Milk ... 83
- Chicken and Green Pepper Mix ... 83
- Chicken Fillets and Mustard Sauce ... 83
- Sweet Sticky Chicken Wings ... 83
- Pozole Blanco ... 83
- Chicken with Nuts ... 84
- Chicken and Hot Sauce ... 84
- Cheesy Turkey and Sauce ... 84
- Coconut Milk Turkey Breast ... 84
- Chicken and Spring Onions ... 85
- Chicken Breast with Avocados ... 85
- Chives Chicken Teriyaki ... 85
- Chicken and Creamy Onions and Peppers ... 85
- Oregano Chicken and Chilies ... 86
- Butter Turkey and Olives ... 86

Meat ... 87
- Pork and Rutabaga ... 87
- Turmeric Beef ... 87
- Adobo Beef ... 87
- Cilantro Beef Tenderloin ... 87
- Beef Brisket ... 88
- Marinara Beef and Chives ... 88
- Thyme and Coriander Brisket ... 88
- Lemon Beef ... 88
- Smoked Pork ... 89
- Steak and Dill Sauce ... 89
- Ribs and Celery ... 89
- Ground Pork and Veggies ... 89
- Sausages and Cabbage ... 90
- Caraway Ribs ... 90
- Mint Lamb Roast ... 90
- Pork and Green Peas ... 90
- Coconut Pork Ribs ... 91
- Garlic Pork Chops ... 91
- Thyme Pork and Beans ... 91
- Ginger Ham ... 91
- Sausage and Zucchini Stew ... 91
- Beef and Cauliflower ... 92
- Beef and Broccoli ... 92
- Pork and Bok Choy ... 92
- Sumac Beef ... 92
- Lamb in Grape Leaves ... 93
- Butter and Lemon Lamb ... 93
- Beef and Asparagus ... 93
- Curry Pork Mix ... 93
- Crushed Tomatoes, Lamb and Chives . 94
- Stevia Pork Mix ... 94
- Chili Lamb Skewers ... 94
- Almond Beef ... 94
- Cajun Lamb ... 94
- Tomato Beef and Spices ... 95
- Simple Beef Steaks ... 95
- Coffee Lamb ... 95
- Turmeric Chops ... 95
- Mustard Beef ... 96
- Lamb and Leeks ... 96
- Pork Shoulder and Zucchinis ... 96
- Beef and Scallions ... 96
- Dill Pork Stew ... 96
- Lamb and Spinach ... 97
- Shredded Beef ... 97
- Beef Curry ... 97
- Lamb Shanks and Olives ... 97
- Beef with Bok Choy ... 98
- Lamb and Brussels Sprouts ... 98
- Basil Lamb and Apples ... 98
- Lamb and Berries Mix ... 98
- Lamb, Celery and Tomatoes ... 98
- Lamb Meatballs ... 99
- Lamb Chops with Dill Butter ... 99
- Pork Meatloaf ... 99
- Chipotle Beef ... 99
- Creamy Ground Beef with Kale ... 100
- Beef Stuffed Mushrooms ... 100
- Pork Tenderloin and Kale ... 100
- Chili Lamb ... 100

Vegetable Meals ... 102
- Butter Green Peas ... 102
- Lemon Asparagus ... 102
- Lime Green Beans ... 102
- Cheese Asparagus ... 102
- Creamy Broccoli ... 102
- Curry Cauliflower ... 103
- Garlic Eggplant ... 103
- Coconut Brussels Sprouts ... 103
- Cauliflower Pilaf with Hazelnuts ... 103
- Cauliflower and Turmeric Mash ... 103

Recipe	Page
Spinach and Olives Mix	104
Red Cabbage and Walnuts	104
Paprika Bok Choy	104
Zucchini Mix	104
Zucchini and Spring Onions	105
Creamy Portobello Mix	105
Eggplant Mash	105
Cheddar Artichoke	105
Squash and Zucchinis	105
Dill Leeks	106
Vegetable Lasagna	106
Cauliflower Rice Mix	106
Vegetable Cream	106
Coconut Okra	107
Pecan Kale Mix	107
Mushroom Soup	107
Artichoke and Asparagus Mix	107
Butter Green Beans	108
Hot Eggplant Mix	108
Zucchini Balls	108
Broccoli Sauté	108
Spinach and Sauce	108
Sesame Zucchini	109
Creamy Avocado	109
Cauliflower Cream Soup	109
Radish Soup	109
Zucchini Dip	109
Celery Dip	110
Bell Peppers and Spinach	110
Green Beans, Leeks and Artichokes	110
Brussel Sprouts Saute	110
Coriander Broccoli	111
Balsamic Cauliflower	111
Eggplant Loaf	111
Kale Chowder	111
Sprouts and Zucchinis	111
Sautéed Cabbage	112
Garlic Kale and Mushrooms	112
Kale Stew	112
Okra Sauté	112
Desserts	**113**
Cocoa Cake	113
Zucchini Cake	113
Lemon Cake	113
Pumpkin Cake	113
Mascarpone Fudge	114
Walnut Cake	114
Vanilla Cake	114
Chocolate Pudding	114
Lime Vanilla Bites	115
Cinnamon Cake	115
Berry Brownies	115
Cream Cheese Cookies	115
Chocolate Pecan Cake	116
Lemon Scones	116
Strawberries Cake	116
Almond Roll	116
Keto Flan	117
Peanut Pie	117
Rutabaga Cake	117
Coffee Cream	118
Cashew Cream Mix	118
Strawberry Cobbler	118
Chocolate Walnut Pie	118
Almond Blondies	119
Green Tea Cupcakes	119
Blueberry Crisp	119
Biscuits	119
Mint Cake	120
Pecan Pie	120
Cinnamon and Blackberry Pie	120
Zucchini Muffins	121
Vanilla Bars	121
Vanilla Pudding	121
Zucchini and Pumpkin Pie	121
Chocolate Muffins	121
Strawberry Jam	122
Espresso Cookie	122
Blackberry Pancake	122
Almond Spread	122
Walnut Squares	123
Avocado Mousse	123
Almond Coffee Cream	123
Avocado and Walnuts Balls	123
Chia Bites	124
Red Berry Gummies	124
Creamy Mousse	124
Cayenne Mousse	124
Vanilla Avocado Cookies	125
Peanut Butter Bars	125
Ricotta and Pecan Cupcakes	125
Appendix : Recipes Index	**126**

Introduction

Keto diet is a trend of nowadays. People on this diet choose to eat more fats and proteins and restrict carbs consumption. The main condition for a low carb diet is to get a certain amount of net carbs every day. This figure shouldn't exceed 7.5 grams of net carbs per serving. It means that the total amount of net carbs per day has to be not more than 15-30 grams; what is about 5-10 % of total calories. There are some exceptions for hyperactive people and sportsmen. In this case, the total amount of consumed net carbs per day should be determined by a doctor or Keto specialist. To count the number of net carbs in your food is very easy: you need to minus fiber and non-digestible sugar alcohol from the total amount of carbs.

Keto diet can be very diverse. There are a huge amount of delicious salads, side dishes, snacks, desserts, and simple but very useful breakfasts.

The most protein we get from meat and high-fat products such as heavy cream, coconut cream, butter, nuts, cheese, etc. What about vegetables and fruits that are full of carbohydrates and sugars? They are also allowed on the Keto diet. Such vegetables and fruits as kale, spinach, broccoli, cauliflower, radish, zucchini, cabbage, blackberries, raspberries, and avocado have a low percent of net carbs and are Keto friendly. It is almost impossible to live without sugars. To vary the diet sometimes you can treat yourself with delicious desserts. Add artificial low-carb sweeteners such as stevia or Erythritol in your meal instead of sugar. The cooked dish will be not only tasty but also very useful.

There are a lot of benefits in the Keto diet. It helps to increase endurance level, fight with skin problems, maintain the level of blood sugar and insulin in your body, support your health while degenerative brain diseases, helps people who suffer from epilepsy, reduce the risks of heart diseases, helps reduce the onset of PMS, and maintain the gut health.

The biggest obstacle to dieting is lack of time. The peculiarity of the crockpot is that you can cook healthy and tasty without making significant efforts. A smart kitchen appliance will cook all by itself. Equipped with "LOW" (200F) and "High" (300F) modes and warming option, crockpot can bring to life almost any of your food desires. You can use the appliance as for cooking during the day as to let it work overnight. Using crockpot you bring newness and diverse in your daily diet. Don't spend the whole day on cooking, better spend time with loved ones; and smart kitchen appliances will cook everything for you by itself!out

Breakfast

Cheesy Egg and Bacon
Prep time: 15 minutes
Cooking time: 8 hours
Servings: 4
Ingredients:
- 4 eggs, beaten
- 1 cup bacon, chopped
- 1 teaspoon sweet paprika
- 1 teaspoon turmeric powder
- ½ teaspoon black pepper
- ½ teaspoon salt
- 1 teaspoon dried oregano
- 1 teaspoon olive oil
- 5 oz Mozzarella cheese, shredded

Directions:
1. Heat up a pan with the oil over medium heat, add the bacon, cook for 5 minutes and transfer to the slow cooker.
2. Add the eggs mixed with the rest of the ingredients, and stir,
3. Close the lid and cook the mix for 8 hours on Low.
4. Divide between plates and serve.

Nutrition value/serving: calories 400, fat 20.5, fiber 1, carbs 6.9, protein 21.9

Coconut Sausage Mix
Prep time: 10 minutes
Cooking time: 4 hours
Servings: 3
Ingredients:
- 6 oz sausages, chopped
- ½ cup coconut cream
- 1 teaspoon turmeric powder
- ½ teaspoon cayenne pepper
- 2 egg, whisked
- 1/2 cup Parmesan, grated
- ¼ teaspoon ground black pepper
- 1 tablespoon fresh parsley, chopped

Directions:
1. In the slow cooker, mix the sausages with the cream and the other ingredients and toss.
2. Close the lid.
3. Cook casserole for 4 hours on High.

Nutrition value/serving: calories 403, fat 29.5, fiber 1.9, carbs 5.9, protein 14.4

Tomato Frittata
Prep time: 10 minutes
Cooking time: 3 hours
Servings: 2
Ingredients:
- 3 eggs, whisked
- 1 tablespoon sweet paprika
- 1 teaspoon basil, dried
- 1 cup tomatoes, chopped
- 1/3 teaspoon salt
- ½ teaspoon cayenne pepper
- 1 tablespoon sour cream

Directions:
1. In the slow cooker, mix the eggs with the paprika, tomatoes and the other ingredients, toss and spread.
2. Close the lid and cook Frittata for 3 hours on Low or until the mixture is set.

Nutrition value/serving: calories 258, fat 9.1, fiber 1.1, carbs 2.8, protein 9.3

Cauliflower Frittata
Prep time: 10 minutes
Cooking time: 5 hours
Servings: 4
Ingredients:
- 1 cup cauliflower florets
- 4 eggs, whisked
- 1/3 cup coconut cream
- ½ teaspoon salt
- ½ teaspoon cumin, ground
- 1 teaspoon oregano, dried
- 2 oz ham, chopped
- 1 teaspoon butter

Directions:
1. In the slow cooker, mix the cauliflower with the eggs and the other ingredients, stir and spread into the pot.
2. Close the lid and cook the frittata for 4 hours on High.
3. The broccoli in cooked frittata should be tender.

Nutrition value/serving: calories 338, fat 10.4, fiber 4.9, carbs 3, protein 5.8

Parsley Eggs
Prep time: 10 minutes
Cooking time: 2 hours
Servings: 4
Ingredients:
- 6 eggs, whisked
- 2 tablespoons Mozzarella, shredded
- 1 teaspoon basil, dried
- 1 teaspoon garam masala
- ½ teaspoon salt
- ½ teaspoon ground black pepper
- 1 tablespoon olive oil
- 1 tablespoon parsley, chopped

Directions:
1. Grease the slow cooker with the oil and combine the eggs with the Mozzarella and the other ingredients inside.
2. Close the lid and cook eggs for 2 hours on High.
3. Then open the lid and with the help of the wooden spatula scramble the eggs.
4. Divide between plates and serve.

Nutrition value/serving: calories 338, fat 11.2, fiber 4.1, carbs 5.8, protein 2.7

Mushroom Eggs
Prep time: 8 minutes
Cooking time: 3 hours
Servings: 3
Ingredients:
- 1 cup white mushrooms, chopped
- 1/3 cup coconut milk
- 1 teaspoon oregano, dried
- ½ teaspoon cayenne pepper
- ½ teaspoon salt
- ½ teaspoon smoked paprika
- 1 teaspoon butter
- 4 eggs, whisked

Directions:
1. In the slow cooker, mix the mushrooms with the milk and the other ingredients except the eggs, stir, close the lid and cook on High for 1 hour.
2. Add the eggs, stir the mix, cook on High for 2 more hours, divide between plates and serve.

Nutrition value/serving: calories 240, fat 9.5, fiber 4.3, carbs 5.1, protein 4.2

Peppers and Eggs Mix
Prep time: 15 minutes
Cooking time: 8 hours
Servings: 5
Ingredients:
- 1 tablespoon smoked paprika
- 2 red bell peppers, chopped
- 2 green bell peppers, chopped
- 1 tablespoon Mozzarella, shredded
- 1 teaspoon turmeric powder
- ½ teaspoon cayenne pepper
- 1 teaspoon salt
- 5 eggs, whisked
- ½ cup heavy cream
- 1 tablespoon chives, chopped
- 1 teaspoon olive oil

Directions:
1. Grease the slow cooker with the oil and combine the peppers with the Mozzarella, eggs and the other ingredients inside.
2. Close the lid, cook on Low for 8 hours, divide between plates and serve.

Nutrition value/serving: calories 301, fat 12.6, fiber 2.2, carbs 8, protein 14.6

Parmesan Eggs
Prep time: 10 minutes
Cooking time: 3.5 hours
Servings: 2
Ingredients:
- 3 eggs, whisked
- 3 oz Parmesan cheese, shredded
- 1 cup spring onions, chopped
- 1 teaspoon sweet paprika
- Cooking spray

Directions:
1. Grease the slow cooker with the cooking spray, combine all the ingredients inside and close the lid.
2. Cook the casserole for 3.5 hours on High.

Nutrition value/serving: calories 254, fat 13.4, fiber 3, carbs 2, protein 26.3

Pork Casserole
Prep time: 10 minutes
Cooking time: 9 hours
Servings: 4
Ingredients:
- 2 cups ground pork, browned
- 2 bell peppers, chopped
- 4 spring onions, chopped

- 1 tablespoon olive oil
- ½ cup heavy cream
- 1 teaspoon ground black pepper
- 1 teaspoon oregano, dried
- 1 tablespoon cilantro, chopped
- 1 tablespoon keto tomato sauce

Directions:
1. Grease the slow cooker with the oil and combine the pork with peppers and the other ingredients inside.
2. Close the lid and cook it on Low for 9 hours.
3. Stir the casserole well before serving.

Nutrition value/serving: calories 404, fat 22.9, fiber 1.3, carbs 6.6, protein 17.5

Coconut Avocado and Chicken Mix

Prep time: 15 minutes
Cooking time: 8 hours
Servings: 4
Ingredients:
- 1 avocado, pitted and roughly chopped
- 1/3 cup spring onions, chopped
- 3 oz Cheddar cheese, shredded
- 1 teaspoon olive oil
- 1 teaspoon turmeric powder
- ½ teaspoon ground black pepper
- ½ teaspoon salt
- ½ cup of coconut milk
- 4 oz chicken fillet, chopped

Directions:
1. In the slow cooker, mix the avocado with spring onions and the other ingredients.
2. Close the lid and cook avocado bake for 8 hours on Low.

Nutrition value/serving: calories 387, fat 22.1, fiber 4.5, carbs 7.9, protein 15.4

Ricotta Eggs

Prep time: 10 minutes
Cooking time: 5 hours
Servings: 4
Ingredients:
- ½ cup spring onions, chopped
- 1 teaspoon white pepper
- 1 teaspoon turmeric powder
- 3 oz Ricotta cheese
- 4 eggs, whisked
- ½ teaspoon butter, melted
- 1 tablespoon cilantro, chopped

Directions:
1. In the slow cooker, mix the eggs with Ricotta and the other ingredients and whisk.
2. Close the lid and cook egg casserole on Low for 5 hours.

Nutrition value/serving: calories 179, fat 6.8, fiber 0.4, carbs 2.6, protein 6.3

Spinach Casserole

Prep time: 10 minutes
Cooking time: 3 hours
Servings: 2
Ingredients:
- 2 cups spinach
- 1 tablespoon spring onions, chopped
- 3 eggs, whisked
- 1/3 cup almond milk
- ½ teaspoon salt
- ½ teaspoon cayenne pepper
- ½ teaspoon olive oil
- 1 oz chorizo, chopped

Directions:
1. In the slow cooker, mix the spinach with spring onions, eggs and the other ingredients, stir and spread into the pot.
2. Close the lid and cooked casserole for 3 hours on High.

Nutrition value/serving: calories 207, fat 13.9, fiber 5.1, carbs 6.1, protein 5.4

Lemon Pancake

Prep time: 10 minutes
Cooking time: 1 hour
Servings: 4
Ingredients:
- 1 teaspoon almond extract
- 1 tablespoon stevia
- ½ cup almond flour
- ¾ cup heavy cream
- ½ teaspoon baking powder
- 1 tablespoon lemon juice
- 1 tablespoon lemon zest, grated
- 2 eggs, whisked
- 1 teaspoon butter, melted

Directions:
1. In the mixing bowl, mix the flour with cream, eggs and the other ingredients except the butter and mix with a hand mixer.
2. Then place melted butter in the slow cooker.

3. Pour the pancake mixture over the butter and flatten it with the help of spatula if needed.
4. Close the slow cooker lid and cook the pancake for 1 hour on High. You can adjust the time of cooking. It can be from 40 minutes and up to 1.5 hours.
Nutrition value/serving: calories 201, fat 11.2, fiber 0.4, carbs 5.7, protein 4

Cinnamon Eggs
Prep time: 10 minutes
Cooking time: 8 hours / 2.5 hours
Servings: 4
Ingredients:
- 1 tablespoon stevia
- 1 teaspoon almond extract
- ½ teaspoon ground cinnamon
- 4 eggs, beaten
- 1/3 cup coconut cream
- Cooking spray

Directions:
1. In the mixer bowl, combine the eggs with the other ingredients except the coking spray.
2. Mix the mixture until homogenous.
3. Then spray the slow cooker pot with cooking spray.
4. Transfer the sweet egg mixture in the slow cooker and close the lid.
5. Cook the breakfast bake for 8 hours on Low or 2.5 hours on High.
Nutrition value/serving: calories 216, fat 11.5, fiber 4.3, carbs 4.9, protein 4.8

Dill and Avocado Frittata
Prep time: 10 minutes
Cooking time: 2 hours
Servings: 4
Ingredients:
- 2 avocados, peeled, pitted and mashed
- 1 teaspoon green curry paste
- 4 eggs, whisked
- 1 tablespoon fresh dill, chopped
- 1 teaspoon butter, softened
- 2 oz Mozzarella, shredded

Directions:
1. Brush the slow cooker with softened butter from inside.
2. Combine the eggs with avocados and the other ingredients, stir and spread into the pot.
3. Close the lid of the slow cooker and cook the frittata for 2 hours on High.
Nutrition value/serving: calories 324, fat 11.7, fiber 0.8, carbs 3.6, protein 10.7

Ham and Kale Bake
Prep time: 10 minutes
Cooking time: 2 hours
Servings: 2
Ingredients:
- 2 ounces Mozzarella, shredded
- ½ cup kale
- 1 cup ham, chopped
- 1 egg, whisked
- ½ teaspoon salt
- ½ teaspoon smoked paprika
- ½ teaspoon olive oil

Directions:
1. Brush the slow cooker with the oil from inside.
2. Combine the kale with ham and the other ingredients and spread into the pan.
3. Close the slow cooker lid and cook the meal for 2 hours on High.
Nutrition value/serving: calories 235, fat 12.3, fiber 0.9, carbs 4.6, protein 20.3

Chili Bake
Prep time: 10 minutes
Cooking time: 8 hours
Servings: 6
Ingredients:
- 2 green chilies, minced
- 1 ½ cup ground pork
- ½ teaspoon salt
- ½ teaspoon cayenne pepper
- ¼ teaspoon chili powder
- 1 egg, beaten
- 1/3 cup Parmesan cheese, shredded
- ½ onion, chopped
- 1 tablespoon keto tomato sauce
- 1 tablespoon olive oil
- 2 tablespoons chives, chopped

Directions:
1. Grease the slow cooker with the oil and mix the chilies with the pork and the other ingredients inside.
2. Close the lid and cook the casserole for 8 hours on Low.
Nutrition value/serving: calories 346, fat 10.6, fiber 5.3, carbs 6.2, protein 10

Cheesy Bacon Casserole
Prep time: 10 minutes
Cooking time: 6 hours
Servings: 4
Ingredients:
- ½ cup Ricotta cheese
- 3 oz Feta, crumbled
- 3 eggs, whisked
- 3 oz bacon, chopped
- 1 teaspoon olive oil
- 1 tablespoon fresh parsley, chopped
- 1 tablespoon chives, chopped
- 1 teaspoon oregano, chopped

Directions:
1. In the slow cooker, mix the cheese with the eggs and the other ingredients.
2. Stir the casserole gently.
3. Close the slow cooker lid and cook it for 6 hours on Low.

Nutrition value/serving: calories 353, fat 18.2, fiber 4.3, carbs 2.5, protein 19

Creamy Asparagus Bake
Prep time: 10 minutes
Cooking time: 2.5 hours
Servings: 6
Ingredients:
- 1 cup asparagus, chopped
- 1 cup spring onions, chopped
- ½ cup heavy cream
- 3 oz Swiss cheese, grated
- 1 teaspoon olive oil
- ½ teaspoon ground black pepper
- ½ teaspoon cayenne pepper
- 1 teaspoon dill, chopped

Directions:
1. In the slow cooker, mix the asparagus with the spring onions and the other ingredients.
2. Stir the bake mixture gently with the help of the wooden spatula.
3. Close the slow cooker lid and cook the casserole for 2.5 hours on High or until the broccoli is tender.

Nutrition value/serving: calories 250, fat 11.1, fiber 4.1, carbs 4.1, protein 9.5

Cauliflower Rice and Turkey Casserole
Prep time: 10 minutes
Cooking time: 3 hours
Servings: 4
Ingredients:
- 1 cup cauliflower, diced
- 1 egg, beaten
- 1 cup turkey breast, skinless, boneless and cut into strips
- ½ teaspoon salt
- ½ teaspoon smoked paprika
- ¾ teaspoon black pepper
- 1 teaspoon curry powder
- 1 tablespoon olive oil
- 1 tablespoon Ricotta cheese
- ½ cup heavy cream
- 2 oz Cheddar cheese, shredded

Directions:
1. In the slow cooker with the rice cauliflower with the turkey and the other ingredients, toss and close the lid.
2. Cook the meal on High for 3 hours.

Nutrition value/serving: calories 331, fat 13.3, fiber 0.8, carbs 2.5, protein 11.5

Sausage and Spinach
Prep time: 15 minutes
Cooking time: 6 hours
Servings: 6
Ingredients:
- 8 oz Italian sausages
- 1/3 cup spinach leaves, torn
- 1 tablespoon dried oregano
- 1 teaspoon sweet paprika
- 1 teaspoon salt
- 1 teaspoon black pepper
- 4 oz Cheddar cheese, shredded
- 1 tablespoon olive oil
- 1/3 cup coconut milk

Directions:
1. In the slow cooker, mix the sausage with the spinach, oregano and the other ingredients, toss and close the slow cooker lid.
2. Cook the casserole for 6 hours on Low.

Nutrition value/serving: calories 377, fat 16.4, fiber 4.5, carbs 6.4, protein 11.2

Creamy Eggs
Prep time: 10 minutes
Cooking time: 7 hours
Servings: 6
Ingredients:
- 1 teaspoon salt
- 5 eggs, beaten
- ¼ cup heavy cream

- 1 teaspoon turmeric powder
- 1 teaspoon coriander, ground
- ½ teaspoon ground black pepper
- 1 tablespoon fresh parsley, chopped
- ¾ teaspoon garlic powder
- ½ teaspoon chili flakes
- 1 tablespoon butter
- 4 oz Mozzarella, shredded

Directions:
1. In the mixing bowl, combine the eggs with the cream and the other ingredients except the butter and the Mozzarella and whisk.
2. Put the butter in the slow cooker.
3. Add the eggs mix, sprinkle the cheese on top, close the lid and cook the casserole for 7 hours on Low. The casserole is cooked, when the egg mixture is set.

Nutrition value/serving: calories 301, fat 23.8, fiber 4.8, carbs 6.3, protein 13.3

Zucchini Casserole

Prep time: 15 minutes
Cooking time: 3.5 hours
Servings: 4
Ingredients:
- 2 zucchinis, roughly cubed
- 1 tablespoon almond flour
- 1 egg, beaten
- 1 teaspoon ground black pepper
- 1 teaspoon coriander, ground
- 1 teaspoon oregano, dried
- 1 teaspoon basil, dried
- 1 teaspoon almond butter, softened
- ½ teaspoon salt
- 1/3 cup ground pork, browned
- 1/3 cup coconut milk

Directions:
1. In the slow cooker, mix the zucchini with the meat, egg and the other ingredients and toss. Close the slow cooker lid.
2. Cook the casserole for 3.5 – 4 hours on High.

Nutrition value/serving: calories 303, fat 14.3, fiber 3.8, carbs 9.1, protein 14.3

Avocado and Zucchini Bake

Prep time: 10 minutes
Cooking time: 2 hours
Servings: 2
Ingredients:
- 2 avocados, peeled, pitted and cubed
- 1 zucchini, grated
- 1 teaspoon turmeric powder
- 1 teaspoon nutmeg, ground
- 3 eggs, beaten
- ½ teaspoon almond extract
- ¾ teaspoon ground cinnamon
- 1 tablespoon stevia extract
- 1 teaspoon butter
- ¾ cup heavy cream

Directions:
1. In the slow cooker, mix the avocado with the zucchini, turmeric and the other ingredients, stir and spread into the slow cooker.
2. Close the lid and cook egg Bake for 2 hours on High.

Nutrition value/serving: calories 214, fat 16.1, fiber 3.7, carbs 9.6, protein 10.5

Almond Avocado Mix

Prep time: 15 minutes
Cooking time: 2 hours
Servings: 4
Ingredients:
- 3 eggs, whisked
- 1 teaspoon almond extract
- 1 avocado, peeled, pitted and mashed
- 1 tablespoon stevia
- 1 cup heavy cream
- ¾ teaspoon ground cardamom

Directions:
1. In the slow cooker, mix the eggs with the avocado and the other ingredients and toss.
2. Close the lid and cook cream bake for 2 hours on High.

Nutrition value/serving: calories 207, fat 7.9, fiber 4.1, carbs 6.6, protein 3.2

Beef Casserole

Prep time: 15 minutes
Cooking time: 3 hours
Servings: 7
Ingredients:
- 1-pound beef, ground
- 5 oz Mozzarella, shredded
- 1 teaspoon sweet paprika
- 1 teaspoon chili powder
- 1 teaspoon oregano, dried
- 2 tablespoons olive oil
- 1 cup of coconut milk
- ½ teaspoon cayenne pepper

- 1 teaspoon smoked paprika
- 1 tablespoon chives, chopped

Directions:
1. Heat up a pan with the oil over medium-high heat, add the meat, paprika, chili and oregano, brown for 5 minutes and transfer to the slow cooker.
2. Add the rest of the ingredients, and close the lid.
3. Cook the casserole for 3 hours on High.

Nutrition value/serving: calories 349, fat 20.6, fiber 4.8, carbs 4.4, protein 24.5

Shrimp Casserole

Prep time: 10 minutes
Cooking time: 2 hours
Servings: 4
Ingredients:
- 7 oz shrimp, cooked and roughly chopped
- ½ cup spring onions, chopped
- 4 eggs, whisked
- 1 tablespoon almond butter, melted
- 1 teaspoon paprika
- ½ teaspoon chili flakes
- 4 oz Mozzarella, shredded

Directions:
1. Brush the slow cooker pot with melted almond butter.
2. Combine the shrimp with spring onions and the other ingredients and toss.
3. Close the slow cooker lid.
4. Cook the casserole for 2 hours on High.

Nutrition value/serving: calories 205, fat 10.7, fiber 0.7, carbs 3.4, protein 11.9

Chili Eggplant Eggs

Prep time: 15 minutes
Cooking time: 1.5 hours
Servings: 2
Ingredients:
- 1 eggplant, cubed
- 1 red chili pepper, minced
- 4 eggs, whisked
- 1 tomato, sliced
- 1 tablespoon fresh parsley
- 2 oz Mozzarella, sliced
- 1 tablespoon butter
- ½ teaspoon chili flakes
- ½ teaspoon salt

Directions:
1. In the slow cooker, mix the eggs with eggplant and the other ingredients and toss.
2. Close the lid and cook the meal on High for 1.5 hours.
3. Divide between plates and serve.

Nutrition value/serving: calories 212, fat 13, fiber 5.5, carbs 11.6, protein 11

Coconut Muffins

Prep time: 10 minutes
Cooking time: 2 hours
Servings: 4
Ingredients:
- 4 eggs, beaten
- 4 teaspoons coconut cream
- 3 tablespoons coconut, shredded
- 4 teaspoons coconut flour
- 1/3 teaspoon stevia
- Cooking spray
- ½ cup water, for cooking

Directions:
1. In a bowl, mix the eggs with the rest of the ingredients except the cooking spray and water and stir.
2. Spray the muffin molds with cooking spray and pour the mixture inside them.
3. Pour the water in the slow cooker and arrange the muffin molds.
4. Close the slow cooker lid and cook muffins for 2 hours on High.
5. Cool them down and serve.

Nutrition value/serving: calories 262, fat 14.7, fiber 3.1, carbs 7, protein 11.6

Lime Nutmeg Roll

Prep time: 15 minutes
Cooking time: 2.15 hour
Servings: 6
Ingredients:
- 1 and ½ cups coconut flour
- 1 tablespoon nutmeg, ground
- 1 tablespoon stevia
- 4 tablespoons butter, softened
- 1 teaspoon baking powder
- 1 teaspoon lime juice
- 1 egg, beaten

Directions:
1. In the mixer bowl, mix up together the flour with nutmeg and the other ingredients and stir until you obtain a dough.
2. Then roll the dough into the log.
3. Cut the log into 6 buns.
4. Line the slow cooker with baking paper.

5. Place the buns in the slow cooker and close the lid.
6. Cook the breakfast buns for 2.15 hour on High.
7. Then open the lid and let the rolls chill till the room temperature.
8. Remove them from the slow cooker and separate into the serving.
Nutrition value/serving: calories 114, fat 10.9, fiber 1.5, carbs 5.6, protein 2.2

Creamy Eggs and Broccoli
Prep time: 10 minutes
Cooking time: 2 hours
Servings: 5
Ingredients:
- 5 eggs
- 2 tablespoons tomato, crushed
- ½ teaspoon salt
- ½ cup broccoli, chopped
- 1 tablespoon chives, chopped
- ¼ teaspoon curry powder
- 1 teaspoon garam masala
- 3 spring onions, chopped
- ¼ cup heavy cream
- 1 teaspoon butter
- 1 teaspoon chili flakes
- 1 tablespoon cilantro, chopped

Directions:
1. Put butter in the slow cooker.
2. Add the eggs and all the other ingredients, toss and close the lid.
3. Cook the mix on High for 2 hours.
4. Divide into bowls and serve for breakfast.

Nutrition value/serving: calories 214, fat 5.4, fiber 2.7, carbs 13.7, protein 6.2

Chili Tomatoes Bowls
Prep time: 10 minutes
Cooking time: 1.15 hour
Servings: 4
Ingredients:
- 4 eggs, beaten
- 4 tomatoes, chopped
- 1 chili pepper, minced
- 1 teaspoon curry powder
- 1 teaspoon sweet paprika
- 2 shallots, chopped
- 1 tablespoon butter
- ½ teaspoon salt
- 1 teaspoon dried parsley

Directions:
1. Put butter in the slow cooker.
2. Add the eggs, tomatoes and all the other ingredients.
3. Stir gently and close the lid. Cook on High for 1 hour and 15 minutes.
4. Divide into bowls and serve.

Nutrition value/serving: calories 201, fat 7.5, fiber 1.4, carbs 6.3, protein 6.5

Stuffed Peppers
Prep time: 15 minutes
Cooking time: 7 hours
Servings: 4
Ingredients:
- 2 yellow sweet peppers, deseeded and halved
- 1 cup ground turkey meat
- ½ teaspoon salt
- ½ teaspoon ground black pepper
- ½ teaspoon garam masala
- 1 tablespoon red curry paste
- 1 teaspoon oregano, dried
- 2 teaspoons butter
- 2 oz Cheddar cheese, shredded
- ¼ cup of water

Directions:
1. In the mixing bowl, mix up together the meat with salt, pepper and the other ingredients except the cheese and water, stir and stuff the peppers with this.
2. Sprinkle the pepper halves with shredded Cheddar cheese.
3. Pour water in the slow cooker.
4. Carefully add sweet pepper halves in the slow cooker and close the lid.
5. Cook the meal for 7 hours on Low.

Nutrition value/serving: calories 359, fat 10.9, fiber 4.3, carbs 5, protein 10.7

Veggie Casserole
Prep time: 15 minutes
Cooking time: 4 hours
Servings: 6
Ingredients:
- 1 cup zucchinis, grated
- ½ cup broccoli, chopped
- 3 oz celery stalk, chopped
- 1 cup kale, chopped
- 1 tablespoon walnuts, chopped
- 2 tablespoons butter
- 1 teaspoon cream cheese

- 3 oz Mozzarella, shredded
- 1 tablespoon almond flour
- 1 teaspoon chili flakes
- 1 teaspoon salt
- ¼ teaspoon ground black pepper
- ½ cup of coconut milk

Directions:
1. Put the vegetables in the slow cooker.
2. Add coconut milk and the rest of the ingredients, toss and spread into the pot.
3. Close the lid, and cook the casserole for 4 hours on High. The cooked casserole should be very soft.

Nutrition value/serving: calories 296, fat 20.7, fiber 5.5, carbs 7.2, protein 11.2

Chicken Meatballs

Prep time: 15 minutes
Cooking time: 6.5 hours
Servings: 4
Ingredients:
- 1 ½ cup ground chicken meat
- 2 tablespoons oregano, chopped
- 1 teaspoon coriander, ground
- 1 egg, beaten
- 1 tablespoon coconut flour
- ½ teaspoon salt
- 2 red chilies, minced
- 1 teaspoon chili flakes
- ¼ cup tomatoes, crushed
- ¾ cup heavy cream
- 1 teaspoon olive oil

Directions:
1. In a bowl, mix the chicken with the oregano and the other ingredients except the cream, oil and tomatoes, stir and make the medium-sized meatballs with the help of the fingertips.
2. Place the rest of the ingredients in the slow cooker.
3. Place the meatballs in the slow cooker to make 1 layer.
4. Close the lid and cook meatballs for 6.5 hours on Low.

Nutrition value/serving: calories 303, fat 15.2, fiber 4.3, carbs 2.8, protein 13.3

Kale Muffins

Prep time: 15 minutes
Cooking time: 7 hours
Servings: 6
Ingredients:
- 2 cups kale, chopped
- 1 teaspoon oregano, dried
- ½ teaspoon cayenne pepper
- ½ teaspoon salt
- 1 teaspoon sweet paprika
- 1 egg, beaten
- 1 teaspoon butter, melted
- 3 spring onions, chopped
- ½ cup of water

Directions:
1. In the bowl, combine the kale with oregano and the other ingredients except the butter and the water and stir.
2. Brush the muffin molds with melted butter and divide the kale into the muffin molds.
3. Transfer the muffin molds in the slow cooker.
4. Add water in the slow cooker and close it.
5. Cook the chicken muffins for 7 hours on Low.

Nutrition value/serving: calories 307, fat 6.8, fiber 4.1, carbs 5.5, protein 14.5

Almond Buns

Prep time: 20 minutes
Cooking time: 1.30 hour
Servings: 4
Ingredients:
- 1 cup almond flour
- ½ cup almonds, crushed
- 1 tablespoon Psyllium Husk powder
- 1 teaspoon baking soda
- 3 tablespoons coconut oil, melted
- 1 tablespoon stevia
- 1 teaspoon almond extract
- 1 tablespoon water

Directions:
1. In a bowl, mix the flour with almonds and the other ingredients except the water, stir and knead the dough you'll obtain.
2. Then make the log from the dough and cut it into 4 pieces.
3. Knead 4 buns from dough pieces.
4. Line the slow cooker pot with baking paper.
5. Place buns into the slow cooker to make the square.
6. Then brush the buns with water, close the slow cooker lid and cook buns for 1.30 minutes on High.

7. Then open the lid, chill the buns to the room temperature and remove from the slow cooker.
Nutrition value/serving: calories 333, fat 12.6, fiber 5.7, carbs 5.3, protein 1.8

Chives and Sprouts Casserole
Prep time: 5 minutes
Cooking time: 7 hours
Servings: 4
Ingredients:
- 5 oz ham, chopped
- 1 cup Brussels sprouts, halved
- 3 eggs, beaten
- ¾ cup organic coconut milk
- 5 oz Parmesan, grated
- 1 tablespoon chives, chopped
- 1 teaspoon ground black pepper

Directions:
1. In the slow cooker, mix the sprouts with the ham and the other ingredients.
2. Close the lid and cook the casserole for 7 hours on Low.
3. When the casserole is cooked, open the lid and stir it one more time.
Nutrition value/serving: calories 304, fat 14.8, fiber 4.9, carbs 4.4, protein 19.4

Coconut Sausages
Prep time: 20 minutes
Cooking time: 3 hours
Servings: 4
Ingredients:
- ½ cup coconut cream
- 1 tablespoon butter, softened
- 1/2 teaspoon coriander, ground
- 1 teaspoon cumin, ground
- ¾ teaspoon salt
- 4 sausages, organic and sliced
- 1 tablespoon coconut oil

Directions:
1. Spread the slow cooker pot with the coconut oil, add the cream, sausages and the other ingredients and toss.
2. Close the lid and cook the breakfast for 3 hours on High.
Nutrition value/serving: calories 209, fat 11.7, fiber 5.4, carbs 8.1, protein 3.3

Feta Eggs
Prep time: 10 minutes
Cooking time: 2 hours
Servings: 2
Ingredients:
- 4 eggs, beaten
- 1 tablespoon chives, chopped
- 1 tablespoon coconut cream
- 1 tablespoon Ricotta cheese
- 2 oz Feta, crumbled
- 1/3 teaspoon salt
- ½ teaspoon white pepper
- 1 teaspoon butter, melted

Directions:
1. In the slow cooker, mix the eggs with cream, chives and the other ingredients and toss.
2. Close the lid and cook egg mix for 2 hours on high.
Nutrition value/serving: calories 266, fat 16.5, fiber 4.5, carbs 4.7, protein 15.4

Creamy Green Tea
Prep time: 7 minutes
Cooking time: 3 hours
Servings: 1
Ingredients:
- 1 teaspoon green tea powder
- 1 cup heavy cream
- ¼ teaspoon ground cinnamon
- ¾ teaspoon vanilla extract
- ½ cup walnuts, chopped

Directions:
1. In the slow cooker, mix the cream with the green tea and the other ingredients and toss.
2. Close the slow cooker lid and cook the mix for 3 hours on Low.
3. Then strain the cooking liquid and transfer it into the serving cup.
Nutrition value/serving: calories 209, fat 11.8, fiber 4.3, carbs 2, protein 0.8

Zucchini Bread
Prep time: 25 minutes
Cooking time: 4 hours
Servings: 8
Ingredients:
- 1 cup zucchinis, grated
- ½ cup coconut cream
- 1 egg, beaten
- 1 teaspoon nutmeg, ground
- 3 tablespoons butter, softened
- 1 teaspoon baking soda
- 1 teaspoon lemon juice

- 2 cups almond flour
- 2 tablespoons cream cheese
- ½ teaspoon salt

Directions:
1. Place all the ingredients in a bowl, stir well and pour into the lined slow cooker.
2. Close the slow cooker lid and cook bread on High for 4 hours.
3. When the time is over, open the lid and chill the bread for 15 minutes.
4. Slice it into the serving.

Nutrition value/serving: calories 209, fat 11.5, fiber 4.2, carbs 6.9, protein 4

Sausages and Peppers Hash

Prep time: 10 minutes
Cooking time: 2.5 hour
Servings: 3
Ingredients:
- 3 pork sausages, organic and sliced
- 2 red bell peppers, cubed
- 2 spring onions, chopped
- 2 tomatoes, cubed
- 2 oz bacon, sliced
- 1 teaspoon butter
- ¼ teaspoon ground black pepper

Directions:
1. Grease the slow cooker with the butter, combine the sausages with peppers and the other ingredients, toss and close the lid.
2. Cook the mix for 2.5 hours on High.

Nutrition value/serving: calories 308, fat 12.9, fiber 4.1, carbs 5.4, protein 9.6

Mixed Veggies Burrito

Prep time: 15 minutes
Cooking time: 8 hours
Servings: 4
Ingredients:
- 1-pound chicken fillet, cut into strips
- 1 red bell pepper, cut into strips
- 1 zucchini, cut into strips
- 1 eggplant, cut into strips
- ½ cup coconut cream
- 1 teaspoon butter
- 1 tablespoon mayonnaise
- ½ avocado, chopped
- 1 tomato, chopped
- 1 teaspoon chili flakes
- 1 teaspoon salt
- 4 keto tortillas

Directions:
1. In the crock pot, mix the chicken with the pepper and the other ingredients except the avocado, mayonnaise and tortillas.
2. Close the lid and cook the ingredients for 8 hours on Low.
3. Spread the chicken mix on each tortilla, also divide the remaining ingredients, roll and serve.

Nutrition value/serving: calories 308, fat 11.5, fiber 3.9, carbs 7.7, protein 19.5

Zucchini Quiche

Prep time: 10 minutes
Cooking time: 7.5 hours
Servings: 6
Ingredients:
- 4 eggs, beaten
- 2 oz zucchinis, grated
- 1 cup spring onions, chopped
- 1 teaspoon ground black pepper
- ½ teaspoon salt
- 1 teaspoon curry powder
- 1 teaspoon oregano, dried

Directions:
1. In the bowl, combine the eggs with the zucchinis and the other ingredients, toss, pour into the slow cooker and spread.
2. Close the lid and cook the quiche for 7.5 hours on Low.
3. Chill the cooked quiche well and then slice it into the servings.

Nutrition value/serving: calories 271, fat 5.7, fiber 4.4, carbs 11.2, protein 8.4

Green Beans Casserole

Prep time: 15 minutes
Cooking time: 9 hours
Servings: 6
Ingredients:
- 1-pound green beans, chopped
- 4 oz Cheddar cheese, shredded
- ½ teaspoon curry powder
- 1 teaspoon garam masala
- 4 oz Mozzarella, sliced
- 1 cup heavy cream
- 1 teaspoon chili flakes
- 1 teaspoon ground nutmeg
- 1 teaspoon olive oil

Directions:
1. Spread the slow cooker bottom with the oil.

2. Combine the green beans with the other ingredients except the Mozzarella and toss.
3. Top the mix with Mozzarella slices and close the lid.
4. Cook casserole for 9 hours on Low.
Nutrition value/serving: calories 362, fat 17.8, fiber 1.2, carbs 5, protein 12.5

Cheddar Beef and Sprouts Casserole
Prep time: 10 minutes
Cooking time: 3 hours
Servings: 8
Ingredients:
- 1 cup Brussels sprouts, trimmed and halved
- 1 cup ground beef
- 3 oz Cheddar cheese, shredded
- 1 tablespoon olive oil
- 1 teaspoon turmeric powder
- 1 teaspoon coriander, ground
- ¼ cup heavy cream
- ½ teaspoon salt

Directions:
1. In the slow cooker, mix the sprouts with the beef and the other ingredients except the cheese.
2. Sprinkle the cheese on top.
3. Close the lid and cook the casserole for 3 hours on High.
Nutrition value/serving: calories 305, fat 10.8, fiber 4.7, carbs 8.1, protein 12.6

Chili Frittata
Prep time: 10 minutes
Cooking time: 2 hours
Servings: 4
Ingredients:
- 1 red chili, minced
- 1 teaspoon chili powder
- 1 cup chives, chopped
- 1 zucchini, cubed
- ½ bell pepper, chopped
- 4 eggs, beaten
- ¾ teaspoon salt
- Cooking spray

Directions:
1. Grease the slow cooker with the cooking spray and combine the eggs with the other ingredients inside.
2. Close the lid.
3. Cook frittata for 2 hours on High.
Nutrition value/serving: calories 232, fat 4.6, fiber 4.4, carbs 7.1, protein 5.8

Basil Sprouts and Eggs
Prep time: 15 minutes
Cooking time: 7 hours
Servings: 6
Ingredients:
- 1 cup Brussels sprouts, trimmed and shredded
- 1 tablespoon basil, chopped
- 1 tablespoon yellow curry paste
- 1 teaspoon ground black pepper
- ½ teaspoon salt
- 1 teaspoon butter
- ½ cup of coconut milk
- 3 eggs, beaten
- ½ teaspoon chili powder

Directions:
1. Spread the slow cooker bottom with the butter.
2. Combine the sprouts with the basil and the other ingredients.
3. Close the slow cooker lid.
4. Cook the meal for 7 hours on Low.
Nutrition value/serving: calories 321, fat 7.9, fiber 3.8, carbs 12.6, protein 4.6

Cilantro Pork Meatballs
Prep time: 15 minutes
Cooking time: 3 hours
Servings: 2
Ingredients:
- ½ cup ground pork
- 1 egg, beaten
- 1 teaspoon ground black pepper
- ½ teaspoon salt
- ½ teaspoon dried basil
- ½ teaspoon oregano, dried
- 1 tablespoon cilantro, chopped
- 1/2 cup coconut milk
- 1 teaspoon coconut oil
- 1 teaspoon chili flakes
- 1 jalapeno pepper, chopped

Directions:
1. In a bowl, mix the pork with the egg and the other ingredients except the oil and the coconut milk, stir and shape medium meatballs.
2. Grease the slow cooker with the oil, add the milk and meatballs.

3. Close the lid and cook meatballs for 3 hours on High. The time of cooking depends on meatballs size.
Nutrition value/serving: calories 202, fat 13.7, fiber 3.8, carbs 3, protein 12.2

Shrimp Omelet

Prep time: 10 minutes
Cooking time: 1.5 hours
Servings: 2
Ingredients:
- 6 eggs, whisked
- 1 cup shrimp, peeled, cooked and chopped
- 1 tomato, cubed
- 1 avocado, peeled, pitted and cubed
- 2 spring onions, chopped
- ½ teaspoon salt
- ¾ teaspoon ground black pepper
- 3 tablespoons cream cheese
- ½ teaspoon butter, melted

Directions:
1. In a bowl, mix the eggs with shrimp and the other ingredients except the butter and stir.
2. put melted butter in the slow cooker.
3. Add the eggs mix and close the lid.
4. Cook the omelet for 1.5 hours on High.

Nutrition value/serving: calories 205, fat 9.2, fiber 3.2, carbs 6.5, protein 4.8

Chia Bowls

Prep time: 7 minutes
Cooking time: 10 hours
Servings: 3
Ingredients:
- 1 teaspoon almond extract
- 2 cups organic almond milk
- 2 tablespoons chia seeds, dried
- 1 teaspoon flax meal seeds
- 1 tablespoon stevia
- 2 pecans, chopped

Directions:
1. In the slow cooker, mix the milk with chia seeds and the other ingredients
2. Close the lid and cook for 10 hours on Low.
3. When the time is over, divide into bowls and serve.

Nutrition value/serving: calories 215, fat 11.1, fiber 5.1, carbs 7.6, protein 4.1

Coconut Porridge

Prep time: 5 minutes
Cooking time: 8 hours
Servings: 2
Ingredients:
- ½ cup flaxseed meal
- 1 teaspoon coconut shred
- ¼ cup almond flour
- 1 cup coconut cream
- 1 ¼ cup of coconut milk

Directions:
1. In the slow cooker, mix the coconut with coconut cream and the other ingredients.
2. Close the slow cooker lid and cook porridge for 8 hours on Low.
3. Stir the mix well before serving.

Nutrition value/serving: calories 222, fat 11.4, fiber 7.9, carbs 13.9, protein 8.7

Berry Pudding

Prep time: 10 minutes
Cooking time: 3 hours
Servings: 6
Ingredients:
- 2 cups of almond milk
- 1/3 cup chia seeds
- 2 tablespoons strawberry, sliced
- 2 tablespoons blackberries
- 2 tablespoons blueberries
- 2 tablespoons stevia

Directions:
1. In the slow cooker, mix the berries with the milk and the rest of the ingredients.
2. Close the slow cooker lid and cook the pudding for 3 hours on Low.
3. When the pudding is cooked, transfer it into the serving ramekins and serve.

Nutrition value/serving: calories 131, fat 5.2, fiber 5.1, carbs 3.7, protein 3.4

Artichoke and Asparagus Mix

Prep time: 15 minutes
Cooking time: 3.5 hours
Servings: 4
Ingredients:
- ½ cup coconut cream
- 1 cup artichoke hearts, chopped
- 1 tablespoon butter, softened
- 1 cup asparagus, chopped
- 1 teaspoon oregano, dried
- ¼ teaspoon salt
- 3 eggs, beaten
- 3 tablespoons cream cheese

- ¼ cup fresh parsley

Directions:
1. In the slow cooker, mix the artichokes with the asparagus and the other ingredients and stir.
2. Close the lid and cook quiche for 3 and ½ hours on High.

Nutrition value/serving: calories 351, fat 10.7, fiber 3.9, carbs 12.3, protein 5.6

Cayenne Sprouts Hash
Prep time: 10 minutes
Cooking time: 3 hours
Servings: 5
Ingredients:
- 1-pound Brussels sprouts, trimmed and quartered
- 4 oz ham, chopped
- 1 egg, whisked
- 1 teaspoon garlic powder
- ¾ teaspoon cayenne pepper
- ¼ cup heavy cream
- Cooking spray

Directions:
1. Spray the slow cooker with cooking spray from inside.
2. Combine the sprouts with the ham and the other ingredients and close the lid.
3. Cook the strata for 3 hours on high.

Nutrition value/serving: calories 309, fat 13.3, fiber 2, carbs 5.6, protein 9.2

Walnuts Yogurt
Prep time: 10 minutes
Cooking time: 12 hours
Servings: 3
Ingredients:
- 2 cups organic almond milk
- 1 cup walnuts, chopped
- 1 tablespoon yogurt starter
- 1 tablespoon stevia

Directions:
1. In the slow cooker, mix the milk with the other ingredients.
2. Close the lid and cook yogurt on Low for 12 hours.
3. When the time is over, the liquid should be thick.
4. Pour yogurt into the serving ramekins.

Nutrition value/serving: calories 175, fat 3.4, fiber 3, carbs 8, protein 0.8

Ham and Tomato Bake
Prep time: 10 minutes
Cooking time: 2.5 hours
Servings: 2
Ingredients:
- 8 oz ham, chopped
- 1/2-pound cherry tomatoes, halved
- 1 teaspoon sweet paprika
- ¼ cup heavy cream
- 1 teaspoon curry powder
- 1 egg, beaten
- ½ teaspoon coconut oil

Directions:
1. Brush the slow cooker bottom with the coconut oil
2. Combine the ham with tomatoes and the other ingredients inside.
3. Close the slow cooker lid.
4. Cook the casserole for 2.5 hours on High.

Nutrition value/serving: calories 280, fat 15.8, fiber 1.5, carbs 5.4, protein 5.8

Beef Meatloaf
Prep time: 15 minutes
Cooking time: 5 hours
Servings: 8
Ingredients:
- 2 cups beef meat, ground
- 1 egg
- 2 tablespoons chives, chopped
- ½ cup tomatoes, cubed
- 1 teaspoon smoked paprika
- 1 teaspoon salt
- 1 teaspoon chili flakes
- 2 tablespoon fresh basil, chopped
- 1 teaspoon keto tomato sauce
- 1 teaspoon Ricotta cheese

Directions:
1. Line the slow cooker bottom with the baking paper.
2. In a bowl, mix the beef with the egg and the other ingredients except the cheese and tomato sauce
3. Mix up together Ricotta cheese and tomato sauce in the shallow bowl.
4. Spread the uncooked meatloaf with the tomato spread.
5. Close the slow cooker lid and cook meatloaf for 5 hours on High.
6. Cool down, slice and serve.

Nutrition value/serving: calories 269, fat 11.8, fiber 4.3, carbs 8.6, protein 14.3

Paprika and Shallots Omelet

Prep time: 10 minutes
Cooking time: 6 hours
Servings: 4
Ingredients:
- 4 eggs, beaten
- 4 tablespoons heavy cream
- ½ teaspoon sweet paprika
- ¾ teaspoon Pink salt
- 1 cup shallots, chopped
- 1 teaspoon curry powder
- Cooking spray

Directions:
1. Spray the slow cooker bottom with the cooking spray.
2. Combine the eggs with shallots and the other ingredients and spread.
3. Close the slow cooker lid and cook the meal for 6 hours on Low or until the omelet is set.

Nutrition value/serving: calories 348, fat 11.1, fiber 5.9, carbs 17.7, protein 10.9

Lunch

Beef and Mushrooms
Prep time: 10 minutes
Cooking time: 8 hours
Servings: 4
Ingredients:
- 1 shallot, chopped
- 2 spring onions, chopped
- 1 cup ground beef
- 1/3 cup white mushrooms, chopped
- ½ cup tomatoes, crushed
- 1 teaspoon butter
- 1 teaspoon dried basil
- 1 teaspoon salt
- ½ teaspoon ground black pepper

Directions:
1. In the slow cooker, mix the beef with the shallot and the other ingredients and toss.
2. Close the slow cooker lid and cook pizza casserole for 8 hours on Low.

Nutrition value/serving: calories 326, fat 16.8, fiber 5.1, carbs 6.3, protein 22.9

Cauliflower Bowls
Prep time: 10 minutes
Cooking time: 3 hours
Servings: 2
Ingredients:
- 1 and ½ cups cauliflower, shredded
- 1/2 cup Mozzarella, shredded
- ½ cup tomatoes, cubed
- 1 teaspoon chili flakes
- 1 teaspoon dried oregano
- 3 eggs, beaten
- 1 teaspoon olive oil

Directions:
1. Place the oil in the bottom of the slow cooker.
2. Combine the cauliflower with the Mozzarella and the other ingredients and toss.
3. Close the slow cooker lid.
4. Cook the hash for 3 hours on High.

Nutrition value/serving: calories 228, fat 11.2, fiber 0.9, carbs 2.5, protein 13.8

Broccoli Soup
Prep time: 10 minutes
Cooking time: 2.5 hours
Servings: 4
Ingredients:
- 8 oz broccoli, shredded
- 4 cups water
- 1 teaspoon sweet paprika
- 1 teaspoon oregano, dried
- 2 spring onions, chopped
- 1/3 cup organic almond milk
- 1 tablespoon chives, chopped
- 1 teaspoon salt

Directions:
1. In the crock pot, mix the broccoli with the water and the other ingredients, toss and close the slow cooker lid.
2. Cook casserole for 2.5 hours on High.

Nutrition value/serving: calories 223, fat 13.2, fiber 3.8, carbs 11.2, protein 10.2

Chicken Soup
Prep time: 10 minutes
Cooking time: 5.5 hours
Servings: 6
Ingredients:
- 4 cups of water
- 1-pound chicken breast, skinless, boneless and cubed
- 1 red chili pepper, minced
- ½ teaspoon coriander, ground
- 1 yellow sweet pepper, chopped
- 1 teaspoon chili powder
- 1 teaspoon salt
- 3 oz avocado, chopped
- 3 tablespoons lemon juice

Directions:
1. In the slow cooker, mix the water with the chicken and the other ingredients except the avocado, close the lid and cook the soup for 5 hours and 30 minutes on High.
2. When the soup is cooked, add chopped avocado.

Nutrition value/serving: calories 346, fat 12.5, fiber 4.9, carbs 4.6, protein 17

Creamy Beef Mix
Prep time: 10 minutes
Cooking time: 9 hours
Servings: 2
Ingredients:
- 10 oz beef loin, roughly cubed
- 1 cup heavy cream
- 1 teaspoon coconut oil, melted
- 1 teaspoon turmeric powder

- 1 teaspoon garam masala
- 1 teaspoon cayenne pepper
- 1 teaspoon salt
- 2 spring onions, chopped
- 1/3 cup cremini mushrooms, diced
- 1 tablespoon fresh parsley

Directions:
1. Heat up a pan with the oil over medium-high heat, add the meat, turmeric, masala and cayenne, toss, and brown for 5 minutes.
2. Then transfer meat in the slow cooker.
3. Add the rest of the ingredients and close the lid.
4. Cook beef stroganoff for 9 hours on Low.

Nutrition value/serving: calories 468, fat 22.3, fiber 0.6, carbs 8.3, protein 29.1

Chili Soup

Prep time: 10 minutes
Cooking time: 7 hours
Servings: 3
Ingredients:
- 2 cups of water
- 1 teaspoon chili powder
- ½ teaspoon salt
- 2 red chilies, minced
- 1/3 cup tomatoes, crushed
- 1 teaspoon curry powder
- 1 teaspoon sweet paprika
- 1 cup ground pork
- 3 spring onions, chopped
- 1 tablespoon chives, chopped

Directions:
1. In the slow cooker, mix the water with the pork and the other ingredients, toss, close the lid and cook on Low for 7 hours.
2. Divide the soup into bowls

Nutrition value/serving: calories 413, fat 29.2, fiber 4.6, carbs 8.7, protein 22.1

Sausage Soup

Prep time: 10 minutes
Cooking time: 4.15 hour
Servings: 5
Ingredients:
- 9 oz Italian sausages, chopped
- 1 teaspoon sweet paprika
- 1 teaspoon salt
- ½ teaspoon ground black pepper
- 1 cup broccoli, chopped
- 3 cups of water
- 1 cup spinach
- 1/3 cup heavy cream
- 1 tablespoon cream cheese

Directions:
1. In the slow cooker, mix the sausage with the paprika and the other ingredients except the cream and cream cheese.
2. Close the slow cooker lid and cook soup for 4 hours on High.
3. Then open the lid and add the remaining ingredients.
4. Cook the meal for 15 minutes more on High.

Nutrition value/serving: calories 362, fat 22.2, fiber 0.9, carbs 6.5, protein 12.1

Chicken Stew

Prep time: 15 minutes
Cooking time: 5.5 hours
Servings: 4
Ingredients:
- 1-pound chicken breast, skinless, boneless and cubed
- 1 tablespoon olive oil
- 1 cup heavy cream
- 1 teaspoon oregano, dried
- 1 teaspoon garam masala
- ½ teaspoon garlic powder
- 1 teaspoon sweet paprika
- ½ cup white mushrooms, sliced

Directions:
1. Heat up a pan with the oil over medium-high heat, add the meat and masala, brown for 5 minutes and transfer to the slow cooker.
2. Add the rest of the ingredients and toss.
3. Close the lid and cook the stew for 5.5 hours on Low.

Nutrition value/serving: calories 449, fat 18.3, fiber 4.9, carbs 8.9, protein 24.7

Shrimp Soup

Prep time: 10 minutes
Cooking time: 3 hours
Servings: 4
Ingredients:
- 1-pound shrimp, peeled and deveined
- 1 ½ cup organic almond milk
- ½ teaspoon turmeric powder
- ¼ cup cauliflower, chopped
- ½ teaspoon salt
- 1 teaspoon minced garlic
- 1 cup water

Directions:

1. In the slow cooker, mix the shrimp with milk and the other ingredients, close the lid and cook on Low for 3 hours.
2. When the soup is cooked, divide into bowls and serve.
Nutrition value/serving: calories 117, fat 6, fiber 0.9, carbs 6.7, protein 6.2

Chicken and Olives Stew
Prep time: 10 minutes
Cooking time: 5 hours
Servings: 4
Ingredients:
- 1-pound chicken breast, skinless, boneless
- 1 tablespoon keto tomato sauce
- ½ cup of coconut milk
- 1 red bell pepper, chopped
- 1 teaspoon basil, dried
- 1 teaspoon sweet paprika
- 1/2 cup black olives, sliced

Directions:
1. In the slow cooker, mix the chicken with the coconut milk and the other ingredients.
2. Close the lid and cook the chicken for 5 hours on High.
3. Divide into bowls and serve
Nutrition value/serving: calories 269, fat 12.6, fiber 1.5, carbs 4.9, protein 14.1

Lemon Lamb and Cauliflower
Prep time: 10 minutes
Cooking time: 8 hours
Servings: 2
Ingredients:
- 1-pound lamb shoulder, boneless and roughly cubed
- 1 cup cauliflower florets
- 1 teaspoon balsamic vinegar
- 1 tablespoon lemon juice
- 1 teaspoon sweet paprika
- 1 teaspoon minced garlic
- 3 spring onions, chopped
- 1 teaspoon dried cilantro
- ½ teaspoon chili flakes
- 1 tablespoon keto tomato sauce
- 1 ½ cup water
- 1 teaspoon salt
- ½ teaspoon cayenne pepper

Directions:
1. In the slow cooker, mix the lamb with the cauliflower, vinegar and the other ingredients and toss.
2. Close the lid and cook the meal on Low for 8 hours.
Nutrition value/serving: calories 405, fat 13.4, fiber 5.3, carbs 12.1, protein 65

Steak and Tomato Salad
Prep time: 10 minutes
Cooking time: 5 hours
Servings: 2
Ingredients:
- 1-pound beef steaks, cut into strips
- 1 cup cherry tomatoes, halved
- 1 cup baby spinach
- 1 tablespoon olive oil
- 1/3 cup vegetable stock
- 1 tablespoon fresh cilantro, chopped
- 2 bell peppers, roughly chopped
- ½ cup spring onions, chopped
- 1 tablespoon lime juice
- 1 teaspoon chili flakes

Directions:
1. In the slow cooker, mix the beef with the tomatoes and the other ingredients.
2. Close the lid and cook meal for 5 hours on High.
3. Divide into bowls and serve.
Nutrition value/serving: calories 347, fat 11.4, fiber 1.7, carbs 9, protein 27.2

Okra Stew
Prep time: 7 minutes
Cooking time: 9 hours
Servings: 4
Ingredients:
- 14 oz okra, chopped
- 3 spring onions, chopped
- 3 cups of water
- 1 celery stalk, chopped
- 1 tablespoon ground paprika
- 1 teaspoon chili flakes
- 1 teaspoon salt
- 1 teaspoon keto tomato sauce
- 1 teaspoon ground black pepper
- 1 tablespoon chives, chopped

Directions:
1. In the slow cooker, mix the okra with the spring onions and the other ingredients.
2. Close the lid and cook the stew for 9 hours on Low.
3. When the stew is cooked, open the lid, mix it up gently and transfer in the serving bowls.

Nutrition value/serving: calories 206, fat 6.6, fiber 3.2, carbs 5.5, protein 8.2

Green Beans Stew
Prep time: 10 minutes
Cooking time: 4 hours
Servings: 3
Ingredients:
- ½ cup of water
- 1 teaspoon dried rosemary
- ½ teaspoon salt
- ½ teaspoon ground black pepper
- 1 teaspoon sweet paprika
- 1 teaspoon oregano, dried
- 1 teaspoon chili powder
- 1 teaspoon thyme
- 1-pound green beans, halved
- 1 teaspoon coconut oil

Directions:
1. In your slow cooker, mix the green beans with the water and the other ingredients, stir and close the lid.
2. Cook the pork stew for 4 hours on High

Nutrition value/serving: calories 271, fat 11.3, fiber 1.7, carbs 5.2, protein 30.4

Lamb and Coconut Stew
Prep time: 15 minutes
Cooking time: 5.10 hours
Servings: 4
Ingredients:
- 2-pound lamb fillet, cubed
- 1 teaspoon cumin, ground
- 3 spring onions, chopped
- 1 tablespoon coconut cream
- 1 cup of water
- ½ cup of coconut milk
- 1 teaspoon salt
- 1 teaspoon turmeric
- ¼ cup spinach, chopped
- 1/2 teaspoon black pepper

Directions:
1. In the slow cooker, mix the lamb with cumin, spring onions and the other ingredients except the spinach, stir and close the lid.
2. Cook stew for 5 hours on High.
3. Then add spinach and stir the stew well.
4. Cook it on High for 10 minutes more.

Nutrition value/serving: calories 257, fat 13.9, fiber 1.1, carbs 2.7, protein 24.7

Chicken and Okra Stew
Prep time: 10 minutes
Cooking time: 7 hours
Servings: 4
Ingredients:
- 1 teaspoon ground black pepper
- ½ teaspoon smoked paprika
- 1 teaspoon turmeric powder
- ¾ cup heavy cream
- 1 teaspoon olive oil
- ½ cup okra, sliced
- ½ cup of water
- 2 spring onions, chopped
- ½ teaspoon salt
- 14 oz chicken breast, skinless, boneless

Directions:
1. Put the oil in a pan and heat up over medium heat.
2. Add the meat, cook for 5 minutes and transfer to the slow cooker.
3. Add the rest of the ingredients and close the lid.
4. Cook the stew for 7 hours on Low.

Nutrition value/serving: calories 344, fat 23.6, fiber 1.3, carbs 12.7, protein 24.4

Calamari Stew
Prep time: 10 minutes
Cooking time: 2 hours
Servings: 3
Ingredients:
- 1-pound calamari rings
- 3 spring onions, chopped
- ½ cup tomatoes, cubed
- 1 chili pepper, chopped
- 1 teaspoon cayenne pepper
- 1 teaspoon chili powder
- ½ teaspoon paprika
- ½ teaspoon salt
- 1/3 cup water

Directions:
1. Put all the ingredients in the slow cooker and stir.
2. Close the slow cooker lid and cook shrimp fajitas for 1.5 hours on High.

Nutrition value/serving: calories 204, fat 3, fiber 1.9, carbs 7.6, protein 35.4

Lemon Pork Stew
Prep time: 15 minutes
Cooking time: 10 hours

Servings: 4
Ingredients:
- 1-pound pork shoulder, boneless and cubed
- 1 red chili pepper, minced
- ½ teaspoon garam masala
- 1 teaspoon salt
- ½ teaspoon dried rosemary
- ½ cup of water
- ¼ cup tomatoes, crushed
- 2 tablespoons lemon zest, grated
- 2 tablespoons lemon juice

Directions:
1. In the slow cooker, mix the pork with the chili, masala and the other ingredients, toss, close the lid and cook on Low for 10 hours.
2. Divide into bowls and serve.

Nutrition value/serving: calories 425, fat 18.7, fiber 2.6, carbs 5.4, protein 22.7

Spinach and Tomato Soup

Prep time: 15 minutes
Cooking time: 3 hours
Servings: 2
Ingredients:
- 3 cups of water
- 1/3 cup tomatillos, chopped
- 2 cups baby spinach
- 1 teaspoon sweet paprika
- ½ teaspoon ground black pepper
- 1 teaspoon salt
- 1 tablespoon dried dill
- 1 tablespoon butter, melted

Directions:
1. In the slow cooker, mix the water with spinach and the other ingredients, toss and close the lid.
2. Cook soup for 3 hours on Low.

Nutrition value/serving: calories 322, fat 5.3, fiber 2.9, carbs 4.8, protein 4.5

French Onion Soup

Prep time: 10 minutes
Cooking time: 4 hours
Servings: 3
Ingredients:
- 3 spring onions, chopped
- ½ cup coconut milk
- ½ cup coconut cream
- ½ teaspoon minced garlic
- 1 teaspoon turmeric powder
- ½ teaspoon ground black pepper
- 7 oz Parmesan, grated
- 2 tablespoon butter
- 1 cup of water

Directions:
1. Melt butter and pour it in the slow cooker.
2. Add the onions and the other ingredients except the cheese.
3. Close the lid and cook soup for 2 hours on High.
4. After this, add grated cheese and stir well.
5. Cook the soup for 2 hours more on Low.

Nutrition value/serving: calories 371, fat 22.2, fiber 5.8, carbs 10, protein 23.9

Spicy Chicken Soup

Prep time: 10 minutes
Cooking time: 3.5 hours
Servings: 4
Ingredients:
- 3 cups of water
- 1 tablespoon cilantro, chopped
- 1 teaspoon dried parsley
- 1 teaspoon chili powder
- ½ teaspoon chives, chopped
- 9 oz chicken breast, skinless and cubed
- 1/3 cup tomatoes, cubed
- 3 oz celery stalk, chopped
- 1 teaspoon salt
- 1 teaspoon chili flakes

Directions:
1. In the slow cooker, mix the chicken with the water and the other ingredients.
2. Close the lid and cook soup on High for 3.5 hours.
3. Divide into bowls and serve.

Nutrition value/serving: calories 328, fat 8.2, fiber 2.2, carbs 8.6, protein 12.4

Cabbage Stew

Prep time: 15 minutes
Cooking time: 7 hours
Servings: 4
Ingredients:
- 1-pound white cabbage, shredded
- 1 cup cherry tomatoes, halved
- 1 ½ cup ground pork
- 1 teaspoon salt
- 1 teaspoon ground black pepper
- 1/2 cup spring onions, chopped
- 1 teaspoon chili flakes

- ¾ tablespoon keto tomatoes sauce
- 1/3 cup water
- 1 tablespoon dill, chopped

Directions:
1. In the slow cooker, mix the cabbage with the tomatoes and the other ingredients.
2. Close the lid and cook the stew for 7 hours on Low.
3. Divide into bowls and serve.

Nutrition value/serving: calories 305, fat 14.7, fiber 1.7, carbs 4.1, protein 8.3

Turkey Soup

Prep time: 15 minutes
Cooking time: 4 hours
Servings: 3
Ingredients:
- 8 oz turkey breast, skinless, boneless and cubed
- 1 tablespoon olive oil
- 1 teaspoon curry powder
- 1 green bell pepper, chopped
- 2 shallots, chopped
- ½ teaspoon salt
- ½ teaspoon hot paprika
- ½ cup whipped cream
- 1 cup of water
- ¾ teaspoon minced garlic
- ¼ teaspoon cayenne pepper

Directions:
1. In the slow cooker, mix the turkey with the oil and the other ingredients, stir, close the lid and cook on High for 4 hours.
2. Divide the soup into bowls and serve.

Nutrition value/serving: calories 329, fat 21.8, fiber 5, carbs 6.1, protein 24.4

Ground Beef Soup

Prep time: 15 minutes
Cooking time: 3.5 hour
Servings: 4
Ingredients:
- 1 cup ground beef
- 1 teaspoon garam masala
- 1 cup tomatoes, crushed
- ½ teaspoon chili flakes
- 1 teaspoon salt
- 2 spring onions, chopped
- 1 red bell pepper, chopped
- 3 and ½ cups of water
- 1 teaspoon olive oil
- 1 teaspoon fresh dill, chopped

Directions:
1. Grease the slow cooker with the oil and combine all the ingredients inside.
2. Close the lid and cook the soup on High for 3 hours and 30 minutes.
3. Divide the soup into bowls and serve.

Nutrition value/serving: calories 325, fat 16.7, fiber 2.5, carbs 5.8, protein 10.5

Coconut Mushroom Mix

Prep time: 20 minutes
Cooking time: 6 hours
Servings: 4
Ingredients:
- 1-pound white mushrooms, sliced
- 3 spring onions, chopped
- 1 teaspoon turmeric powder
- 1 teaspoon coriander, ground
- ½ cup heavy cream
- 1 teaspoon ground black pepper
- 1 teaspoon salt
- 1 tablespoon olive oil
- ½ teaspoon thyme

Directions:
1. In the slow cooker, mix the mushrooms with the spring onions and the other ingredients, close the lid and cook for 6 hours on Low.
2. Divide into bowls and serve.

Nutrition value/serving: calories 323, fat 9.3, fiber 3.6, carbs 12.2, protein 4.7

Salmon Stew

Prep time: 10 minutes
Cooking time: 3 hours
Servings: 4
Ingredients:
- ¼ teaspoon minced ginger
- 1 teaspoon turmeric powder
- 1 teaspoon cumin, ground
- ¾ teaspoon ground cinnamon
- 1 cup heavy cream
- 2 tablespoons butter
- 8 oz celery stalk, roughly chopped
- 14 oz salmon fillet, roughly chopped

Directions:
1. In the slow cooker, mix the salmon with the celery and the other ingredients and toss.
2. Close the slow cooker lid and cook the stew for 3 hours on High.

Nutrition value/serving: calories 315, fat 13.2, fiber 3.1, carbs 7.1, protein 12.6

Walnut Beef Mix

Prep time: 15 minutes
Cooking time: 7 hours
Servings: 2
Ingredients:
- 2 cups ground beef
- ½ cup walnuts, chopped
- 3 garlic cloves, chopped
- 1/2 cup tomatoes, cubed
- 1 teaspoon ground black pepper
- 1/3 teaspoon salt
- 1 teaspoon sweet paprika
- 1 teaspoon chili flakes
- 1 teaspoon olive oil
- 1 cup baby spinach

Directions:
1. In the slow cooker, mix the beef with walnuts, garlic and the other ingredients and toss.
2. Close the lid and cook the meal for 7 hours on Low.

Nutrition value/serving: calories 435, fat 23.8, fiber 2.4, carbs 7.9, protein 19.7

Tomato Chili

Prep time: 7 minutes
Cooking time: 5 hours
Servings: 4
Ingredients:
- 1 teaspoon chili powder
- 1-pound tomatoes, roughly cubed
- 1 jalapeno pepper, chopped
- 2 spring onions, chopped
- 1 cup kale, chopped
- 1 teaspoon oregano, dried
- 1 teaspoon ground black pepper
- 1 teaspoon salt
- 1 green bell pepper, chopped
- 1/3 cup vegetable stock

Directions:
1. In the slow cooker, mix the tomatoes with the kale and the other ingredients.
2. Then close the slow cooker lid and cook on Low for 5 hours.
3. Divide into bowls and serve.

Nutrition value/serving: calories 239, fat 8.5, fiber 1.8, carbs 6.8, protein 4.1

Eggplant Stew

Prep time: 15 minutes
Cooking time: 4.5 hour
Servings: 6
Ingredients:
- 1-pound eggplant, roughly cubed
- 1 cup tomatoes, cubed
- 1 cup spring onions, chopped
- 1 teaspoon chili powder
- 1 tablespoon chives
- 1 teaspoon dried oregano
- 1 tablespoon Italian seasoning
- 1 teaspoon salt
- 1 teaspoon keto tomato sauce
- 1 teaspoon butter
- ¾ cup of water

Directions:
1. In the slow cooker, mix the eggplant with tomatoes, spring onions and the other ingredients.
2. Close the lid and cook the mix on Low for 4.5 hours.

Nutrition value/serving: calories 230, fat 7.8, fiber 6.8, carbs 7.2, protein 12.9

Ginger and Broccoli Soup

Prep time: 15 minutes
Cooking time: 2 hours
Servings: 4
Ingredients:
- 1 cup spinach, chopped
- 1 cup broccoli florets
- 1 teaspoon minced ginger
- ¼ cup coconut cream
- 2 cups of water
- 1 teaspoon butter
- 1 teaspoon turmeric powder
- 1 teaspoon yellow curry paste
- 1 teaspoon minced garlic
- 1 tablespoon chives, chopped

Directions:
1. In the slow cooker, mix the broccoli with spinach and the other ingredients.
2. Close the lid and cook soup on High for 2 hours.
3. After this, blend the soup with the help of the hand blender until you get a smooth creamy texture.
4. Divide into bowls and serve.

Nutrition value/serving: calories 121, fat 3.9, fiber 3.8, carbs 4.4, protein 2.5

Salmon Skewers

Prep time: 10 minutes
Cooking time: 2 hours

Servings: 2
Ingredients:
- 10 oz salmon fillet, boneless and cubed
- 1 cup small mushroom caps
- 1 teaspoon salt
- 1 tablespoon lemon juice
- ½ teaspoon chili flakes
- 2 tablespoons olive oil
- ½ teaspoon paprika

Directions:
1. In a bowl, mix the salmon with the other ingredients and toss.
2. Arrange the salmon and mushrooms on skewers and put them in the slow cooker.
3. Close the slow cooker lid and cook chicken skewers for 2 hours on Low.

Nutrition value/serving: calories 251, fat 17.9, fiber 1.3, carbs 3.8, protein 11.4

Coconut Halibut

Prep time: 10 minutes
Cooking time: 7 hours
Servings: 4
Ingredients:
- 14 oz halibut fillet, cut into serving steaks
- 1 teaspoon turmeric powder
- ½ cup coconut cream
- 1 teaspoon sweet paprika
- 1 garlic clove, peeled, crushed
- ½ teaspoon ground black pepper
- 1 teaspoon butter

Directions:
1. In the slow cooker, mix the halibut with the cream and the other ingredients.
2. Close the slow cooker lid and cook the fish for 7 hours on Low.

Nutrition value/serving: calories 226, fat 11.2, fiber 1, carbs 2.8, protein 17.9

Zucchini and Shrimp

Prep time: 10 minutes
Cooking time: 2 hours
Servings: 4
Ingredients:
- 1 cup zucchini, roughly cubed
- 1-pound shrimp, peeled and deveined
- 1/2 cup coconut cream
- 1 tablespoon butter
- 1 teaspoon dried oregano
- 1 teaspoon salt

Directions:
1. In the slow cooker, mix the zucchini with the shrimp and the other ingredients.
2. Stir gently and close the slow cooker lid.
3. Cook the meal for 2 hours on High.
4. Divide between plates and serve.

Nutrition value/serving: calories 203, fat 7.7, fiber 1.2, carbs 6.1, protein 12.1

Zucchini Stew

Prep time: 15 minutes
Cooking time: 3 hours
Servings: 4
Ingredients:
- 1-pound zucchini, roughly cubed
- 3 spring onions, chopped
- 1 cup cherry tomatoes, halved
- 1 teaspoon dried basil
- ½ teaspoon sweet paprika
- 1 cup veggie stock
- 1 tablespoon chives, chopped

Directions:
1. In the slow cooker, mix the zucchinis with the spring onions and the other ingredients, toss and close the lid.
2. Cook the meal for 3 hours on High.

Nutrition value/serving: calories 207, fat 11.6, fiber 4.2, carbs 8.5, protein 7.7

Ground Beef and Leeks

Prep time: 15 minutes
Cooking time: 3 hours
Servings: 4
Ingredients:
- 2 cups ground beef
- 2 leeks, sliced
- 1 cup cherry tomatoes, halved
- 1 cup keto tomato sauce
- 1 ½ cup white mushrooms, chopped
- ¼ cup fresh parsley, chopped
- 1 tablespoon olive oil
- ½ teaspoon oregano, dried
- 1 teaspoon salt

Directions:
1. Heat up a pan with the oil over medium-high heat, add the meat, brown for 5 minutes and transfer to the slow cooker.
2. Add the rest of the ingredients and toss.
3. Close the slow cooker lid and cook the lunch for 3 hours on High.

Nutrition value/serving: calories 403, fat 19.9, fiber 1.9, carbs 7.5, protein 18.1

Lemongrass Short Ribs

Prep time: 15 minutes
Cooking time: 6 hours
Servings: 6
Ingredients:
- 16 oz beef short ribs, boneless
- 2 tablespoons lemon juice
- 2 tablespoons lemon zest, grated
- 1 tablespoon lemongrass, crushed
- ½ cup fresh cilantro, chopped
- 1 cup of water
- 1 tablespoon Keto tomato sauce
- 1 teaspoon minced garlic
- 1 teaspoon butter
- 1 teaspoon salt

Directions:
1. Place the short ribs in the slow cooker.
2. Add the rest of the ingredients and toss.
3. Close the lid and cook the meat for 6 hours on High.
4. Divide between plates and serve.

Nutrition value/serving: calories 358, fat 30.7, fiber 1., carbs 8.7, protein 24.9

Cinnamon Beef

Prep time: 20 minutes
Cooking time: 10 hours
Servings: 4
Ingredients:
- 1 ½ pound beef sirloin, sliced
- ½ cup keto tomato sauce
- 1 teaspoon cinnamon powder
- 1 teaspoon turmeric
- 1 teaspoon garlic powder
- 1 teaspoon salt
- 1 tablespoon olive oil

Directions:
1. In the slow cooker, mix the beef with the cinnamon and the other ingredients
2. Close the lid and cook beef for 10 hours on Low.
3. When the meat is cooked, remove it from the liquid and slice into the servings.

Nutrition value/serving: calories 352, fat 14.3, fiber 0.5, carbs 1.3, protein 51.9

Leeks Soup

Prep time: 10 minutes
Cooking time: 3.5 hours
Servings: 6
Ingredients:
- 4 leeks, sliced
- 3 and ½ cups of water
- 3 spring onions, chopped
- 1 teaspoon butter, soft
- ½ cup heavy cream
- 1 teaspoon salt
- 1 teaspoon ground black pepper
- ½ teaspoon oregano, dried

Directions:
1. In the slow cooker, mix the leeks with the water and the other ingredients except the cream.
2. Close the lid and cook soup for 3 hours on High.
3. When the time is over, open the lid and add heavy cream blend with an immersion blender.
4. Close the lid and cook the soup for 30 minutes more on High.
5. Divide into bowls and serve.

Nutrition value/serving: calories 232, fat 11.7, fiber 2.2, carbs 3.5, protein 7.4

Pork Stew

Prep time: 10 minutes
Cooking time: 3.5 hours
Servings: 4
Ingredients:
- 1-pound pork chops
- 1 tablespoon sweet paprika
- 2 leeks, sliced
- ½ cup of water
- 1/3 cup coconut milk
- 1 teaspoon curry powder
- 1 teaspoon salt
- 1 teaspoon chili powder

Directions:
1. In the slow cooker, mix the pork chops with the paprika and the other ingredients, toss and close the lid.
2. Cook the stew on High for 3 hours and 30 minutes.
3. Divide into bowls and serve.

Nutrition value/serving: calories 303, fat 19.2, fiber 1.2, carbs 7, protein 18.3

Cauliflower Rice and Tomatoes

Prep time: 15 minutes
Cooking time: 2 hours
Servings: 4

Ingredients:
- 2 cups cauliflower, riced
- 1 cup cherry tomatoes, halved
- 1/2 cup veggie stock
- 1 teaspoon turmeric
- 1 teaspoon smoked paprika
- 1 teaspoon salt
- 1 teaspoon butter
- ½ cup of coconut milk

Directions:
1. In the slow cooker, mix the cauliflower with tomatoes and the other ingredients.
2. After this, close the lid of the slow cooker and cook the meal for 2 hours on high.
3. When the time is over, open the slow cooker lid, stir, divide into bowls and serve.

Nutrition value/serving: calories 207, fat 11.5, fiber 2.5, carbs 5.5, protein 7.1

Roast and Peppers

Prep time: 15 minutes
Cooking time: 5.5 hours
Servings: 4
Ingredients:
- 1-pound beef chuck roast, chopped
- 1 tablespoon keto tomato sauce
- 1 cup of water
- 1 green bell pepper, chopped
- 1 red bell pepper, chopped
- 1 orange bell pepper, chopped
- 1 teaspoon sweet paprika
- ½ teaspoon ground nutmeg
- 1 teaspoon olive oil

Directions:
1. Pour olive oil in a skillet, heat up over medium heat, add the meat, brown for 5 minutes and transfer to the slow cooker.
2. Add the rest of the ingredients, toss and close the lid.
3. Cook the pot roast for 5.5 hours on High.

Nutrition value/serving: calories 308, fat 12.9, fiber 1.4, carbs 7.4, protein 20.4

Kale and Shrimp

Prep time: 10 minutes
Cooking time: 2 hours
Servings: 2
Ingredients:
- 2 cups kale, chopped
- 1 cup of veggie stock
- 1-pound shrimp, peeled and deveined
- 1 teaspoon dried dill
- 1 teaspoon turmeric powder
- 1 teaspoon curry powder
- 1 teaspoon salt

Directions:
1. In the slow cooker, mix the kale with shrimp and the other ingredients, toss and close the lid.
2. Cook meat for 2 hours on High.
3. Divide into bowls and serve.

Nutrition value/serving: calories 300, fat 7.1, fiber 1.1, carbs 7.6, protein 5.3

Bacon and Zucchinis

Prep time: 10 minutes
Cooking time: 5 hours
Servings: 4
Ingredients:
- 1-pound zucchinis, roughly cubed
- 5 oz bacon, chopped
- 1 teaspoon sweet paprika
- 1 teaspoon minced garlic
- 1 teaspoon salt
- 1 teaspoon ground black pepper
- 1/2 cup Cheddar cheese, shredded
- ¼ cup heavy cream
- 1 teaspoon butter

Directions:
1. Grease the slow cooker with the butter and arrange all the ingredients except the cheese.
2. Sprinkle the cheese on top.
3. Close the lid and cook it for 5 hours on Low.

Nutrition value/serving: calories 312, fat 13.2, fiber 0.7, carbs 3.6, protein 14.6

Sausage Stew

Prep time: 10 minutes
Cooking time: 3.5 hours
Servings: 4
Ingredients:
- 7 oz sausages, sliced
- 3 spring onions, chopped
- 1 tomato, chopped
- 1 tablespoon Cajun seasonings
- 1 cup of water
- 1 cup keto tomato sauce
- 1 teaspoon minced garlic
- 1 teaspoon olive oil

Directions:

1. In the slow cooker, combine the sausages with the spring onions and the other ingredients and toss.
2. Close the lid and cook gumbo for 3 hours and 30 minutes.
Nutrition value/serving: calories 329, fat 24, fiber 1.5, carbs 3.4, protein 17.5

Garlic Chicken Mix
Prep time: 15 minutes
Cooking time: 3 hours
Servings: 2
Ingredients:
- 1-pound chicken breast, skinless, boneless and roughly cubed
- 1 jalapeno pepper, chopped
- 1 poblano pepper, chopped
- 2 spring onions, chopped
- 1 cup cherry tomatoes, halved
- 1 teaspoon chili flakes
- ½ teaspoon salt
- 1 teaspoon coriander, ground
- 1 cup of water
- 4 garlic cloves, minced

Directions:
1. In the slow cooker, mix the chicken with jalapeno and poblano pepper and the other ingredients and toss.
2. Close the lid and cook chicken on High for 3 hours.
3. Stir the meal well before serving.
Nutrition value/serving: calories 285, fat 5.1, fiber 4, carbs 11.4, protein 32.3

Shrimp and Tomatoes
Prep time: 20 minutes
Cooking time: 2 hours
Servings: 7
Ingredients:
- 1-pound shrimp, peeled and deveined
- 1 avocado, peeled, pitted
- 1 teaspoon chili flakes
- 1 teaspoon salt
- 1 teaspoon chili powder
- 1 cup cherry tomatoes, halved
- 1 cup fresh cilantro, chopped

Directions:
1. In the slow cooker, mix the shrimp with the avocado and the other ingredients, put the lid on and cook on High for 2 hours.
2. Divide into bowls and serve.

Nutrition value/serving: calories 280, fat 5.7, fiber 3.6, carbs 6.5, protein 7.7

Spiced Chicken
Prep time: 15 minutes
Cooking time: 3.5 hours
Servings: 3
Ingredients:
- 3 chicken thighs, boneless, skinless
- 1 teaspoon cumin, ground
- 1 teaspoon coriander, ground
- 1 teaspoon nutmeg, ground
- 1 jalapeno pepper, sliced
- 1 teaspoon minced garlic
- 1 teaspoon ground cinnamon
- ½ teaspoon chili flakes
- 1/3 cup water
- 1 teaspoon olive oil

Directions:
1. In the slow cooker, mix the chicken with cumin, coriander and the rest of the ingredients.
2. Close the lid and cook chicken for 3.5 hours on High.
3. Divide into bowls and serve.
Nutrition value/serving: calories 301, fat 12.4, fiber 1.5, carbs 8.8, protein 22.8

Sugar Snap Peas Soup
Prep time: 15 minutes
Cooking time: 3 hours
Servings: 4
Ingredients:
- 2 cups sugar snap peas
- ½ cup celery stalk, chopped
- 1 teaspoon garlic, diced
- 3 cups of water
- 1 teaspoon chili powder
- 1 teaspoon salt
- 1 tablespoon chives, chopped
- ½ teaspoon thyme
- 1 teaspoon olive oil

Directions:
1. Grease the slow cooker with the oil and combine all the ingredients inside.
2. Close the lid and cook soup for 3 hours on High.
Nutrition value/serving: calories 226, fat 5.8, fiber 1.8, carbs 6.3, protein 6.3

Ginger Lamb
Prep time: 15 minutes

Cooking time: 5 hours
Servings: 2
Ingredients:
- 1-pound lamb fillet, chopped
- ½ teaspoon fresh ginger
- 1 tablespoon butter, soft
- 2 scallions, minced
- 1 cup coconut cream
- ½ cup water
- 1 teaspoon paprika
- ½ teaspoon cumin
- 1 teaspoon salt
- ½ teaspoon ground coriander

Directions:
1. Heat up a pan with the butter over medium-high heat, add the lamb, brown for 5 minutes and transfer to the slow cooker.
2. Add the rest of the ingredients, toss and close the lid.
3. Cook the meat for 5 hours on High.
4. Divide into bowls and serve.

Nutrition value/serving: calories 456, fat 19, fiber 0.9, carbs 2.8, protein 65

Balsamic Beef

Prep time: 15 minutes
Cooking time: 9 hours
Servings: 3
Ingredients:
- 3 tablespoons balsamic vinegar
- 1 teaspoon tahini paste
- ½ teaspoon minced garlic
- 1 teaspoon olive oil
- 1/3 teaspoon grated ginger
- ½ teaspoon white pepper
- 1 tablespoon coconut cream
- 1-pound beef sirloin, chopped

Directions:
1. In the slow cooker, mix the beef with the vinegar and the other ingredients.
2. Close the lid and cook the beef for 9 hours on High.
3. Divide into bowls and serve.

Nutrition value/serving: calories 392, fat 13, fiber 4.4, carbs 3.1, protein 46.4

Side Dishes

Spinach Mix
Prep time: 10 minutes
Cooking time: 4 hours
Servings: 4
Ingredients:
- 3 cups spinach, chopped
- 1 cup organic coconut milk
- 4 oz Parmesan, grated
- 1 teaspoon olive oil
- 1 cup fresh cilantro, chopped

Directions:
1. In the slow cooker, mix the spinach with the milk and the other ingredients, toss and close the lid.
2. Cook the dip on Low for 4 hours.

Nutrition value/serving: calories 241, fat 7.5, fiber 2.4, carbs 5.5, protein 5.4

Tomato and Spaghetti Squash
Prep time: 10 minutes
Cooking time: 3 hours
Servings: 4
Ingredients:
- 10 oz spaghetti squash, halved
- 1 cup cherry tomatoes, halved
- 1 teaspoon sweet paprika
- 2 oz Parmesan
- 1 teaspoon butter
- ½ teaspoon garlic powder
- ½ teaspoon turmeric powder
- ½ cup of water

Directions:
1. Pour water in the slow cooker.
2. Add spaghetti squash and cook it on High for 3 hours.
3. When the squash is soft, it is cooked.
4. Shred the vegetable with the help of the fork.
5. In the shallow bowl, mix the spaghetti squash with the remaining ingredients, toss and serve.

Nutrition value/serving: calories 178, fat 4.4, fiber 3.1, carbs 5.8, protein 5.1

Hot Green Beans
Prep time: 10 minutes
Cooking time: 1 hour
Servings: 5
Ingredients:
- 1-pound green beans, chopped
- 1 teaspoon chili powder
- 1 teaspoon hot paprika
- 1 teaspoon curry powder
- 1 tablespoon sesame oil
- 1 tablespoon Erythritol
- 1 cup of water

Directions:
1. In the slow cooker, mix the green beans with chili powder and the other ingredients, close the lid and cook on High for 1 hour.
2. Divide between plates and serve.

Nutrition value/serving: calories 56, fat 3.1, fiber 3.2, carbs 9.6, protein 1.8

Butter Zucchini
Prep time: 5 minutes
Cooking time: 15 minutes
Servings: 3
Ingredients:
- 1 cup zucchinis, sliced
- 1 teaspoon oregano, dried
- 1 teaspoon turmeric powder
- 2 tablespoons butter
- 1/3 cup heavy cream
- 1 teaspoon salt

Directions:
1. In the slow cooker, mix the zucchinis with the oregano and the other ingredients, toss and close the lid.
2. Cook the green peas for 15 minutes on High.

Nutrition value/serving: calories 134, fat 5.9, fiber 2.6, carbs 7.6, protein 3

Dill Broccoli
Prep time: 10 minutes
Cooking time: 1.5 hour
Servings: 4
Ingredients:
- 2 cups broccoli florets
- 2 tablespoons fresh dill, chopped
- 2 tablespoons butter
- 1 teaspoon basil, dried
- 1 teaspoon oregano, dried
- ½ cup heavy cream
- ¼ teaspoon ground nutmeg

Directions:
1. In the slow cooker, mix the broccoli with the dill and the other ingredients.

2. Close the lid and cook the vegetables on High for 1.5 hours on High.
3. When the time is over, divide between plates and serve.
Nutrition value/serving: calories 120, fat 6.5, fiber 1.5, carbs 4, protein 4.7

Tomato and Radish
Prep time: 10 minutes
Cooking time: 4 hours
Servings: 4
Ingredients:
- 2 cups radish, trimmed and halved
- 2 cups cherry tomatoes, halved
- 1 teaspoon oregano, dried
- ½ cup of water
- 1 teaspoon salt
- 1 teaspoon butter

Directions:
1. In the slow cooker, mix the radishes with the tomatoes and the other ingredients.
2. Close the lid and cook radish on Low for 4 hours.
3. Divide between plates and serve.
Nutrition value/serving: calories 109, fat 3.2, fiber 1.2, carbs 2.4, protein 0.4

Balsamic Leeks
Prep time: 10 minutes
Cooking time: 4.5 hours
Servings: 2
Ingredients:
- 1 cup leeks, roughly sliced
- 1 tablespoon rosemary, chopped
- 1 tablespoon balsamic vinegar
- ¾ teaspoon ground thyme
- ¼ cup of water
- 1 teaspoon olive oil

Directions:
1. In the slow cooker, mix the leeks with the rosemary and the other ingredients.
2. Close the slow cooker lid and cook side dish for 4.5 hours on High.
Nutrition value/serving: calories 162, fat 3.1, fiber 2.9, carbs 4.6, protein 4.1

Rosemary Cauliflower
Prep time: 10 minutes
Cooking time: 3 hours
Servings: 7
Ingredients:
- 1-pound cauliflower florets
- 1 teaspoon turmeric powder
- 1 tablespoon rosemary, chopped
- 1 teaspoon curry powder
- 2 tablespoons butter
- 3 tablespoons almond milk

Directions:
1. In the slow cooker, mix the cauliflower with the turmeric and the other ingredients, toss and put the lid on.
2. Cook the vegetables for 3 hours on High.
3. Divide between plates and serve.
Nutrition value/serving: calories 111, fat 4.5, fiber 1.7, carbs 4.3, protein 1.2

Butter Mushrooms
Prep time: 10 minutes
Cooking time: 3.5 hours
Servings: 2
Ingredients:
- 1 cup cremini mushrooms
- 3 tablespoons butter, melted
- 1 tablespoon turmeric powder
- 1 teaspoon black pepper
- 1 teaspoon coriander, ground
- 1 teaspoon salt

Directions:
1. In the slow cooker, mix the mushrooms with the other ingredients.
2. Cook the side dish for 3.5 hours on Low.
Nutrition value/serving: calories 214, fat 11.4, fiber 3.2, carbs 2.3, protein 1.1

Paprika Green Beans
Prep time: 10 minutes
Cooking time: 1 hour
Servings: 2
Ingredients:
- 2 teaspoons sweet paprika
- 7 oz green beans, halved
- 1 tablespoon butter
- ¼ cup of water
- 1 teaspoon salt
- ½ teaspoon cumin, ground
- 1 teaspoon black pepper
- 1 teaspoon apple cider vinegar

Directions:
1. In the slow cooker, mix the green beans with the paprika and the other ingredients, toss and close the lid.
2. Cook the green beans on High for 1 hour.
3. Divide between plates and serve.

Nutrition value/serving: calories 200, fat 7.9, fiber 4.9, carbs 7.1, protein 6.3

Spicy Kale

Prep time: 10 minutes
Cooking time: 2.5 hours
Servings: 3
Ingredients:
- 2 cups kale, chopped
- 4 oz Mozzarella balls, sliced
- 1/3 cup coconut cream
- 1 teaspoon keto tomato sauce

Directions:
1. In the slow cooker, mix the kale with the remaining ingredients.
2. Close the lid and cook spinach on Low for 2.5 hours.

Nutrition value/serving: calories 202, fat 8.5, fiber 0.5, carbs 1.5, protein 6.6

Mushroom and Kale

Prep time: 8 minutes
Cooking time: 3 hours
Servings: 2
Ingredients:
- 1 tablespoon chives, chopped
- 1 cup kale, chopped
- 1 cup mushrooms, sliced
- 1/3 cup coconut milk
- 1 tablespoon almond butter
- ½ teaspoon salt
- 1 teaspoon curry powder

Directions:
1. In the slow cooker, mix the kale with mushrooms and the other ingredients.
2. Close the lid and cook for 3 hours on Low.
3. Divide between plates and serve.

Nutrition value/serving: calories 225, fat 11.5, fiber 5.1, carbs 9.1, protein 11.2

Creamy Green Beans

Prep time: 10 minutes
Cooking time: 2 hours
Servings: 4
Ingredients:
- 2 cups green beans, trimmed and halved
- 1 tablespoon tahini paste
- 1 teaspoon turmeric powder
- 1 red chili, minced
- ½ teaspoon salt
- 1 teaspoon olive oil
- 1/3 cup heavy cream

Directions:
1. Put green beans in the slow cooker.
2. Add the rest of the ingredients and put the lid on.
3. Cook the mix for 2 hours on High.
4. Put in the serving bowls.

Nutrition value/serving: calories 134, fat 5.9, fiber 3.1, carbs 6.3, protein 6.7

Artichoke and Broccoli Mix

Prep time: 10 minutes
Cooking time: 5 hours
Servings: 4
Ingredients:
- 4 tablespoons lemon juice
- 2 artichokes, trimmed and halved
- 1 cup broccoli florets
- 1 teaspoon tahini paste
- ½ teaspoon sweet paprika
- 3 tablespoons olive oil
- ½ teaspoon salt
- ½ garlic clove, minced
- 1/4 cup water

1. In the slow cooker, mix the artichokes with the broccoli and the other ingredients and close the lid.
2. Cook the vegetable for 5 hours on Low.
3. Divide between plates and serve.

Nutrition value/serving: calories 142, fat 11.2, fiber 4.6, carbs 9.5, protein 3

Collard Greens and Mushrooms

Prep time: 10 minutes
Cooking time: 3.5 hours
Servings: 4
Ingredients:
- 9 oz collard greens, trimmed, chopped
- 2 spring onions, chopped
- 1 cup white mushrooms, sliced
- 1 cup of water
- 1 teaspoon salt
- 1 teaspoon chili powder
- 1 teaspoon olive oil

Directions:
1. In the slow cooker, mix the greens with mushrooms and the other ingredients and close the slow cooker lid.
2. Cook the greens for 3.5 hours on High.
3. Divide into bowls and serve.

Nutrition value/serving: calories 184, fat 7.5, fiber 4.8, carbs 7.6, protein 5.8

Lime Zucchini Noodles
Prep time: 10 minutes
Cooking time: 1 hour and 30 minutes
Servings: 4
Ingredients:
- 7 oz zucchini noodles
- 1 tablespoon balsamic vinegar
- 1 tablespoon lime juice
- ¼ teaspoon sweet paprika
- ½ teaspoon salt
- 1/3 cup water
- 1 teaspoon butter

Directions:
1. In the slow cooker, mix the noodles with the vinegar and the other ingredients.
2. Put the lid on and cook noodles for 1.5 hours on Low.
3. Divide between plates and serve.

Nutrition value/serving: calories 120, fat 5.1, fiber 5.3, carbs 0.1, protein 3.4

Swiss Chard Mix
Prep time: 10 minutes
Cooking time: 2.5 hours
Servings: 4
Ingredients:
- 11 oz Swiss chard, chopped
- 5 oz bacon, chopped
- 1 tablespoon butter
- 1 teaspoon turmeric powder
- 1 teaspoon coriander, ground
- ½ cup of water
- ½ teaspoon ground black pepper

Directions:
1. In the slow cooker, mix the chard with the bacon and the other ingredients,
2. Close the slow cooker lid and cook the casserole for 2.5 hours on High.

Nutrition value/serving: calories 283, fat 14.7, fiber 1.4, carbs 4.5, protein 14.2

Green Beans and Tomato Casserole
Prep time: 15 minutes
Cooking time: 6 hours
Servings: 6
Ingredients:
- 8 oz green beans, chopped
- 3 oz tomatoes, cubed
- 4 oz Mozzarella, shredded
- 1 tablespoon Ricotta cheese
- ¼ cup keto tomato sauce
- 1 tablespoon butter, melted
- 1 teaspoon oregano, dried
- ½ teaspoon smoked paprika
- ¼ cup heavy cream

Directions:
1. Pour butter in the slow cooker.
2. Combine the green beans with tomatoes and the other ingredients except the Mozzarella and toss.
3. Then pour the Mozzarella and close the slow cooker lid.
4. Cook the casserole for 6 hours on Low.

Nutrition value/serving: calories 249, fat 11.7, fiber 1.5, carbs 7.5, protein 14.6

Parsley and Tomato Green Beans
Prep time: 10 minutes
Cooking time: 7 hours
Servings: 3
Ingredients:
- 1 ½ cup green beans, trimmed and halved
- 2 tablespoons fresh parsley, chopped
- 1 tablespoon rosemary, chopped
- 1/3 cup keto tomato sauce
- 1 teaspoon chili pepper
- 1 teaspoon butter
- 1 teaspoon salt
- 1 teaspoon black pepper

Directions:
1. In the slow cooker, mix the green beans with the parsley and the other ingredients.
2. Close the slow cooker lid and cook chili on Low for 7 hours.
3. Divide between plates and serve.

Nutrition value/serving: calories 228, fat 12.7, fiber 5.1, carbs 11.1, protein 14.6

Paprika Peppers
Prep time: 20 minutes
Cooking time: 3 hours
Servings: 4
Ingredients:
- 1 cup red bell peppers, cut into strips
- 1 cup green bell peppers, cut into strips
- 1 teaspoon keto tomato sauce
- 1 teaspoon hot paprika

- 1 teaspoon salt
- 2 spring onions, chopped
- ½ teaspoon ground black pepper
- ½ cup of coconut milk

Directions:
1. In the slow cooker, mix the peppers with the paprika and the other ingredients and close the lid.
2. Cook the peppers for 3 hours on Low.

Nutrition value/serving: calories 206, fat 7.4, fiber 3.7, carbs 10.2, protein 4.5

Cabbage and Tomatoes

Prep time: 10 minutes
Cooking time: 2 hours
Servings: 4
Ingredients:
- 1-pound white cabbage, shredded
- ½ pound cherry tomatoes, halved
- ½ cup keto tomato sauce
- ½ jalapeno pepper
- 1 teaspoon cumin, ground
- 1 teaspoon coriander, ground
- 1 teaspoon garlic, diced
- 1 teaspoon chili flakes
- 1 teaspoon salt
- ½ teaspoon olive oil

Directions:
1. In the slow cooker, mix the cabbage with the tomatoes and the other ingredients.
2. Close the lid and cook it for 2 hours on High.

Nutrition value/serving: calories 129, fat 1.2, fiber 3.8, carbs 4.1, protein 4.5

Zucchini and Cabbage

Prep time: 10 minutes
Cooking time: 1 hour and 30 minutes
Servings: 3
Ingredients:
- 10 oz zucchini, trimmed
- 1 cup cabbage, shredded
- ¼ cup heavy cream
- 1 teaspoon chili powder
- ½ teaspoon turmeric
- ½ teaspoon butter
- 1 teaspoon garam masala

Directions:
1. In the slow cooker, mix the zucchinis with the cabbage and the other ingredients.
2. Close the lid and cook side dish for 1 hour and 30 minutes on High.

Nutrition value/serving: calories 164, fat 8.1, fiber 2.2, carbs 5.3, protein 4.1

Zucchini and Radish Mix

Prep time: 15 minutes
Cooking time: 2 hours
Servings: 4
Ingredients:
- 2 zucchinis, trimmed and sliced
- 1 cup radishes, halved
- ¼ cup of veggie stock
- 1 tablespoon butter
- ½ teaspoon salt
- ½ teaspoon ground black pepper
- 1 tablespoon chives, chopped

Directions:
1. In the slow cooker, combine all the ingredients and toss gently.
2. Close the slow cooker lid and cook a meal for 2 hours on Low.

Nutrition value/serving: calories 157, fat 6.1, fiber 1.2, carbs 3.7, protein 6.5

Thyme Mushrooms

Prep time: 15 minutes
Cooking time: 2 hours
Servings: 4
Ingredients:
- 10 oz mushrooms, halved
- 1 tablespoon thyme
- ½ cup chicken stock
- 1 teaspoon black pepper
- ½ teaspoon salt

Directions:
1. In the slow cooker, mix all the ingredients, toss and close the lid.
2. Cook the mix for 2 hours on High.
3. When the side dish is cooked, shake it well.

Nutrition value/serving: calories 158, fat 3.3, fiber 1, carbs 2.9, protein 1

Mint Peppers

Prep time: 10 minutes
Cooking time: 8 hours
Servings: 5
Ingredients:
- ½ cup crushed tomatoes
- 2 green bell peppers, roughly chopped
- 2 red bell peppers, roughly chopped
- 2 teaspoons mint, dried
- 1 teaspoon curry powder

- ½ teaspoon turmeric
- 1 teaspoon chili flakes
- ¼ cup of water

Directions:
1. In the slow cooker, mix the peppers with tomatoes and the other ingredients.
2. Close the slow cooker lid and cook for 8 hours on Low.
3. Divide into bowls and serve.

Nutrition value/serving: calories 31, fat 0.4, fiber 2.3, carbs 8.1, protein 1.7

Garlic Green Beans

Prep time: 10 minutes
Cooking time: 3.5 hours
Servings: 4
Ingredients:
- 1-pound green beans, trimmed and halved
- 4 teaspoons minced garlic
- 4 teaspoons olive oil
- 1 tablespoon salt
- 1 teaspoon chili powder
- 1 teaspoon dried oregano
- 1/2 cup veggie stock

Directions:
1. In the slow cooker, mix the green beans with the garlic and the other ingredients and close the lid.
2. Cook the artichokes on High for 3.5 hours.

Nutrition value/serving: calories 217, fat 4.9, fiber 7.4, carbs 7.6, protein 4.5

Asparagus and Onion Mix

Prep time: 10 minutes
Cooking time: 3 hours
Servings: 4
Ingredients:
- 1 cup spring onions, chopped
- 12 oz asparagus, chopped
- ½ cup heavy cream
- 1 teaspoon salt
- 1 teaspoon ground black pepper
- 1 tablespoon chives, chopped

Directions:
1. In the slow cooker, mix the asparagus with the spring onions and the other ingredients, toss and close the lid.
2. Cook the casserole for 3 hours on High.

Nutrition value/serving: calories 233, fat 7, fiber 2.6, carbs 7.3, protein 4.7

Tofu and Green Beans

Prep time: 15 minutes
Cooking time: 7.5 hours
Servings: 6
Ingredients:
- 1 teaspoon cumin seeds
- ½ teaspoon sweet paprika
- 1 teaspoon salt
- 1 teaspoon keto tomato sauce
- 1 teaspoon chili flakes
- 1 teaspoon rosemary, dried
- 7 oz firm tofu, cubed
- 7 oz green beans, halved
- ½ cup crushed tomatoes
- 1 chili pepper, chopped
- 1 tablespoon almond butter

Directions:
1. In the slow cooker, combine the tofu with green beans and the other ingredients.
2. Close the lid and cook for 7.5 hours on Low.

Nutrition value/serving: calories 132, fat 3.3, fiber 3.5, carbs 7.4, protein 5.3

Lime Cauliflower

Prep time: 10 minutes
Cooking time: 4 hours
Servings: 2
Ingredients:
- 1 ½ cup cauliflower, shredded
- 1 teaspoon sweet paprika
- ½ teaspoon chili flakes
- ½ teaspoon salt
- ½ teaspoon ground black pepper
- 1/2 cup coconut cream
- 1 teaspoon lime juice
- 1 teaspoon lime zest, grated
- 1 teaspoon butter

Directions:
1. In the slow cooker, mix the cauliflower with the paprika, chili and the other ingredients
2. Close the lid and cook for 4 hours on High.

Nutrition value/serving: calories 158, fat 4, fiber 2.5, carbs 5.4, protein 6.9

Oregano Green Beans

Prep time: 10 minutes
Cooking time: 6 hours
Servings: 4

Ingredients:
- 2 cups green beans, trimmed and halved
- ½ cup coconut cream
- 1 teaspoon turmeric powder
- 1 teaspoon rosemary, dried
- 1 teaspoon salt
- ¾ teaspoon dried oregano

Directions:
1. In the slow cooker, mix the peas with the cream and the other ingredients.
2. Close the slow cooker lid and cook for 6 hours on Low.
3. Divide between plates and serve.

Nutrition value/serving: calories 167, fat 4.5, fiber 4, carbs 10.9, protein 5.2

Masala Broccoli

Prep time: 10 minutes
Cooking time: 6 hours
Servings: 4
Ingredients:
- 2 cups broccoli florets
- 1 tablespoon garam masala
- 2 spring onions, chopped
- 1 teaspoon curry powder
- ½ teaspoon chili pepper
- ½ cup organic almond milk

Directions:
1. In the slow cooker, mix the broccoli with the masala and the other ingredients.
2. Close the lid and cook korma for 6 hours on low.
3. Divide between plates and serve.

Nutrition value/serving: calories 102, fat 8, fiber 2.9, carbs 7.4, protein 2.3

Curry Mushrooms

Prep time: 10 minutes
Cooking time: 4 hours
Servings: 2
Ingredients:
- 1-pound white mushrooms, halved
- 1 cup of coconut milk
- 1 teaspoon curry paste
- 1 teaspoon garam masala
- 1 teaspoon coriander, ground
- 1 teaspoon dill, chopped
- 1 teaspoon olive oil

Directions:
1. In the slow cooker, mix the mushrooms with coconut milk, curry paste and the other ingredients, toss and close the lid.
2. Cook the side dish for 4 hours on High.

Nutrition value/serving: calories 213, fat 7.9, fiber 4.1, carbs 7.5, protein 4.5

Celery Puree

Prep time: 10 minutes
Cooking time: 3 hours
Servings: 3
Ingredients:
- 1 cup celery stalks, chopped
- 2 tablespoons butter
- 1 teaspoon sweet paprika
- 1 teaspoon chives, chopped
- ½ cup of water

Directions:
1. Put celery and water in the slow cooker.
2. Close the lid and cook it for 3 hours on High.
3. Then drain water and mash until you get soft mash.
4. Add the rest of the ingredients, whisk and serve.

Nutrition value/serving: calories 151, fat 6.8, fiber 2.2, carbs 8, protein 0.6

Coconut Celery

Prep time: 15 minutes
Cooking time: 2 hours
Servings: 2
Ingredients:
- 7 oz celery stalks, roughly chopped
- 1 teaspoon fresh parsley
- 1/3 cup coconut cream
- ½ teaspoon salt

Directions:
1. In the slow cooker, mix the celery stalks with the other ingredients.
2. Then close the lid and cook the vegetable for 2 hours on High.
3. Divide between plates and serve.

Nutrition value/serving: calories 67, fat 2.8, fiber 2.8, carbs 9.7, protein 2

Rosemary Bok Choy

Prep time: 8 minutes
Cooking time: 8 hours
Servings: 4
Ingredients:
- 8 oz bok choy, chopped
- 1 cup spring onions, chopped
- 1 teaspoon curry powder
- ½ jalapeno pepper, chopped

- 1 tablespoon keto tomato sauce
- ½ cup chicken stock
- 1 teaspoon almond butter
- 1 tablespoon rosemary

Directions:
1. In the slow cooker, mix the bok choy with the spring onions and the other ingredients.
2. Close the slow cooker lid and cook the mix for 8 hours on Low.
3. Divide between plates and serve.

Nutrition value/serving: calories 49, fat 2.6, fiber 2, carbs 5.4, protein 2.7

Coconut Radish Mix

Prep time: 10 minutes
Cooking time: 4 hours
Servings: 2
Ingredients:
- 1 cup radishes, halved
- ½ cup coconut cream
- 1 tablespoon dried rosemary
- 1 tablespoon butter
- 1 teaspoon black pepper
- ½ teaspoon salt

Directions:
1. In the slow cooker, mix the radishes with the cream and the other ingredients.
2. Close the lid and cook the mix for 4 hours on Low.

Nutrition value/serving: calories 82, fat 6.2, fiber 2.5, carbs 6.8, protein 1

Okra and Artichokes

Prep time: 10 minutes
Cooking time: 6 hours
Servings: 4
Ingredients:
- 9 oz okra, sliced
- 2 artichokes, trimmed and quartered
- 1 jalapeno, sliced
- 2 tablespoons chives, chopped
- 1 teaspoon ground black pepper
- ¾ cup heavy cream

Directions:
1. In the slow cooker, mix the okra with the artichokes and the other ingredients,
2. Close the slow cooker lid and cook the mix for 6 hours on Low.

Nutrition value/serving: calories 182, fat 5.6, fiber 2.7, carbs 7.4, protein 10.6

Red Cabbage Sauté

Prep time: 15 minutes
Cooking time: 7 hours
Servings: 4
Ingredients:
- 1-pound red cabbage, shredded
- ½ cup of veggie stock
- 1 teaspoon sweet paprika
- 1 teaspoon curry powder
- 1 teaspoon black pepper
- 1 bay leaf
- 1 teaspoon salt

Directions:
1. In the slow cooker, mix all the ingredients and toss.
2. Close the lid and cook red cabbage for 7 hours on Low.
3. Mix up the cabbage well before serving.

Nutrition value/serving: calories 200, fat 7.1, fiber 4.3, carbs 9.9, protein 3.2

Broccoli and Cauliflower Bake

Prep time: 15 minutes
Cooking time: 8 hours
Servings: 4
Ingredients:
- 2 cups broccoli florets
- 2 cups cauliflower florets
- 4 eggs, beaten
- 5 oz Cheddar cheese, shredded
- ½ cup coconut milk
- 1 teaspoon turmeric powder
- ½ teaspoon salt

Directions:
1. In the slow cooker, mix the broccoli with cauliflower and the other ingredients except the cheese and toss.
2. Sprinkle the cheese on top.
3. Close the lid and cook the mix for 8 hours on Low.

Nutrition value/serving: calories 242, fat 17.6, fiber 1.8, carbs 4.8, protein 12.4

Nutmeg Artichokes

Prep time: 10 minutes
Cooking time: 2.5 hours
Servings: 2
Ingredients:
- 2 artichokes, trimmed and halved
- 3 tablespoons coconut cream

- 1 teaspoon ground cinnamon
- ¾ teaspoon ground nutmeg
- ½ teaspoon salt
- 1/3 cup organic almond milk

Directions:
1. In the slow cooker, mix the artichokes with the cream and the other ingredients.
2. Close the lid and cook the pudding on High for 2.5 hours.

Nutrition value/serving: calories 202, fat 5.2, fiber 4.7, carbs 9.2, protein 7.4

Eggplants and Olives

Prep time: 20 minutes
Cooking time: 4 hours
Servings: 7
Ingredients:
- 3 eggplants, trimmed and roughly cubed
- ½ cup black olives, pitted and halved
- 1/2 cup keto marinara sauce
- 1 tablespoon cilantro, chopped
- 1 teaspoon salt
- 1 teaspoon dried oregano

Directions:
1. In the slow cooker, mix the eggplants with the olives and the other ingredients.
2. Close the lid and cook the dish for 4 hours on High.

Nutrition value/serving: calories 207, fat 9.3, fiber 5.9, carbs 16.1, protein 16.6

Green Beans and Radishes

Prep time: 7 minutes
Cooking time: 3 hours
Servings: 2
Ingredients:
- 1 cup radishes, halved
- 1 teaspoon rosemary, dried
- 1 teaspoon oregano, dried
- 1/2-pound green beans, trimmed and halved
- 1 teaspoon garlic powder
- ¾ teaspoon salt
- 1 tablespoon coconut oil
- Cooking spray

Directions:
1. Spray the slow cooker with cooking spray from inside and combine all the veggies inside.
2. Close the lid and cook the mix for 3 hours on High.

Nutrition value/serving: calories 120, fat 4.9, fiber 2.1, carbs 7.5, protein 1.9

Swiss Chard Saute

Prep time: 10 minutes
Cooking time: 2 hours
Servings: 2
Ingredients:
- 2 cups Swiss chard, trimmed, chopped
- ¼ cup cream cheese
- 1 teaspoon butter
- ½ teaspoon salt
- ½ teaspoon turmeric
- 1 teaspoon garlic powder
- 1 teaspoon white pepper
- 1 teaspoon basil, dried

Directions:
1. In the slow cooker, mix the chard with the cream cheese and the other ingredients.
2. Close the lid.
3. Cook the side dish for 2 hours on High.

Nutrition value/serving: calories 225, fat 12.4, fiber 0.8, carbs 3.9, protein 7.5

Glazed Leeks

Prep time: 10 minutes
Cooking time: 1.5 hours
Servings: 2
Ingredients:
- 3 leeks, roughly sliced
- 1 teaspoon sweet paprika
- 1 teaspoon butter, melted
- 1 teaspoon stevia
- ½ teaspoon ground nutmeg

Directions:
1. In the slow cooker, mix the leeks with paprika and the other ingredients and close the lid.
2. Cook the parsnip for 1.5 hours on High.

Nutrition value/serving: calories 115, fat 4.2, fiber 2.7, carbs 4.4, protein 4.4

Oregano Beans and Cucumber

Prep time: 5 minutes
Cooking time: 2 hours
Servings: 4
Ingredients:
- 1 ½ cup green beans, trimmed and halved
- 1 cup cucumber, sliced
- 1 teaspoon mint, dried

- 1 tablespoon dried oregano
- ½ cup chicken stock
- 1 teaspoon salt

Directions:
1. In the slow cooker, mix the green beans with all the other ingredients.
2. Close the slow cooker lid and cook the side dish for 2 hours on Low.
3. Serve the snap beans right away.

Nutrition value/serving: calories 117, fat 2.2, fiber 1.9, carbs 3.8, protein 1

Chard and Radishes

Prep time: 5 minutes
Cooking time: 4 hours
Servings: 4
Ingredients:
- 2 cups red chard, torn
- 1 cup radishes, halved
- 1 teaspoon sweet paprika
- ¼ cup butter
- 1 teaspoon salt
- ¼ teaspoon ground ginger
- 1/4 cup veggie stock

Directions:
1. In the slow cooker, mix the chard with radishes and the other ingredients
2. Close the slow cooker lid and cook the beet greens for 4 hours on High.
3. Mix up the mix carefully before serving.

Nutrition value/serving: calories 122, fat 4.7, fiber 2.1, carbs 6.5, protein 4.5

Bok Choy and Radishes

Prep time: 10 minutes
Cooking time: 5 hours
Servings: 2
Ingredients:
- 1 cup bok choy, chopped
- 1 tablespoon balsamic vinegar
- 1 cup radishes, halved
- 1 teaspoon olive oil
- 3 tablespoons coconut cream
- 1 teaspoon salt
- 1 tablespoon lime juice
- 1 teaspoon paprika

Directions:
1. In the slow cooker, mix the bok choy with the radishes and the other ingredients, toss and close the lid.
2. Cook the side dish for 5 hours on Low.
3. Divide between plates and serve.

Nutrition value/serving: calories 121, fat 3.6, fiber 1.5, carbs 3.7, protein 1.5

Mushroom Stew

Prep time: 15 minutes
Cooking time: 3.5 hours
Servings: 4
Ingredients:
- 1 cup white mushrooms, chopped
- 1 green bell pepper, chopped
- 1 red bell pepper, chopped
- 1 cup radishes, halved
- 1 cup avocado, peeled, pitted and cubed
- 1 tomato, chopped
- 1 teaspoon butter
- 1 teaspoon ground coriander
- 1/3 cup chicken stock
- 1 teaspoon salt

Directions:
1. In the slow cooker, mix the mushrooms with the peppers and the other ingredients.
2. Close the slow cooker lid and cook the stew on High for 3.5 hours.

Nutrition value/serving: calories 215, fat 5.2, fiber 3.8, carbs 7.5, protein 1.1

Herbed Mushrooms

Prep time: 20 minutes
Cooking time: 2 hours
Servings: 4
Ingredients:
- 1 cup white mushrooms, halved
- 4 tablespoons lemon juice
- 1 tablespoon chives, chopped
- 1 tablespoon oregano, chopped
- 1 tablespoon basil, chopped
- ½ teaspoon salt
- ½ teaspoon peppercorns
- 1/4 cup veggie stock

Directions:
1. In the slow cooker, mix the mushrooms with the lemon juice and the other ingredients.
2. Cook on High for 2 hours.

Nutrition value/serving: calories 212, fat 4.2, fiber 3.6, carbs 7.2, protein 0.6

Leeks and Cauliflower Mash

Prep time: 10 minutes
Cooking time: 4 hours
Servings: 2
Ingredients:

- 1 cup leeks, chopped
- 1 cup cauliflower florets
- 1 tablespoon coconut cream
- 1 teaspoon turmeric powder
- 1 teaspoon curry powder
- ½ teaspoon ground black pepper
- ½ teaspoon salt
- ½ cup of water

Directions:
1. Put leeks, cauliflower, salt and water in the slow cooker.
2. Close the lid and cook for 4 hours on Low.
3. Then drain water.
4. Mash the mix, add the rest of the ingredients, whisk and serve.

Nutrition value/serving: calories 189, fat 4.3, fiber 5.4, carbs 9.5, protein 6.5

Cherry Tomatoes Sauté

Prep time: 10 minutes
Cooking time: 3 hours
Servings: 4
Ingredients:
- 2 cups cherry tomatoes, halved
- 1/2 cup veggie stock
- 1 teaspoon salt
- 1 teaspoon chili flakes
- 1 teaspoon dried oregano
- ¼ teaspoon ground nutmeg
- 1 tablespoon keto tomato sauce

Directions:
1. In the slow cooker, mix the tomatoes and the other ingredients.
2. Then close the slow cooker lid and cook soybeans on High for 2 hours.
3. Divide between plates and serve.

Nutrition value/serving: calories 201, fat 7, fiber 1.7, carbs 8.8, protein 7.9

Ginger Peppers

Prep time: 10 minutes
Cooking time: 1 hour
Servings: 2
Ingredients:
- 4 red bell peppers, cut into strips
- 1 teaspoon ground ginger
- 1/2 cup veggie stock
- 1 teaspoon sweet paprika
- 1 teaspoon butter
- ½ teaspoon salt

Directions:
1. In the slow cooker, mix the peppers with the ginger and the other ingredients.
2. Close the lid and cook for 1 hour on High.

Nutrition value/serving: calories 162, fat 3.9, fiber 0.1, carbs 4.3, protein 2.3

Mozzarella Zucchinis and Leeks

Prep time: 15 minutes
Cooking time: 5 hours
Servings: 5
Ingredients:
- 1 cup zucchinis, roughly cubed
- 1 cup leeks, sliced
- 1 oz Mozzarella, shredded
- 1 tablespoon chives, chopped
- ½ teaspoon ground black pepper
- ¾ cup coconut cream

Directions:
1. In the slow cooker, mix the zucchinis and leeks with the other ingredients, toss and close the lid.
2. Cook the squash cubes for 5 hours on Low.

Nutrition value/serving: calories 162, fat 10.6, fiber 1, carbs 5.6, protein 3.9

Hot Tomatoes

Prep time: 10 minutes
Cooking time: 6 hours
Servings: 4
Ingredients:
- 2 cups tomatoes, roughly cubed
- 1 jalapeno pepper
- 1 teaspoon chili powder
- 1 teaspoon hot paprika
- ¾ cup chicken stock
- 1 teaspoon salt
- ½ teaspoon dried basil
- ½ teaspoon dried oregano
- ¾ teaspoon ground ginger
- 1 teaspoon lemon juice

Directions:
1. In the slow cooker, mix the tomatoes with jalapeno pepper, chili powder and the other ingredients and toss.
2. Close the lid and cook on Low for 6 hours.
3. Serve warm.

Nutrition value/serving: calories 146, fat 1.5, fiber 0.9, carbs 2.7, protein 0.6

Smashed Cauliflower
Prep time: 15 minutes
Cooking time: 7 hours
Servings: 6
Ingredients:
- 3 cups cauliflower florets, chopped
- 1 tablespoon cream cheese
- 1 oz Parmesan, grated
- 1 teaspoon hot paprika
- 1 teaspoon oregano, dried
- 2 tablespoons walnuts, chopped
- 2 cups of water

Directions:
1. Put the cauliflower and water and close the lid.
2. Cook the cauliflower 7 hours on Low.
3. After this, drain water and transfer the cauliflower to a bowl.
4. Mash with the help of the masher or fork, add the rest of the ingredients, toss and serve.

Nutrition value/serving: calories 143, fat 4.3, fiber 3.4, carbs 5.5, protein 3.6

Tomato and Eggplant Salad
Prep time: 10 minutes
Cooking time: 2 hours
Servings: 3
Ingredients:
- 1 large eggplant, roughly sliced
- 1-pound cherry tomatoes, halved
- 1 teaspoon balsamic vinegar
- 1 teaspoon fresh basil, chopped
- ¼ teaspoon salt
- ½ teaspoon black pepper
- ¼ teaspoon turmeric
- 3 tablespoons heavy cream
- 1 teaspoon butter

Directions:
1. Spread the slow cooker bottom with butter and combine all the ingredients inside.
2. Close the slow cooker lid and cook the eggplant slices for 2 hours on High.

Nutrition value/serving: calories 206, fat 7.1, fiber 5.7, carbs 6.3, protein 7

Garlic Eggplant Mix
Prep time: 10 minutes
Cooking time: 3 hours
Servings: 4
Ingredients:
- 8 oz eggplant, roughly cubed
- 2 shallots, chopped
- 1 teaspoon garlic powder
- 2 garlic cloves, diced
- 1 tablespoon apple cider vinegar
- 3 tablespoons avocado oil
- 1 teaspoon capers
- ½ teaspoon salt
- ¼ cup of vegetable stock

Directions:
1. In the slow cooker, mix the eggplant with the shallots and eth other ingredients, stir, close the slow cooker lid and cook for 3 hours on high.
2. Open the lid and mix up the cooked meal one more time.

Nutrition value/serving: calories 129, fat 4.5, fiber 3.6, carbs 8.3, protein 1.5

Radish and Tomato Salad
Prep time: 10 minutes
Cooking time: 1 hour
Servings: 4
Ingredients:
- 1 cup cherry tomatoes, halved
- 1 cup lettuce, chopped
- 1 cup radish, halved
- 1 tablespoon balsamic vinegar
- 1 teaspoon olive oil
- 1 teaspoon salt
- 1 tablespoon chives, chopped
- 1 teaspoon lemon juice
- 1 teaspoon sesame oil

Directions:
1. In the slow cooker, mix the radish with tomatoes, olive oil and balsamic vinegar and toss.
2. Close the lid and cook the vegetables for 1 hour on High.
3. Transfer to a salad bowl, add the rest of the ingredients, toss and serve.

Nutrition value/serving: calories 55, fat 5.3, fiber 0.8, carbs 2.1, protein 0.6

Paprika Spaghetti Squash
Prep time: 10 minutes
Cooking time: 4.5 hours
Servings: 3
Ingredients:
- 1-pound spaghetti squash, shredded

- 1 teaspoon ground paprika
- 1 teaspoon smoked paprika
- 1 teaspoon salt
- 1 tablespoon rosemary, chopped
- ½ teaspoon curry powder
- 1 teaspoon onion powder
- 1 teaspoon garlic powder
- 1/3 cup chicken stock

Directions:
1. In the slow cooker, mix the squash with paprika and the other ingredients, toss and close the lid.
2. Cook it for 4.5 hours on Low.
3. Divide between plates and serve.

Nutrition value/serving: calories 186, fat 5.1, fiber 2.8, carbs 6.5, protein 7.4

Rhubarb and Zucchini Mix

Prep time: 15 minutes
Cooking time: 6 hours
Servings: 4
Ingredients:
- 2 cups rhubarb, chopped
- 1 cup zucchini, sliced
- 1 teaspoon coriander, ground
- 1 teaspoon curry powder
- 1 teaspoon garam masala
- 7 oz Cheddar cheese, shredded
- 4 tablespoons coconut cream
- 1 teaspoon butter
- 1 teaspoon olive oil
- ½ teaspoon salt
- ¼ cup fresh cilantro, chopped

Directions:
1. In the slow cooker, mix the rhubarb with the zucchini and the other ingredients, toss and close the slow cooker lid.
2. Cook the mix for 6 hours on Low.

Nutrition value/serving: calories 200, fat 10.2, fiber 1.2, carbs 4.3, protein 7.6

Snacks and Appetizers

Chicken Bites

Prep time: 15 minutes
Cooking time: 4 hours
Servings: 4
Ingredients:
- 1-pound chicken fillet, roughly cubed
- 1 teaspoon turmeric powder
- 1 teaspoon yellow curry paste
- 1 oz Parmesan, grated
- ¼ cup butter

Directions:
1. In the slow cooker, mix the chicken with the curry paste and the other ingredients and toss.
2. Close the lid and the chicken tenders for 4 hours on High.

Nutrition value/serving: calories 336, fat 13.7, fiber 2.6, carbs 3.5, protein 16.5

Paprika Almonds

Prep time: 10 minutes
Cooking time: 6 hours
Servings: 2
Ingredients:
- 1 cup almonds
- 1 tablespoon sweet paprika
- 1/3 cup water
- ½ teaspoon Vanilla extract
- ¾ teaspoon ground ginger

Directions:
1. In the slow cooker, mix the almonds with the other ingredients, toss and close the lid.
2. Cook the almonds for 6 hours on Low. Mix up the almonds every 1 hour.

Nutrition value/serving: calories 126, fat 4.3, fiber 2.1, carbs 9.1, protein 5.2

Mixed Nuts

Prep time: 15 minutes
Cooking time: 3 hours
Servings: 6
Ingredients:
- 1 cup almonds
- 1 cup walnuts
- 1 cup sunflower seeds
- 1/4 cup water
- 2 tablespoons poppy seeds
- 1 teaspoon sweet paprika
- 1 teaspoon lemon zest, grated

Directions:
1. In the slow cooker, mix the almonds with walnuts and the other ingredients, toss and close the lid.
2. Cook for 3 hours on High.
3. Divide into bowls and serve.

Nutrition value/serving: calories 137, fat 7.9, fiber 2.3, carbs 5.1, protein 7.2

Beef and Zucchini Wraps

Prep time: 15 minutes
Cooking time: 4 hours
Servings: 6
Ingredients:
- 6 keto tortillas
- 2 zucchinis, roughly cubed
- 1-pound beef sirloin, chopped
- 1 teaspoon sweet paprika
- 5 tablespoons cream cheese
- 1 teaspoon butter
- 1 teaspoon garam masala

Directions:
1. In the slow cooker, mix the zucchinis with the other ingredients except the tortillas, stir and close the slow cooker lid.
2. Cook beef for 4 hours on High.
3. Divide this on each tortilla, wrap and serve.

Nutrition value/serving: calories 278, fat 8.3, fiber 4.3, carbs 8.8, protein 23.7

Cauliflower Bites

Prep time: 10 minutes
Cooking time: 3 hours
Servings: 5
Ingredients:
- 2 cups cauliflower florets
- ¾ cup coconut cream
- 4 oz Parmesan, grated
- 1 teaspoon turmeric powder
- 1 teaspoon paprika
- 1 teaspoon butter, melted

Directions:
1. In the slow cooker, mix the cauliflower with the cream and the other ingredients and close the lid.

2. Cook the cauliflower bites for 3 hours on High.
Nutrition value/serving: calories 202, fat 6.6, fiber 5,.4, carbs 2.9, protein 9.2

Cheese Sticks
Prep time: 20 minutes
Cooking time: 2.5 hours
Servings: 8
Ingredients:
- 4 eggs, beaten
- 1 cup Cheddar cheese, shredded
- 1 tablespoon fresh dill, chopped
- 1 tablespoon chives, chopped
- 1 teaspoon turmeric powder
- 1 teaspoon butter, softened
- 1/3 cup almond flour
- 1 teaspoon salt

Directions:
1. In the mixing bowl, mix up together beaten eggs, cheese and the other ingredients. You should get a soft homogenous mixture.
2. Line the bottom of the slow cooker with the baking paper.
3. Transfer the cheese mixture in the slow cooker and flatten well.
4. Close the lid and bake it for 2.5 hours on High.
5. Then chill the cooked mixture very well and cut into the serving sticks.

Nutrition value/serving: calories 304, fat 8.3, fiber 4.5, carbs 1.6, protein 7

Eggplant Bread
Prep time: 15 minutes
Cooking time: 7 hours
Servings: 4
Ingredients:
- 2 eggplants, chopped
- 2 eggs, beaten
- 3 tablespoons coconut cream
- 1 teaspoon garam masala
- 2 tablespoons almond flour
- ½ teaspoon baking soda
- 1 teaspoon lime juice
- ½ teaspoon ground black pepper
- 1 teaspoon butter, melted

Directions:
1. Line the slow cooker bottom with the baking paper.

2. In the mixing bowl, mix up together eggs with the eggplants and the other ingredients, and stir really well.
3. Transfer the eggplant bread mixture in the slow cooker and flatten it well.
4. Close the lid and cook zucchini bread for 7 hours on Low.

Nutrition value/serving: calories 186, fat 12.1, fiber 4.6, carbs 11.2, protein 7.5

Almond Granola
Prep time: 10 minutes
Cooking time: 1.5 hour
Servings: 6
Ingredients:
- 1/3 cup coconut shred
- 1/4 cup almonds, chopped
- 2 eggs, whisked
- 1 tablespoon almond flour
- 1 teaspoon Erythritol
- 1 teaspoon ground cinnamon

Directions:
1. In the slow cooker, mix the almonds with the coconut and the other ingredients, stir and spread into the pot.
2. Cook granola on High for 1 hour.
3. Then mix up the granola mixture well and cook it for 30 minutes more.
4. Chill the cooked granola well and store it in the glass jar.

Nutrition value/serving: calories 203, fat 12.3, fiber 3.1, carbs 5.9, protein 4.7

Chili Walnuts
Prep time: 10 minutes
Cooking time: 2 hours
Servings: 3
Ingredients:
- 1 cup walnuts
- 1 teaspoon hot paprika
- 1 teaspoon salt
- 1 egg white
- ½ teaspoon chili powder

Directions:
1. Whisk the egg white, paprika, salt and chili until you get foam.
2. Coat walnuts in the egg white mixture.
3. Line the slow cooker bottom with baking paper and arrange coated walnuts.
4. Cook them for 2 hours on High.

Nutrition value/serving: calories 270, fat 10.1, fiber 4.7, carbs 6.3, protein 5.8

Pork Bites

Prep time: 15 minutes
Cooking time: 4 hours
Servings: 4
Ingredients:
- 1 cup pork stew meat, cubed
- 1 teaspoon keto tomato sauce
- 1 teaspoon chili flakes
- ¼ cup heavy cream
- 1 teaspoon olive oil
- ½ teaspoon salt

Directions:
1. In the slow cooker, mix the pork cubes with tomato paste and the other ingredients, close the lid and cook for 4 hours on High.
2. Divide into bowls and serve

Nutrition value/serving: calories 283, fat 20.2, fiber 3.3, carbs 1.4, protein 14.5

Turkey Meatballs

Prep time: 15 minutes
Cooking time: 4 hours
Servings: 3
Ingredients:
- ½ cup ground turkey meat
- 1 egg, whisked
- 1 teaspoon oregano, dried
- 1 teaspoon curry powder
- ½ teaspoon ground black pepper
- ¼ teaspoon salt
- ¾ cup of coconut milk

Directions:
1. In the mixing bowl, mix up together the meat with the egg and the other ingredients except the coconut milk, stir and shape small meatballs out of this mix.
2. Pour the coconut milk in the slow cooker, add the meatballs and toss gently.
3. Cook the meatballs for 4 hours on High.

Nutrition value/serving: calories 273, fat 16.7, fiber 1.5, carbs 4.1, protein 11.8

Tomato Salmon Meatballs

Prep time: 15 minutes
Cooking time: 3 hours
Servings: 2
Ingredients:
- 6 oz salmon fillet, minced
- 1 tablespoon keto tomato sauce
- 1 teaspoon almond flour
- ½ teaspoon turmeric
- ¾ teaspoon salt
- ¼ teaspoon sweet paprika
- ¼ cup organic almond milk
- 1 teaspoon butter

Directions:
1. In a bowl, mix the salmon meat with the keto tomato sauce and the other ingredients except the milk and butter, stir and make small meatballs.
2. Place them in the slow cooker, add butter and almond milk. Close the lid of the slow cooker.
3. Cook the appetizer for 3 hours on High

Nutrition value/serving: calories 301, fat 9.7, fiber 2.7, carbs 5.4, protein 15.8

Pecans Bowls

Prep time: 7 minutes
Cooking time: 1 hour
Servings: 6
Ingredients:
- 6 pecans
- 1 teaspoon butter, melted
- 1 tablespoon keto tomato sauce
- ½ teaspoon olive oil

Directions:
1. In the slow cooker, mix the pecans with the keto tomato sauce and the other ingredients, toss and close the lid.
2. Cook pecans for 1 hour on High. Stir the pecans after 30 minutes of cooking and divide them into bowls at the end.

Nutrition value/serving: calories 126, fat 11.2, fiber 1.5, carbs 2, protein 1.5

Sausage Dip

Prep time: 10 minutes
Cooking time: 4 hours
Servings: 5
Ingredients:
- 1 cup Italian sausages, crumbled
- 1 tablespoon chives, chopped
- 1 teaspoon Italian seasoning
- 1 teaspoon sweet paprika
- 1 cup Cheddar cheese, shredded
- 1 cup Mozzarella cheese, shredded
- ¼ cup heavy cream

Directions:
1. In the slow cooker, mix the sausages with chives and the other ingredients and stir.
2. Close the lid and cook dip for 4 hours on Low.

Nutrition value/serving: calories 304, fat 24.9, fiber 5.4, carbs 6.5, protein 13.8

Butter Pork Ribs
Prep time: 15 minutes
Cooking time: 7 hours
Servings: 4
Ingredients:
- 10 oz pork ribs
- 3 tablespoons butter, soft
- 1/3 cup coconut cream
- 1 teaspoon turmeric powder
- ½ teaspoon salt
- 1 teaspoon garlic powder

Directions:
1. In the slow cooker, mix the pork with soft butter and the other ingredients.
2. Close the lid and cook the pork ribs for 7 hours on Low.

Nutrition value/serving: calories 321, fat 14.8, fiber 4.5, carbs 6.5, protein 19.7

Chicken Dip
Prep time: 15 minutes
Cooking time: 4 hours
Servings: 4
Ingredients:
- 1 cup ground chicken
- 1 teaspoon chives, chopped
- ½ cup keto tomato sauce
- 1 tablespoon olive oil
- 1 teaspoon basil, dried
- ¼ teaspoon minced garlic
- 3 oz Parmesan, grated

Directions:
1. In the slow cooker, mix the chicken with the tomato sauce and the other ingredients, whisk and close the lid.
2. Cook the dip for 4 hours on High, divide into bowls and serve.

Nutrition value/serving: calories 236, fat 7.2, fiber 5.1, carbs 6.5, protein 17

Chia Chicken Bites
Prep time: 15 minutes
Cooking time: 2.5 hours
Servings: 4
Ingredients:
- 10 oz chicken breast, skinless, boneless
- 2 tablespoons chia seeds
- 1 egg, beaten
- ½ teaspoon chives, chopped
- ½ teaspoon garlic powder
- ½ teaspoon salt
- 1 teaspoon cayenne pepper
- 1 teaspoon garam masala
- 1/3 cup butter

Directions:
1. In the slow cooker, mix the chicken with the chia seeds and the other ingredients and toss.
2. Close the lid and cook the appetizer for 2.5 hours on High.

Nutrition value/serving: calories 281, fat 20.5, fiber 5.6, carbs 11.9, protein 17.5

Cocktail Shrimp
Prep time: 8 minutes
Cooking time: 2 hours
Servings: 4
Ingredients:
- 10 oz shrimp, peeled and deveined
- ½ cup crushed tomatoes
- 1 teaspoon olive oil
- 1 teaspoon sweet paprika
- 1 teaspoon chili pepper
- 1 teaspoon onion powder

Directions:
1. In the slow cooker, mix the shrimp with the other ingredients.
2. Close the lid and cook sausages for 2 hours on High.

Nutrition value/serving: calories 235, fat 11.3, fiber 1.1, carbs 3.1, protein 11.6

Coconut Mushrooms Caps
Prep time: 10 minutes
Cooking time: 6 hours
Servings: 4
Ingredients:
- 1 cup cremini mushroom caps
- ¼ cup spring onions, chopped
- 1 teaspoon sweet paprika
- 1 teaspoon garlic powder
- 2 tablespoons olive oil
- 1 teaspoon salt
- 1 teaspoon black pepper
- ½ teaspoon ground turmeric
- ¾ cup coconut cream

Directions:
1. In the slow cooker, mix the mushroom caps with the spring onions, paprika and the other ingredients and toss.

2. Close the lid and cook mushroom caps for 6 hours on Low.
Nutrition value/serving: calories 246, fat 22.1, fiber 4.4, carbs 12.2, protein 1.3

Mozzarella Broccoli Bites
Prep time: 15 minutes
Cooking time: 4 hours
Servings: 8
Ingredients:
- 1-pound broccoli florets
- 1 cup Mozzarella, shredded
- 1 teaspoon turmeric powder
- 1 tablespoon butter, melted
- 1 teaspoon salt
- 1 teaspoon chili powder
- 2 egg, beaten

Directions:
1. In a bowl, mix the broccoli with the other ingredients except the butter and toss.
2. Grease the slow cooker with the butter and arrange the broccoli bites inside.
3. Close the lid and cook the appetizer for 4 hours on High.
4. Arrange on a platter and serve.
Nutrition value/serving: calories 264, fat 4.9, fiber 3.5, carbs 12.3, protein 4.6

Bacon Dip
Prep time: 15 minutes
Cooking time: 4 hours
Servings: 4
Ingredients:
- 1 cup bacon, cooked and crumbled
- 1/4 cup spring onions, chopped
- 1 teaspoon ground black pepper
- 1 teaspoon smoked paprika
- ½ teaspoon salt
- 1/3 cup coconut cream

Directions:
1. In the slow cooker, mix the bacon with spring onions and the other ingredients.
2. Close the slow cooker lid and cook meatballs for 4 hours on High.
Nutrition value/serving: calories 319, fat 22, fiber 4.3, carbs 12.3, protein 20.4

Chili Dip
Prep time: 15 minutes
Cooking time: 1.5 hour
Servings: 8
Ingredients:
- 2 red chili peppers, minced
- 1 teaspoon hot paprika
- 1 teaspoon curry powder
- 1 tablespoon cream cheese
- ½ cup Cheddar cheese, shredded
- ¼ cup crushed tomatoes
- 1 teaspoon butter

Directions:
1. In the slow cooker, mix the chili peppers with the paprika and the other ingredients and whisk.
2. Close the slow cooker lid and cook the dip for 1.5 hours on High.
Nutrition value/serving: calories 124, fat 3.4, fiber 3.6, carbs 3.6, protein 2.2

Shrimp Tortillas
Prep time: 10 minutes
Cooking time: 2 hours
Servings: 2
Ingredients:
- 2 keto tortillas
- 1 cup shrimp, peeled and deveined
- ½ cup spring onions, chopped
- 1 teaspoon oregano, dried
- 1 teaspoon keto tomato sauce
- ½ teaspoon ground coriander
- ¾ teaspoon salt
- 3 tablespoons butter

Directions:
1. In the slow cooker, mix the shrimp with the spring onions and the other ingredients except the tortillas.
2. Close the lid and cook meat on High for 2 hours.
3. Stuff the tortillas with the shrimp mix, wrap and serve.
Nutrition value/serving: calories 230, fat 12.4, fiber 2.3, carbs 5.1, protein 11.8

Smoked Hazelnuts
Prep time: 15 minutes
Cooking time: 2.5 hours
Servings: 6
Ingredients:
- 1 tablespoon butter
- 1 tablespoon smoked paprika
- 1 teaspoon turmeric powder
- ½ cup hazelnuts, chopped

Directions:

1. In the slow cooker, mix the hazelnuts with the paprika and the other ingredients and toss.
2. Close the lid and cook the mixture for 2.5 hours on Low.
3. Divide into bowls and serve.

Nutrition value/serving: calories 218, fat 8.5, fiber 1.4, carbs 6.9, protein 3.9

Tomato Chicken Wings
Prep time: 20 minutes
Cooking time: 6.5 hours
Servings: 4
Ingredients:
- 4 chicken wings
- 1 tablespoon lime juice
- 1 tablespoon Keto tomato sauce
- ½ teaspoon balsamic vinegar
- ½ teaspoon salt
- ½ teaspoon chili flakes
- ¾ teaspoon smoked paprika
- 1/3 cup water
- 1 teaspoon coconut butter

Directions:
1. In the slow cooker, mix the chicken wings with lime juice and the other ingredients
2. Close the lid and cook chicken wings for 6.5 hours on Low.
3. Serve the chicken wings as an appetizer.

Nutrition value/serving: calories 306, fat 15.2, fiber 4.9, carbs 12.9, protein 23.8

Worcestershire Chicken
Prep time: 10 minutes
Cooking time: 4 hours
Servings: 5
Ingredients:
- 1 tablespoon Worcestershire sauce
- 1-pound chicken breast, skinless, boneless and cubed
- 1 tablespoon keto tomato sauce
- 1 teaspoon chili powder
- 1 teaspoon coriander, ground
- 1/3 teaspoon garlic powder
- 2 tablespoons butter, softened

Directions:
1. In the slow cooker, mix the chicken with the sauce and the other ingredients.
2. Close the lid and cook a snack for 4 hours on High.
3. Transfer the mix to bowls and serve.

Nutrition value/serving: calories 302, fat 20.7, fiber 4.3, carbs 12.7, protein 12.1

Almond Bars
Prep time: 10 minutes
Cooking time: 45 minutes
Servings: 6
Ingredients:
- 1 oz dark chocolate, melted
- 2 tablespoons peanut butter
- 1/2 cup almonds, chopped
- 1 teaspoon vanilla extract
- 1 tablespoon chia seeds, dried
- 1 tablespoon coconut flakes

Directions:
1. In the lined slow cooker, mix all the ingredients, whisk and spread.
2. Close the lid, cook on High for 45 minutes and cool down.
3. Cut into bars and serve cold as a snack.

Nutrition value/serving: calories 109, fat 7.3, fiber 3.8, carbs 5.2, protein 2.8

Paprika Dip
Prep time: 15 minutes
Cooking time: 1 hour
Servings: 5
Ingredients:
- 1 cup coconut cream
- 1 green bell pepper, chopped
- 1 red bell pepper, chopped
- 1 teaspoon smoked paprika
- ½ teaspoon salt
- ½ teaspoon chili pepper
- ½ teaspoon garam masala

Directions:
1. In the slow cooker, mix the cream with peppers and the other ingredients, whisk, close the lid and cook on High for 1 hour.
2. Chill the cooked dip well before serving.

Nutrition value/serving: calories 42, fat 3.2, fiber 1.4, carbs 3.3, protein 0.8

Turkey Bites and Sauce
Prep time: 15 minutes
Cooking time: 3.5 hours
Servings: 3
Ingredients:
- 1-pound turkey breast, skinless, boneless and cubed
- 1 tablespoon butter
- ½ teaspoon ground coriander

- 1 teaspoon oregano, dried
- 1 teaspoon curry powder
- 1/3 cup keto tomato sauce

Directions:
1. In the slow cooker, mix the turkey with the butter, coriander and the other ingredients, stir and close the lid.
2. Cook the mix for 3.5 hours on High.
3. Divide into bowls and serve.

Nutrition value/serving: calories 277, fat 11.2, fiber 5.3, carbs 8.4, protein 14.2

Masala Hazelnuts

Prep time: 20 minutes
Cooking time: 2 hours
Servings: 4
Ingredients:
- 1 tablespoon avocado oil
- 1 cup hazelnuts
- 1 teaspoon garam masala
- 1 teaspoon coriander, ground
- ¼ cup water
- 1 teaspoon chili powder
- 1 teaspoon cayenne pepper
- ½ teaspoon salt

Directions:
1. In the slow cooker, mix the hazelnuts with the oil and the other ingredients and close the lid.
2. Cook the nuts for 2 hours on High.
3. Spread the hazelnuts on a lined baking sheet, cool down and serve as a snack.

Nutrition value/serving: calories 109, fat 5.1, fiber 1.3, carbs 2.2, protein 1.7

Pizza Dip

Prep time: 7 minutes
Cooking time: 5 hours
Servings: 4
Ingredients:
- 1 cup keto tomato sauce
- ½ cup Mozzarella, shredded
- 2 oz Parmesan, grated
- 1 teaspoon oregano, dried
- 1 teaspoon chili powder
- ½ teaspoon garlic powder
- 1 teaspoon butter

Directions:
1. In the slow cooker, mix the tomato sauce with the cheese and the other ingredients and close the lid.
2. Cook the dip on Low for 5 hours.
3. Mix and serve.

Nutrition value/serving: calories 167, fat 4.9, fiber 2.3, carbs 3.1, protein 5.9

Salmon Spread

Prep time: 8 minutes
Cooking time: 2 hours
Servings: 6
Ingredients:
- 1 teaspoon hot paprika
- 6 oz salmon fillets, boneless, skinless and minced
- ¼ cup coconut cream
- 2 tablespoons Ricotta cheese
- ½ cup Cheddar cheese, shredded
- ½ teaspoon Italian seasoning

Directions:
1. In the slow cooker, mix the salmon with paprika, cream and the remaining ingredients, whisk and close the lid.
2. Cook the mass on Low for 2 hours.
3. Divide into bowls and serve.

Nutrition value/serving: calories 209, fat 7.2, fiber 2.7, carbs 11.4, protein 4.3

Balsamic Beef Meatballs

Prep time: 15 minutes
Cooking time: 4 hours
Servings: 4
Ingredients:
- 1 cup ground beef
- 1 teaspoon salt
- ½ teaspoon ground black pepper
- 1 egg, whisked
- 1 tablespoon balsamic vinegar
- 1 teaspoon oregano, dried
- 1 teaspoon coriander, ground
- 1 teaspoon lime juice
- ¼ teaspoon lime zest
- 1/3 cup crushed tomatoes
- 1 teaspoon olive oil

Directions:
1. In a bowl, mix the beef with salt, pepper and the other ingredients except the tomatoes and oil, stir and shape medium meatballs out of this mix.
2. Grease the slow cooker with the oil and add the crushed tomatoes inside.
3. Add the meatballs, close the lid and cook on High for 4 hours.

Nutrition value/serving: calories 243, fat 6.8, fiber 3.8, carbs 12.5, protein 7.9

Hot Ham

Prep time: 15 minutes
Cooking time: 12. 5 hours
Servings: 7
Ingredients:
- 18 oz ham
- 1 teaspoon garlic powder
- 1 teaspoon chili flakes
- 1 teaspoon hot paprika
- 1 teaspoon cumin, ground
- 1 tablespoon avocado oil
- 1 tablespoon mustard
- 1 teaspoon minced garlic
- ½ cup of water
- 1 teaspoon keto tomato sauce
- ½ teaspoon salt

Directions:
1. In the slow cooker, mix the ham with garlic powder and the other ingredients
2. Close the lid and cook the ham for 12 hours on Low.
3. When the ham is cooked, shred it with the help of 2 forks.
4. Cook pulled ham for 30 minutes on high.

Nutrition value/serving: calories 312, fat 7, fiber 3.4, carbs 12.2, protein 12.7

Sausage Bites and Sauce

Prep time: 10 minutes
Cooking time: 3 hours
Servings: 6
Ingredients:
- 1-pound smoked sausages, sliced
- ½ cup keto tomato sauce
- 1 teaspoon butter
- 1 teaspoon chili powder
- ½ teaspoon minced garlic
- 1 teaspoon coriander, ground
- 1 teaspoon sweet paprika

Directions:
1. In the slow cooker, mix the sausages with tomato sauce and the other ingredients, toss, close the lid and cook for 3 hours on High.
2. Transfer in the serving bowls serve.

Nutrition value/serving: calories 307, fat 22.9, fiber 4.8, carbs 12.5, protein 9.9

Cheddar Dip

Prep time: 10 minutes
Cooking time: 4 hours
Servings: 6
Ingredients:
- 1 teaspoon butter
- 3 spring onions, chopped
- 1 cup Cheddar cheese, shredded
- ½ cup of coconut cream
- 1 teaspoon minced jalapeno pepper
- 1 tablespoon Italian seasoning

Directions:
1. In the slow cooker, mix the cheese with the butter and the other ingredients and whisk.
2. Close the lid and cook the dip on Low for 4 hours.

Nutrition value/serving: calories 234, fat 9.6, fiber 3.4, carbs 8.3, protein 9.2

Shrimp Skewers

Prep time: 15 minutes
Cooking time: 3 hours
Servings: 5
Ingredients:
- 1-pound shrimp, peeled and deveined
- 2 tablespoons chives, chopped
- 1 tablespoon butter
- 1 teaspoon Italian seasoning
- 1 teaspoon salt
- ¼ cup heavy cream

Directions:
1. In a bowl, mix the shrimp with chives, butter, seasoning and salt, toss and thread them on skewers
2. Put the skewers in the slow cooker, add the cream on top and cook the appetizer for 3 hours on High.

Nutrition value/serving: calories 320, fat 18.9, fiber 3.1, carbs 10.8, protein 27.3

Chives Wings

Prep time: 8 minutes
Cooking time: 2.5 hours
Servings: 4
Ingredients:
- 1-pound chicken wings
- ½ cup keto tomato sauce
- ¼ cup chives, chopped
- 1 teaspoon turmeric powder
- 2 tablespoons butter
- 1 teaspoon chili pepper

Directions:
1. In the slow cooker, mix the chicken with tomato sauce and the other ingredients.

2. After this, close the lid and cook chicken wings for 2.5 hours on High.
Nutrition value/serving: calories 250, fat 14.2, fiber 1.1, carbs 12.1, protein 22.9

Creamy Dip

Prep time: 10 minutes
Cooking time: 1.5 hours
Servings: 6
Ingredients:
- 5 oz bacon, chopped
- 1 teaspoon turmeric powder
- 1/3 cup heavy cream
- 1 cup Mozzarella, shredded
- 1 teaspoon white pepper
- ½ teaspoon coriander, ground
- 1 teaspoon dried basil

Directions:
1. In the slow cooker, mix bacon with turmeric and the other ingredients, toss and close the lid.
2. Cook the cheese dip for 1.5 hours on High.

Nutrition value/serving: calories 220, fat 16.2, fiber 3, carbs 1.4, protein 8.8

Tofu Bites

Prep time: 10 minutes
Cooking time: 2 hours
Servings: 4
Ingredients:
- 3 oz firm tofu, cubed
- 1/3 cup coconut cream
- 1 tablespoon balsamic vinegar
- ½ teaspoon salt
- 1 teaspoon chili powder

Directions:
1. In the slow cooker, mix the tofu with the cream and the other ingredients, close the lid and cook for 1.5hours on High.
2. Serve as a snack.

Nutrition value/serving: calories 214, fat 7.5, fiber 4.4, carbs 3.3, protein 11.1

Fish Bites

Prep time: 10 minutes
Cooking time: 2.5 hours
Servings: 4
Ingredients:
- 1-pound salmon fillet, boneless and cubed
- ½ teaspoon sweet paprika
- 3 tablespoons coconut oil
- ½ cup keto tomato sauce

Directions:
1. In the slow cooker, mix the salmon with the paprika and the other ingredients.
2. Close the lid and cook the fish bites for 2.5 hours on High.

Nutrition value/serving: calories 224, fat 13.8, fiber 2.8, carbs 2.1, protein 8.1

Cauliflower Popcorn

Prep time: 10 minutes
Cooking time: 6 hours
Servings: 4
Ingredients:
- 1 cup cauliflower florets
- ½ cup Parmesan, grated
- 1 teaspoon black pepper
- 1 teaspoon salt
- 1 teaspoon chili powder
- 1/3 cup heavy cream

Directions:
1. Put cauliflower florets in the slow cooker.
2. Add the rest of the ingredients, toss and close the lid.
3. Cook cauliflower popcorn for 6 hours on Low.

Nutrition value/serving: calories 210, fat 8.5, fiber 3.9, carbs 2.2, protein 4.3

Cayenne Chorizo

Prep time: 7 minutes
Cooking time: 3 hours
Servings: 4
Ingredients:
- 8 oz chorizo, chopped
- 1 teaspoon cayenne pepper
- 2 tablespoons keto tomato sauce
- 1 tablespoon olive oil
- 1 teaspoon sweet paprika
- 1 teaspoon curry powder
- ½ teaspoon salt
- ¾ cup of water

Directions:
1. In the slow cooker, mix the chorizo with the cayenne and the other ingredients.
2. Close the slow cooker lid and cook the chorizo for 3 hours on High.

Nutrition value/serving: calories 227, fat 14.7, fiber 3.2, carbs 5.7, protein 13.8

Milky Chicken Sticks

Prep time: 10 minutes
Cooking time: 4 hours
Servings: 2
Ingredients:
- 8 oz chicken fillets, boneless and cut into strips
- 1 teaspoon lemon juice
- ½ teaspoon ground black pepper
- 1/2 teaspoon lemon zest, grated
- ¾ cup organic coconut milk
- 1 teaspoon butter

Directions:
1. In the slow cooker, mix the chicken with the lemon juice and the other ingredients.
2. Close the lid and cook chicken slices for 4 hours on High.

Nutrition value/serving: calories 234, fat 11.6, fiber 4.7, carbs 5.6, protein 13.4

Oregano Dip

Prep time: 5 minutes
Cooking time: 2 hours
Servings: 4
Ingredients:
- ½ cup Cheddar cheese, shredded
- 1 tablespoon dried oregano
- ½ teaspoon cayenne pepper
- 2 tablespoon butter
- 1 teaspoon smoked paprika
- ¼ cup coconut cream

Directions:
1. Put the cheese, oregano and the other ingredients in the slow cooker.
2. Close the lid and cook the dip of High for 2 hours.

Nutrition value/serving: calories 204, fat 12.4, fiber 1, carbs 2.9, protein 11.4

Cayenne Shrimps

Prep time: 10 minutes
Cooking time: 2 hours
Servings: 4
Ingredients:
- 1 oz Parmesan, grated
- ¾ teaspoon cayenne pepper
- 1 teaspoon turmeric powder
- 1 teaspoon curry powder
- 1 tablespoon butter
- ½ cup organic almond milk
- 9 oz shrimps, peeled

Directions:
1. In the slow cooker, mix the shrimp with the Parmesan and the other ingredients, stir and close the lid
2. Cook the shrimp for 2 hours on High.
3. Divide into bowls and serve.

Nutrition value/serving: calories 184, fat 10.7, fiber 1.2, carbs 3.3, protein 19

Masala Green Beans Bowl

Prep time: 10 minutes
Cooking time: 3.5 hours
Servings: 4
Ingredients:
- ½ cup of water
- ½ teaspoon ground coriander
- ½ teaspoon garam masala
- ½ teaspoon salt
- 1 tablespoon butter
- 1 cup green beans, trimmed and halved

Directions:
1. In the slow cooker, mix the snap peas with the other ingredients.
2. After this, close the slow cooker lid.
3. Cook the mix for 3.5 hours on Low and serve.

Nutrition value/serving: calories 36, fat 3, fiber 0.6, carbs 3.5, protein 4.3

Shrimp Meatballs

Prep time: 15 minutes
Cooking time: 3 hours
Servings: 4
Ingredients:
- 1 cup shrimp, cooked, peeled and minced
- 1 egg white
- 1 teaspoon salt
- ½ teaspoon ground black pepper
- ½ teaspoon turmeric
- 1 teaspoon oregano, dried
- ¼ cup of water
- 1 teaspoon avocado oil
- ¼ cup spring onions, chopped

Directions:
1. In the mixing bowl, combine the shrimp with egg white and the other ingredients except the oil and water, stir and make small meatballs.
2. Transfer the meatballs in the slow cooker.
3. Add coconut oil and water.
4. Close the lid and cook meatballs for 3 hours on Low.

Nutrition value/serving: calories 195, fat 7.3, fiber 2.5, carbs 1.4, protein 12.6

Garlic Pork Slices
Prep time: 10 minutes
Cooking time: 8 hours
Servings: 10
Ingredients:
- 1-pound pork belly
- 2 teaspoons minced garlic
- 1 teaspoon garlic powder
- 1 teaspoon ground black pepper
- ½ teaspoon salt
- 1 tablespoon avocado oil
- 1/3 cup water
- 1 tablespoon apple cider vinegar

Directions:
1. In the slow cooker, mix the pork with garlic and the other ingredients and close the lid.
2. Cook the snack for 8 hours on Low.
3. Then remove the pork belly from the slow cooker and dry it gently with the help of the paper towel.
4. Slice the cooked pork belly into the slices.

Nutrition value/serving: calories 314, fat 12.4, fiber 5.2, carbs 12.7, protein 21

Zucchini Bites
Prep time: 10 minutes
Cooking time: 1 hour
Servings: 6
Ingredients:
- 2 zucchinis, trimmed and roughly cubed
- 1 teaspoon turmeric powder
- 1 tablespoon yellow curry powder
- 1 tablespoon minced garlic
- ½ teaspoon salt
- 2 tablespoons butter

Directions:
1. In the slow cooker mix the zucchinis with the turmeric and the other ingredients and close the lid.
2. Cook the zucchini rounds for 1 hour on High.

Nutrition value/serving: calories 46, fat 4, fiber 0.8, carbs 2.7, protein 0.9

Fish and Seafood

Poached Trout
Prep time: 10 minutes
Cooking time: 2.5 hours
Servings: 4
Ingredients:
- 1 cup of water
- 1 oz spring onions, chopped
- 1 teaspoon coriander, ground
- 1 teaspoon peppercorns
- 1 teaspoon salt
- 1 bay leaf
- 1 teaspoon dried oregano
- 3 spring onions, chopped
- 4 trout fillets (5 oz each)
- ½ teaspoon ground black pepper

Directions:
1. Pour water in the slow cooker.
2. Add all the ingredients except the trout, close the lid and cook for 2 hours on High.
3. Add the fish and close the lid.
4. Cook the salmon on Low for 30 minutes.
5. Divide into bowls and serve.

Nutrition value/serving: calories 305, fat 12.4, fiber 3.2, carbs 3.2, protein 32.7

Seafood Bowls
Prep time: 10 minutes
Cooking time: 3 hours
Servings: 4
Ingredients:
- 5 oz scallops
- 4 oz shrimps, peeled
- ½ pound salmon, boneless and cubed
- 1 teaspoon lemongrass, minced
- 1 teaspoon salt
- 1 teaspoon cayenne pepper
- 1/3 cup crushed tomatoes
- 1 teaspoon cumin seeds
- 1 tablespoon avocado oil
- 1 teaspoon smoked paprika
- 1 oz fennel bulb, chopped
- 1 teaspoon lemon rind, chopped
- 1 teaspoon onion powder
- ½ cup of water

Directions:
1. Preheat the skillet well and add olive oil.
2. Add fennel and the other ingredients except the seafood, stir, cook for 5 minutes and transfer to the slow cooker.
3. Add the remaining ingredients, close the lid and cook on High for 1 hour and on Low for 2 hours.

Nutrition value/serving: calories 246, fat 5.3, fiber 3.6, carbs 5.6, protein 26.4

Salmon Soup
Prep time: 8 minutes
Cooking time: 3 hours
Servings: 4
Ingredients:
- 2 cups of water
- 1 cup coconut cream
- 1 teaspoon garlic powder
- 2 garlic cloves, chopped
- 1 teaspoon lemongrass
- ½ teaspoon chili flakes
- 8 oz salmon, skinless, boneless and cubed
- 1 teaspoon salt

Directions:
1. In the slow cooker, mix the water with cream and the other ingredients except the fish and close the lid.
2. Cook the stock for 2 hours on High.
3. After this, open the slow cooker lid and add the salmon.
4. Close the lid and cook the soup for 1 hour on Low.

Nutrition value/serving: calories 209, fat 12.1, fiber 2.1, carbs 5.9, protein 7.9

Shrimp Bake
Prep time: 10 minutes
Cooking time: 2 hours
Servings: 2
Ingredients:
- 1-pound shrimp, peeled and deveined
- 2 tablespoons lime juice
- 1 teaspoon salt
- 1 teaspoon apple cider vinegar
- 1 tablespoon butter
- ¾ cup heavy cream
- 2 oz Provolone cheese, shredded

Directions:
1. In the slow cooker, mix the shrimp with the lime juice and the other ingredients except the cheese.
2. Toss, sprinkle the cheese on top and cook on High for 2 hours.

Nutrition value/serving: calories 290, fat 5.2, fiber 0.2, carbs 2.5, protein 18.8

Shrimp and Salmon Skewers
Prep time: 10 minutes
Cooking time: 1.5 hour
Servings: 4
Ingredients:
- 9 oz shrimps, peeled
- 9 ounces salmon fillets, boneless and cubed
- 1 teaspoon garlic powder
- 1 teaspoon ginger powder
- 1 tablespoon lime juice
- 1/3 teaspoon oregano, dried
- 1 tablespoon sesame oil
- 1 teaspoon heavy cream
- ¾ cup of water

Directions:
1. String the shrimps and salmon into the skewers one-by-one.
2. After this, pour water in the slow cooker.
3. Arrange the shrimp and salmon skewers in the slow cooker, and add the rest of the ingredients as well.
4. Close the lid and cook shrimps for 1.5 hours on High.
5. Then transfer the cooked shrimp skewers on the plates and sprinkle with slow cooker gravy.

Nutrition value/serving: calories 185, fat 5, fiber 3.3, carbs 5.4, protein 14.7

Shrimp Salad
Prep time: 10 minutes
Cooking time: 30 minutes
Servings: 4
Ingredients:
- ¼ cup cherry tomatoes
- 1 cup kale, chopped
- ½ cup avocado, peeled, pitted and cubed
- 7 oz shrimps, peeled and deveined
- 1 teaspoon basil, dried
- 3 tablespoons butter
- 1 tablespoon olive oil
- 1 tablespoon fresh parsley, chopped
- ¾ cup heavy cream
- 1 teaspoon ground black pepper
- ½ teaspoon salt

Directions:

1. In the slow cooker, mix the shrimp with tomatoes and the other ingredients, close the lid and cook for 30 minutes on High.
2. Divide into bowls and serve.

Nutrition value/serving: calories 249, fat 11.3, fiber 0.5, carbs 2.7, protein 8.3

Shrimp and Fennel Soup
Prep time: 10 minutes
Cooking time: 2 hours
Servings: 6
Ingredients:
- ½ cup fennel, shredded
- 12 oz shrimps, peeled
- ½ teaspoon sweet paprika
- 1 teaspoon turmeric powder
- ½ teaspoon salt
- ½ teaspoon cayenne pepper
- 1 teaspoon coriander seeds
- 2 cups of water
- 2 cups of coconut milk
- 1 teaspoon chili powder
- 1 cup spinach, chopped

Directions:
1. In the slow cooker, mix the shrimp with fennel and the other ingredients and toss.
2. Divide into bowls and serve.

Nutrition value/serving: calories 275, fat 20.3, fiber 3.4, carbs 5.3, protein 16

Italian Shrimp Tortillas
Prep time: 10 minutes
Cooking time: 2 hours
Servings: 2
Ingredients:
- 2 keto tortillas
- ½ teaspoon Cajun seasoning
- 1 teaspoon Italian seasoning
- 1 tablespoon chives, chopped
- 2 tablespoons fresh cilantro, chopped
- 2 oz Cheddar cheese, shredded
- 7 oz shrimps, peeled
- ½ cup heavy cream
- ½ teaspoon ground coriander
- 1 teaspoon salt
- 1 jalapeno pepper, sliced

Directions:
1. In the slow cooker, mix the shrimp with the seasonings and the other ingredients and close the lid.
2. Cook shrimps on High for 2 hours.

3. After this, fill keto tortillas with shrimps and serve.
Nutrition value/serving: calories 220, fat 6.2, fiber 2.4, carbs 8.7, protein 6.5

Creamy Tuna

Prep time: 10 minutes
Cooking time: 4 hours
Servings: 6
Ingredients:
- 1-pound tuna fillet, boneless and cubed
- 1 red chili pepper, minced
- 1 tablespoon butter
- 2 shallots, chopped
- ½ cup heavy cream
- 1 cup Mozzarella cheese, shredded
- 1 teaspoon salt
- 1 teaspoon paprika
- 1 teaspoon basil, dried

Directions:
1. Put butter in the bottom of slow cooker.
2. Add the tuna and the other ingredients and toss.
3. Close the lid and cook for 4 hours on High.

Nutrition value/serving: calories 205, fat 12.7, fiber 3.7, carbs 9.7, protein 21.9

Salmon and Radish Soup

Prep time: 10 minutes
Cooking time: 2.5 hours
Servings: 4
Ingredients:
- 1 cup radishes, halved
- 10 oz salmon, chopped
- 1 teaspoon lime juice
- 1 teaspoon lime zest, grated
- ½ cup of coconut milk
- 2 cups of water
- 1 teaspoon salt
- 1 teaspoon garlic, diced
- ½ teaspoon chives, chopped

Directions:
1. In the slow cooker, mix the salmon with radishes and the other ingredients.
2. Close the lid and cook the liquid for 2.5 hours on High.
3. Divide into bowls and serve.

Nutrition value/serving: calories 209, fat 11.6, fiber 1.7, carbs 5.4, protein 8.5

Cajun Shrimp

Prep time: 10 minutes
Cooking time: 3 hours
Servings: 4
Ingredients:
- 1-pound shrimps, peeled
- 1 tomato, chopped
- 1 tablespoon keto tomato sauce
- 2 green bell peppers, chopped
- 1/3 teaspoon Cajun seasoning
- 1 teaspoon basil, dried
- 1 teaspoon oregano, dried
- 1 teaspoon salt
- ½ teaspoon ground black pepper
- ½ cup of water

Directions:
1. Pour water in the slow cooker.
2. Add shrimp and the other ingredients.
3. Close the lid and cook liquid for 2 hours on High.
4. Divide into bowls and serve.

Nutrition value/serving: calories 150, fat 2.1, fiber 1.2, carbs 5.1, protein 26.5

Balsamic Salmon

Prep time: 10 minutes
Cooking time: 1 hour
Servings: 3
Ingredients:
- 1-pound salmon fillet, sliced
- ½ teaspoon garlic powder
- ½ teaspoon salt
- ¼ teaspoon cayenne pepper
- 3 tablespoons balsamic vinegar
- 1/3 cup water
- ½ teaspoon olive oil

Directions:
1. In the slow cooker, mix the salmon with garlic powder, salt and the other ingredients and toss gently.
2. Close the lid and cook salmon for 1 hour on High.
3. Serve the salmon with the balsamic sauce.

Nutrition value/serving: calories 226, fat 10.1, fiber 4.1, carbs 8.6, protein 20.5

Tomato Shrimps

Prep time: 10 minutes
Cooking time: 1 hour
Servings: 2
Ingredients:
- 8 oz king shrimps, peeled

- 1/4 cup keto tomato sauce
- 1 tablespoon sweet paprika
- 1 green chili pepper, chopped
- 2 tablespoons butter
- ¼ cup of water
- ½ teaspoon chili powder

Directions:
1. Pour water in the slow cooker.
2. Add the shrimp and the other ingredients, stir and close the lid.
3. Cook for 1 hour on High and serve.

Nutrition value/serving: calories 174, fat 12.7, fiber 0.8, carbs 2.6, protein 12.7

Oregano Salmon

Prep time: 15 minutes
Cooking time: 1.5 hours
Servings: 2
Ingredients:
- 2 salmon steaks (2 fillets 6 oz each)
- 1 tablespoon oregano, dried
- 1 teaspoon smoked paprika
- 2 tablespoons olive oil
- 6 tablespoons water
- ½ teaspoon salt
- ½ teaspoon balsamic vinegar

Directions:
1. In the slow cooker, mix the salmon with the oregano and the other ingredients.
2. Close the lid and cook salmon for 1.5 hours on High.

Nutrition value/serving: calories 222, fat 12.1, fiber 0.7, carbs 1.5, protein 14.7

Crab Dip

Prep time: 15 minutes
Cooking time: 2 hours
Servings: 3
Ingredients:
- 1 cup crabmeat
- 1 cup Cheddar cheese, shredded
- ½ cup of coconut milk
- 2 spring onions, chopped
- 1 teaspoon olive oil
- 1 teaspoon paprika
- 1 teaspoon oregano, dried
- ½ teaspoon salt
- ½ teaspoon dried cilantro

Directions:
1. In the slow cooker, mix the crabmeat with the cheese and the other ingredients and whisk.
2. Close the lid and cook the dip for 2 hours on High.
3. Mix up it well with the help of the spoon.

Nutrition value/serving: calories 210, fat 13.1, fiber 1.2, carbs 4.2, protein 22.2

Ginger Mackerel

Prep time: 15 minutes
Cooking time: 1.5 hours
Servings: 6
Ingredients:
- 2-pound mackerel
- 1 teaspoon fresh ginger, minced
- 1 teaspoon ground cumin
- 1 teaspoon salt
- 1 teaspoon black pepper
- 1 teaspoon turmeric powder
- 1 teaspoon lemon juice
- ½ teaspoon lemon rind, grated
- ½ cup of coconut milk
- 1 teaspoon coconut oil

Directions:
1. In the slow cooker, mix the mackerel with the ginger, cumin and the other ingredients.
2. Close the slow cooker lid and cook fish for 1.5 hours on High.
3. Divide between plates and serve.

Nutrition value/serving: calories 321, fat 25.8, fiber 1.1, carbs 2.7, protein 20.2

Creamy Sea Bass

Prep time: 15 minutes
Cooking time: 2 hours
Servings: 4
Ingredients:
- 1-pound sea bass fillets, boneless
- 1 teaspoon garlic powder
- ½ teaspoon Italian seasoning
- ½ teaspoon salt
- ¼ cup heavy cream
- 1 tablespoon butter

Directions:
1. In the slow cooker, mix the sea bass with the other ingredients.
2. Close the slow cooker lid and cook for 2 hours on High.

Nutrition value/serving: calories 231, fat 14.9, fiber 4.3 carbs 7.4, protein 24.2

Oregano Crab

Prep time: 10 minutes

Cooking time: 40 minutes
Servings: 4
Ingredients:
- 1 tablespoon dried oregano
- 2 cups crab meat
- ½ cup spring onions, chopped
- ¾ teaspoon minced garlic
- 1 tablespoon lemon juice
- ½ cup of coconut milk

Directions:
1. In the slow cooker, mix the crab with oregano and the other ingredients and close the lid
2. Cook for 40 minutes on High, divide into bowls and serve.

Nutrition value/serving: calories 151, fat 3.4, fiber 1, carbs 6.8, protein 5.2

Parmesan Salmon
Prep time: 10 minutes
Cooking time: 2.5 hours
Servings: 3
Ingredients:
- 7 oz salmon fillets, boneless
- 1 teaspoon cayenne pepper
- 1 teaspoon chili pepper
- ½ cup coconut cream
- 3 oz Parmesan, grated
- 2 tablespoons lime juice
- 1 teaspoon minced garlic
- ¼ cup fresh chives, chopped

Directions:
1. In the slow cooker, mix the salmon with the coconut cream and the other ingredients and close the lid.
2. Cook on High for 2 hours and 30 minutes and serve.

Nutrition value/serving: calories 279, fat 16.5, fiber 1.2, carbs 7.5, protein 18.8

Balsamic Mussels
Prep time: 15 minutes
Cooking time: 2 hours
Servings: 4
Ingredients:
- 1-pound mussels
- 1 tablespoon Balsamic vinegar
- ½ teaspoon stevia extract
- 1 teaspoon lemon zest
- 1 teaspoon lemon juice
- 2 tablespoon sesame oil
- ¼ cup butter
- 4 tablespoons coconut cream

Directions:
1. In the slow cooker, mix the mussels with vinegar, stevia and the other ingredients.
2. Close the slow cooker lid and cook the catfish for 2 hours on High.
3. Divide into bowls and serve.

Nutrition value/serving: calories 279, fat 20.1, fiber 4.5, carbs 5.2, protein 6.1

Spicy Tuna
Prep time: 10 minutes
Cooking time: 1 hour
Servings: 3
Ingredients:
- 12 oz tuna fillet
- 1 tablespoon olive oil
- 1 teaspoon hot paprika
- 1 red chili pepper minced
- ½ teaspoon black pepper
- ½ teaspoon salt
- 1 jalapeno pepper, chopped
- 1/3 cup coconut oil
- 1 garlic clove, chopped

Directions:
1. Put the oil in the slow cooker.
2. Add the fish and the other ingredients and toss gently.
3. Close the lid and cook the oil mixture on High for 1 hour.
4. Divide between plates and serve.

Nutrition value/serving: calories 309, fat 12.8, fiber 0.4, carbs 0.9, protein 19.1

Turmeric Calamari
Prep time: 10 minutes
Cooking time: 6 hours
Servings: 5
Ingredients:
- 1-pound calamari rings
- 1 teaspoon turmeric
- 1 teaspoon hot paprika
- 2 tablespoons coconut cream
- ½ teaspoon minced garlic
- 1 tablespoon heavy cream
- ½ teaspoon ground coriander
- ½ teaspoon salt
- ½ teaspoon black pepper

Directions:
1. In the slow cooker, mix the calamari with the turmeric and the other ingredients and close the lid.

2. Cook the seafood for 6 hours on Low.
3. When the time is over, stir the mix and serve.
Nutrition value/serving: calories 200, fat 4.8, fiber 2.2, carbs 3.6, protein 14.4

Thyme Sea bass
Prep time: 10 minutes
Cooking time: 4 hours
Servings: 4
Ingredients:
- 11 oz sea bass, trimmed
- 2 tablespoons coconut cream
- 3 oz spring onions, chopped
- 1 teaspoon fennel seeds
- ½ teaspoon dried thyme
- 1 teaspoon olive oil
- 1/3 cup water
- 1 teaspoon apple cider vinegar
- ½ teaspoon salt

Directions:
1. In the slow cooker, mix the sea bass with the cream and the other ingredients.
2. Close the lid and cook sea bass for 4 hours on Low.

Nutrition value/serving: calories 304, fat 11.4, fiber 0.9, carbs 6.2, protein 0.7

Shrimp and Zucchini
Prep time: 15 minutes
Cooking time: 2 hours
Servings: 6
Ingredients:
- 1-pound shrimp, peeled and deveined
- 2 zucchinis, roughly cubed
- 1 cup cherry tomatoes, halved
- ½ cup Mozzarella cheese, shredded
- 4 tablespoons cream cheese
- 1 tablespoon butter, melted
- 1 teaspoon salt
- 1 tablespoon keto tomato sauce
- ¾ cup of water

Directions:
1. In the slow cooker, mix the shrimp with zucchinis and the other ingredients except the cheese and toss.
2. Sprinkle the cheese on top, close the lid and cook on High for 2 hours.

Nutrition value/serving: calories 223, fat 8.9, fiber 0.8, carbs 3.2, protein 19.3

Lemon Cod
Prep time: 15 minutes
Cooking time: 2 hours
Servings: 4
Ingredients:
- 20 oz cod fillet
- Juice of 1 lemon
- Zest of 1 lemon, grated
- 2 oz Parmesan, grated
- 1 tablespoon chives, chopped
- 1 teaspoon turmeric powder
- ½ teaspoon salt
- ½ teaspoon ground black pepper
- 1 teaspoon butter
- 1/3 cup organic almond milk

Directions:
1. In the slow cooker, mix the cod with lemon juice, zest and the other ingredients.
2. Close the lid and cook the sauce for 2 hours on High.
3. Divide between plates and serve.

Nutrition value/serving: calories 212, fat 5.6, fiber 4.4, carbs 6.6, protein 30.2

Cinnamon Mackerel
Prep time: 10 minutes
Cooking time: 3 hours
Servings: 4
Ingredients:
- 1 ½ pound mackerel, trimmed
- 1 tablespoon avocado oil
- 1 teaspoon garlic powder
- 1/3 cup coconut milk
- ½ teaspoon salt
- ½ teaspoon basil, dried
- 1 teaspoon cumin, ground
- ¾ teaspoon ground cinnamon

Directions:
1. In the slow cooker, mix the mackerel with the oil and the other ingredients and close the lid.
2. Cook the fish for 3 hours on High.
3. Divide between plates and serve.

Nutrition value/serving: calories 228, fat 8.8, fiber 0.9, carbs 2.2, protein 11.2

Parsley Salmon
Prep time: 15 minutes
Cooking time: 2 hours
Servings: 4
Ingredients:
- 10 oz salmon fillet
- 2 tablespoons parsley, chopped

- ½ cup coconut cream
- ½ teaspoon salt
- ½ teaspoon chili flakes
- 1 teaspoon turmeric powder
- 2 oz Parmesan, grated
- 3 tablespoons coconut oil

Directions:
1. In the slow cooker, mix the salmon with the parsley and the other ingredients.
2. Close the lid and cook the meal for 2 hours on High.

Nutrition value/serving: calories 283, fat 22.2, fiber 0.8, carbs 2.3, protein 21.2

Cheesy Tuna

Prep time: 10 minutes
Cooking time: 9 hours
Servings: 4
Ingredients:
- 1 cup coconut cream
- 1 tablespoon Ricotta cheese
- 1 teaspoon salt
- ½ teaspoon white pepper
- 10 ounces tuna fillet, boneless and cubed
- 1 teaspoon olive oil
- 1 garlic clove, crushed
- 1 teaspoon fennel seeds
- 1/2 cup Cheddar, shredded

Directions:
1. In the slow cooker, mix the tuna with the cream and the other ingredients.
2. Close the lid and cook snapper for 9 hours on Low.

Nutrition value/serving: calories 211, fat 4.3, fiber 3.3, carbs 7.8, protein 21

Spiced Shrimp

Prep time: 10 minutes
Cooking time: 1 hour
Servings: 2
Ingredients:
- 8 oz shrimp, peeled and deveined
- 1 teaspoon chili powder
- 1 teaspoon nutmeg, ground
- 1 teaspoon coriander, ground
- ½ teaspoon minced garlic
- 1 tablespoon olive oil
- 2 tablespoon coconut cream
- ½ teaspoon salt
- 2 tablespoons water

Directions:
1. In the slow cooker, mix the shrimp with chili powder, nutmeg and the other ingredients.
2. Close the lid.
3. Cook for 1 hour on High.

Nutrition value/serving: calories 200, fat 11.7, fiber 4.9, carbs 4.7, protein 9.6

Seafood Stew

Prep time: 15 minutes
Cooking time: 7 hours
Servings: 4
Ingredients:
- 2 tablespoons olive oil
- 1 cup mussels
- 1 cup salmon fillet, boneless and cubed
- 1 cup shrimp, peeled and deveined
- 3 spring onions, chopped
- ½ green bell pepper, chopped
- 1 garlic clove, diced
- ¾ teaspoon chili flakes
- ¼ teaspoon ground black pepper
- ¼ cup crushed tomatoes
- ½ teaspoon dried thyme

Directions:
1. In the slow cooker, mix the mussels with the salmon and the other ingredients.
2. Stir the mixture and close the lid.
3. Cook the meal for 7 hours on Low.
4. Divide into bowls and serve.

Nutrition value/serving: calories 260, fat 15.1, fiber 1.9, carbs 6.2, protein 25.1

Shrimp and Green Beans

Prep time: 15 minutes
Cooking time: 3 hours
Servings: 5
Ingredients:
- 1-pound shrimp, peeled and deveined
- ¼ pound green beans, trimmed and halved
- 1 teaspoon salt
- 1 teaspoon chili flakes
- 1 teaspoon paprika
- ½ teaspoon garam masala
- 1 teaspoon coriander, ground
- 1 teaspoon basil, dried
- ¾ cup crushed tomatoes
- 1 tablespoon olive oil
- 3 spring onions, chopped
- 1 green bell pepper, chopped
- 1 cup of water

Directions:

1. In the slow cooker, mix the shrimp with green beans, salt and the other ingredients.
2. Close the lid and cook for 3 hours on High.
3. Divide into bowls and serve.
Nutrition value/serving: calories 202, fat 7.6, fiber 3, carbs 8.6, protein 12.4

Salmon and Spinach Bake
Prep time: 10 minutes
Cooking time: 6 hours
Servings: 2
Ingredients:
- 1-pound salmon fillet, chopped
- 1/3 cup spinach, chopped
- ½ cup Cheddar cheese, shredded
- ¾ cup organic coconut milk
- 1 teaspoon butter
- ½ teaspoon ground thyme
- ½ teaspoon salt
- 1/3 cup of water

Directions:
1. In the slow cooker mix the salmon with spinach and the other ingredients, toss and close the lid.
2. Cook the salmon bake for 6 hours on Low.
Nutrition value/serving: calories 423, fat 16.1, fiber 1.9, carbs 3.8, protein 17.4

Chili Squid
Prep time: 15 minutes
Cooking time: 2.5 hours
Servings: 4
Ingredients:
- 16 oz squid tubes, trimmed (4 squid tubes)
- 1 cup spring onions, chopped
- 1 teaspoon salt
- ½ teaspoon chili powder
- ½ teaspoon hot paprika
- 1 tablespoon butter
- 1/3 cup heavy cream
- 1 teaspoon ground black pepper
- 1 tablespoon dried dill

Directions:
1. In the slow cooker, mix the squid with spring onions and the other ingredients.
2. Close the slow cooker lid and cook for 2.5 hours on High.
Nutrition value/serving: calories 244, fat 8.2, fiber 3.8, carbs 7.1, protein 13.2

Calamari Rings and Broccoli
Prep time: 15 minutes
Cooking time: 4.5 hours
Servings: 6
Ingredients:
- 1 1/2-pound calamari rings
- 1 cup broccoli florets
- 1 jalapeno pepper, minced
- 1 tablespoon keto tomato sauce
- 1/3 cup heavy cream
- ½ teaspoon salt
- ½ teaspoon chili powder
- 1 teaspoon cumin, ground
- 2 garlic cloves, diced
- 1 tablespoon butter

Directions:
1. In the slow cooker, mix the calamari with broccoli and the other ingredients, toss and close the lid.
2. Cook the meal on Low for 4.5 hours.
Nutrition value/serving: calories 210, fat 6.1, fiber 2.2, carbs 4.7, protein 18.1

Tilapia and Tomatoes
Prep time: 15 minutes
Cooking time: 2 hours
Servings: 2
Ingredients:
- 8 oz tilapia fillet (2 servings)
- 1 and ½ cups cherry tomatoes, halved
- 1 tablespoon keto tomato sauce
- 1 tablespoon butter, melted
- 3 tablespoons coconut cream
- ½ teaspoon lemongrass
- ½ teaspoon salt
- ¼ teaspoon chili flakes

Directions:
1. In the slow cooker, mix the tilapia with tomatoes and the other ingredients.
2. Close the slow cooker lid and cook tilapia for 2 hours on High.
Nutrition value/serving: calories 308, fat 12.2, fiber 0.5, carbs 1.9, protein 32.3

Tuna and Cabbage Mix
Prep time: 10 minutes
Cooking time: 3 hours
Servings: 4
Ingredients:
- 2 oz cabbage, shredded
- 11 oz tuna, drained, chopped

- 2 tablespoons keto tomato sauce
- 1/3 cup water
- 1 teaspoon salt
- 1 tablespoon butter
- 1 teaspoon turmeric powder

Directions:
1. In the slow cooker, mix the cabbage with the tuna and the other ingredients, and close the lid.
2. Cook cabbage for 3 hours on High.
3. Divide into bowls and serve.

Nutrition value/serving: calories 227, fat 8.3, fiber 0.8, carbs 3.2, protein 15.9

Mozzarella Fish

Prep time: 15 minutes
Cooking time: 2 hours
Servings: 4
Ingredients:
- 1-pound salmon fillet
- ½ cup heavy cream
- ½ cup Mozzarella, shredded
- 1 teaspoon oregano, dried
- ½ teaspoon turmeric powder
- 1 teaspoon butter
- ½ teaspoon ground black pepper
- ½ teaspoon smoked paprika
- ½ teaspoon ground nutmeg

Directions:
1. Put salmon fillet in the slow cooker.
2. Add the rest of the ingredients except the cheese.
3. Top the mix with the Mozzarella, and close the lid.
4. Cook fish gratin for 2 hours on High.

Nutrition value/serving: calories 241, fat 14.9, fiber 1.7, carbs 3.3, protein 24.2

Marinara Shrimp

Prep time: 10 minutes
Cooking time: 1 hour
Servings: 2
Ingredients:
- 10 oz shrimp, peeled and deveined
- 3 tablespoons keto marinara sauce
- 2 tablespoons coconut flour
- 1 tablespoon coconut cream

Directions:
1. In the slow cooker, mix the shrimp with the other ingredients and close the lid.
2. Cook the fish for 1 hour on High.

Nutrition value/serving: calories 212, fat 4.7, fiber 5.3, carbs 7.7, protein 26.9

Butter Salmon and Avocado

Prep time: 10 minutes
Cooking time: 1.5 hours
Servings: 1
Ingredients:
- 6 oz salmon fillet
- 1/3 cup butter
- 2 avocados, peeled, pitted and cubed
- 1 teaspoon garam masala
- 1 teaspoon coriander, ground
- 1 teaspoon lemon juice
- 1 teaspoon apple cider vinegar
- ¼ teaspoon salt

Directions:
1. In the slow cooker, mix the salmon with the butter and the other ingredients and close the lid.
2. Cook salmon for 1.5 hours on High.

Nutrition value/serving: calories 370, fat 11.9, fiber 0, carbs 0.2, protein 12.7

Mustard Shrimp

Prep time: 10 minutes
Cooking time: 2 hours
Servings: 2
Ingredients:
- 1-pound shrimp, peeled and deveined
- 2 tablespoons Dijon mustard
- ½ cup of coconut water
- 1 teaspoon turmeric powder
- ½ teaspoon salt
- 1 teaspoon olive oil

Directions:
1. In the slow cooker, mix the shrimp with the mustard and the other ingredients.
2. Close the lid.
3. Cook the fish on Low for 2 hours.

Nutrition value/serving: calories 172, fat 4.4, fiber 0.6, carbs 1.3, protein 32.4

Salmon and Asparagus

Prep time: 15 minutes
Cooking time: 3.5 hours
Servings: 4
Ingredients:
- 1-pound salmon fillet, boneless
- ¼ pound asparagus, trimmed and halved
- 1 cup coconut cream
- 1 teaspoon dried basil

- ½ teaspoon salt
- 1 teaspoon dried parsley
- Cooking spray

Directions:
1. In the slow cooker, mix the salmon with the asparagus, cream and the other ingredients and close the lid.
2. Cook the fish loaf for 3.5 hours on Low.

Nutrition value/serving: calories 204, fat 9.2, fiber 2.8, carbs 6.7, protein 23

Avocado and Shrimp

Prep time: 15 minutes
Cooking time: 2 hours
Servings: 2
Ingredients:
- 1 avocado, peeled, pitted and cubed
- 8 oz shrimps, raw, peeled
- 1 teaspoon basil, dried
- 1 teaspoon coriander, ground
- 1 teaspoon butter, softened
- ½ teaspoon minced garlic
- ½ teaspoon chili flakes
- 1/3 cup water
- ½ teaspoon onion powder

Directions:
1. In the slow cooker, mix the shrimp with avocado, basil and the other ingredients and toss.
2. Close the lid and cook the meal on High for 2 hours.

Nutrition value/serving: calories 279, fat 13.9, fiber 6.8, carbs 12.1, protein 12.5

Tilapia and Radish Bites

Prep time: 15 minutes
Cooking time: 2.5 hours
Servings: 2
Ingredients:
- 1 ½ cups radishes, halved
- 1 teaspoon sweet paprika
- ½ teaspoon dried rosemary
- ¼ teaspoon ground black pepper
- ½ teaspoon salt
- 9 oz tilapia fillet, boneless and cubed
- 2 oz Cheddar cheese, sliced
- ¼ cup veggie stock

Directions:
1. In the slow cooker, mix the radishes with the fish and the other ingredients and toss.
2. Close the lid and cook the fish for 2.5 hours on High.

Nutrition value/serving: calories 251, fat 8.4, fiber 0.2, carbs 1.3, protein 6.6

Balsamic Scallops

Prep time: 10 minutes
Cooking time: 2 hours
Servings: 4
Ingredients:
- 8 scallops
- 1 tablespoon balsamic vinegar
- 1 teaspoon hot paprika
- ½ teaspoon salt
- 2 tablespoons olive oil
- ½ teaspoon dried rosemary

Directions:
1. In the slow cooker, mix the scallops with the vinegar and the other ingredients, toss and close the lid.
2. Cook bacon scallops for 2 hours on High.

Nutrition value/serving: calories 215, fat 6.2, fiber 0.1, carbs 1.8, protein 7.1

Lemon Crab Legs

Prep time: 10 minutes
Cooking time: 3 hours
Servings: 4
Ingredients:
- 12 oz King crab legs
- 1/3 cup butter
- Juice of 1 lemon
- Zest of 1 lemon, grated
- 1 tablespoon yellow curry paste
- ¼ cup of water
- 1 teaspoon minced garlic
- ½ teaspoon salt

Directions:
1. In the slow cooker, mix the crab with the butter and the other ingredients.
2. Close the lid and cook the crab legs for 3 hours on Low.

Nutrition value/serving: calories 165, fat 7.8, fiber 0, carbs 4.2, protein 5.6

Cod Patties

Prep time: 20 minutes
Cooking time: 1 hour
Servings: 3
Ingredients:
- 8 oz cod fillets, boneless, finely chopped
- 1 egg, beaten

- 1 teaspoon cilantro, dried
- 1 teaspoon Italian seasoning
- ¼ cup fresh basil, blended
- ½ teaspoon salt
- ¼ teaspoon chili powder
- 1/3 cup coconut milk
- 1 tablespoon butter
- 1 tablespoon almond flour

Directions:
1. In the mixing bowl, mix up together the cod with cilantro, seasoning, flour, basil, salt and chili powder, stir and shape medium patties out of this mix.
2. Toss the butter in the skillet and bring it to boil.
3. Add the patties and cook for 1 minute over medium high heat.
4. Transfer the patties in the slow cooker and add coconut milk.
5. Close the lid and cook patties for 1 hour on High.

Nutrition value/serving: calories 301, fat 21, fiber 4.7, carbs 5.8, protein 19.3

Cod Soup

Prep time: 10 minutes
Cooking time: 2 hours
Servings: 4
Ingredients:
- ½ cup cream
- 2 cups of water
- 12 oz cod, boneless and cubed
- 1 cup cherry tomatoes, halved
- 1 oz bacon, chopped, roasted
- 1 teaspoon salt
- 1 teaspoon ground black pepper
- 1/3 cup fresh cilantro, chopped

Directions:
1. In the slow cooker, mix the cod with the cream and the other ingredients, close the lid and cook on High for 2 hours.
2. Divide into bowls and serve.

Nutrition value/serving: calories 342, fat 5.6, fiber 4.3, carbs 3.8, protein 19.7

Salmon and Cauliflower Chowder

Prep time: 15 minutes
Cooking time: 2.5 hours
Servings: 2
Ingredients:
- 1-pound salmon fillet, boneless and cubed
- ¼ cup cauliflower florets
- 1 teaspoon turmeric powder
- 1 teaspoon basil, dried
- 1 cayenne pepper, chopped
- 1 teaspoon salt
- ½ teaspoon ground black pepper
- 2 tablespoon lemon juice
- 3 tablespoons coconut cream
- 1 ½ cup of water
- 2 tablespoons fresh parsley, chopped

Directions:
1. In the slow cooker, mix the salmon with cauliflower and the other ingredients and toss.
2. Close the lid and cook the ingredients for 2.5 hours on High.
3. Divide into bowls and serve.

Nutrition value/serving: calories 185, fat 6.9, fiber 2.1, carbs 7.5, protein 11.6

Coconut Catfish

Prep time: 6 minutes
Cooking time: 6.5 hours
Servings: 6
Ingredients:
- 13 oz catfish, chopped
- ½ cup of coconut milk
- 1 tablespoon Cajun seasoning
- 1 teaspoon curry powder
- 1 teaspoon salt
- ½ teaspoon chili flakes
- 1 bay leaf
- 1 garlic clove, peeled
- 1/3 teaspoon coriander, ground

Directions:
1. In the slow cooker, mix the catfish with coconut milk, seasoning and the other ingredients.
2. Close the lid and cook the stew for 6.5 hours on Low.
3. Transfer in the serving bowls and enjoy.

Nutrition value/serving: calories 299, fat 13.4, fiber 4.5, carbs 7.9, protein 12

Saffron Tilapia

Prep time: 15 minutes
Cooking time: 2 hours
Servings: 4
Ingredients:
- 15 oz tilapia fillet
- 1 cup coconut cream

- 1 teaspoon coconut oil
- ¼ teaspoon cumin
- ¼ teaspoon turmeric
- ¼ teaspoon ginger
- ¼ teaspoon paprika
- ¼ teaspoon saffron
- ¾ teaspoon ground black pepper
- 1 teaspoon salt

Directions:
1. In the slow cooker, mix the tilapia with cream and the other ingredients and toss gently.
2. Close the lid and cook fish for 2 hours on High.

Nutrition value/serving: calories 274, fat 13.3, fiber 4.3, carbs 7.5, protein 20.5

Caraway Cod

Prep time: 7 minutes
Cooking time: 5 hours
Servings: 2
Ingredients:
- 8 oz cod fillet
- 1 teaspoon caraway seeds
- ½ teaspoon salt
- ½ teaspoon cayenne pepper
- 1 teaspoon coriander, ground
- 1 tablespoon lime juice
- 1 tablespoon coconut cream
- 3 tablespoons avocado oil

Directions:
1. In the slow cooker, mix the cod with caraway seeds, salt, pepper and the other ingredients.
2. Close the lid and cook cod for 5 hours on Low.

Nutrition value/serving: calories 290, fat 23.4, fiber 4.7, carbs 11.7, protein 20.7

Chili Shrimp and Okra

Prep time: 10 minutes
Cooking time: 2.5 hours
Servings: 4
Ingredients:
- 1 teaspoon chili pepper
- ½ teaspoon chili flakes
- ½ teaspoon salt
- 1-pound shrimp, peeled and deveined
- 1 cup okra, sliced
- 2 tablespoons lemon juice
- 2 tablespoons butter, soft
- ¾ cup of water

Directions:
1. In the slow cooker, combine the shrimp with chili pepper, flakes and the other ingredients.
2. Cook the mix on Low for 2.5 hours.

Nutrition value/serving: calories 203, fat 11.6, fiber 3.9, carbs 8.1, protein 13.8

Nutmeg Halibut

Prep time: 10 minutes
Cooking time: 1 hour
Servings: 2
Ingredients:
- 2 halibut fillets
- 1 teaspoon lemon juice
- 1 teaspoon nutmeg, ground
- 1 tablespoon butter, melted
- ¾ teaspoon coriander, ground
- 1 tablespoon apple cider vinegar
- ¼ cup heavy cream

Directions:
1. In the slow cooker, mix the halibut with lemon juice, nutmeg and the other ingredients.
2. Close the lid and cook the fish for 1 hour on High.

Nutrition value/serving: calories 224, fat 6.8, fiber 0.1, carbs 5.1, protein 6.1

Lime Cod and Shrimps

Prep time: 10 minutes
Cooking time: 3 hours
Servings: 4
Ingredients:
- 1-pound cod fillet, boneless and cubed
- ½ pound shrimp, peeled and deveined
- Juice of 1 lime
- 1 teaspoon Italian seasoning
- 1 teaspoon dried rosemary
- 1/3 teaspoon cayenne pepper
- ½ teaspoon ginger
- ¾ teaspoon ground cinnamon
- 1 tablespoon butter

Directions:
1. In the slow cooker, mix the cod with shrimp, lime juice and the other ingredients, toss and close the lid.
2. Cook fish for 3 hours on High.
3. Divide into bowls and serve.

Nutrition value/serving: calories 220, fat 6, fiber 3.4, carbs 4.8, protein 20.4

Fish and Salsa Bowl

Prep time: 15 minutes
Cooking time: 2 hours
Servings: 5
Ingredients:
- 1-pound white fish fillets, boneless and cubed
- 1 cup keto salsa
- ½ teaspoon Italian seasoning
- ½ cup red cabbage, shredded
- ½ teaspoon paprika
- 2 tablespoons olive oil
- 1 tablespoon chives, chopped

Directions:
1. In the slow cooker, mix the fish with the salsa and the other ingredients.
2. Close the lid and cook on High for 2 hours.
3. Divide into bowls and serve.

Nutrition value/serving: calories 238, fat 16.3, fiber 1.9, carbs 5.8, protein 11.8

Shrimp Curry

Prep time: 10 minutes
Cooking time: 1.5 hours
Servings: 4
Ingredients:
- 1-pound shrimp, peeled and deveined
- 1 tablespoon red curry paste
- 1 teaspoon curry powder
- 1 cup of coconut milk
- 1 tablespoon curry paste
- 1/3 jalapeno pepper, chopped
- ½ teaspoon garlic powder
- 1 teaspoon olive oil
- ½ cup spring onions, chopped

Directions:
1. In the slow cooker, mix the shrimp with curry paste and the other ingredients.
2. Close the lid and cook the curry for 1.5 hours on High.

Nutrition value/serving: calories 261, fat 13.8, fiber 1.7, carbs 6, protein 21

Sage Halibut

Prep time: 10 minutes
Cooking time: 4.5 hours
Servings: 5
Ingredients:
- 5 halibut fillets, boneless
- ¼ cup coconut cream
- ½ teaspoon black pepper
- 1 teaspoon turmeric powder
- 1 teaspoon salt
- ½ teaspoon sage
- 1/3 cup butter

Directions:
1. In the slow cooker, mix the fish with coconut cream and the other ingredients.
2. Close the lid and cook the fish on Low for 4.5 hours.

Nutrition value/serving: calories 278, fat 19, fiber 4.1, carbs 6.2, protein 20.7

Sea Bass and Celery

Prep time: 8 minutes
Cooking time: 3.5 hours
Servings: 2
Ingredients:
- 2 sea bass fillets, boneless
- 1 cup celery stalks, peeled and cubed
- ½ teaspoon black pepper
- 1 teaspoon salt
- 1 tablespoon paprika
- ¼ teaspoon chili powder
- 1/3 cup sour cream

Directions:
1. In the slow cooker, mix the sea bass with the celery and the other ingredients and close the lid.
2. Cook the cod on High for 3.5 hours.

Nutrition value/serving: calories 263, fat 9.5, fiber 4.4, carbs 7.7, protein 21.8

Herbed Shrimp

Prep time: 10 minutes
Cooking time: 1.5 hours
Servings: 4
Ingredients:
- 1-pound shrimp, peeled and deveined
- 1 tablespoon oregano, chopped
- ½ teaspoon dried basil
- ½ teaspoon nutmeg, ground
- 1 tablespoon chives, chopped
- 1 tablespoon sage, chopped
- 1 tablespoon cilantro, chopped
- 1 teaspoon curry powder
- ½ teaspoon paprika
- 1 cup organic almond milk

Directions:
1. In the slow cooker, mix the shrimp with the oregano, basil and the other ingredients.

2. Close the lid and cook curry shrimps on High for 1.5 hours.
Nutrition value/serving: calories 212, fat 3.9, fiber 2.8, carbs 4.6, protein 20.4

Stevia Salmon

Prep time: 10 minutes
Cooking time: 4.5 hours
Servings: 3
Ingredients:
- 8 oz salmon fillet
- 1 tablespoon stevia
- 1 teaspoon saffron powder
- 1 teaspoon garam masala
- 2 tablespoons butter, melted
- ½ teaspoon ground black pepper
- ¼ teaspoon salt

Directions:
1. In the slow cooker mix the salmon with the stevia, saffron and the other ingredients, and close the lid.
2. Cook the salmon steaks for 4.5 hours on Low.

Nutrition value/serving: calories 232, fat 14.7, fiber 3.1, carbs 5.4, protein 15.3

Poultry

Nutmeg Chicken
Prep time: 15 minutes
Cooking time: 5.5 hours
Servings: 8
Ingredients:
- 3-pound whole chicken
- 2 teaspoons ground nutmeg
- 1 teaspoon ground paprika
- 1 teaspoon ground black pepper
- ½ teaspoon salt
- ½ teaspoon chili flakes
- 1 tablespoon Erythritol

Directions:
1. Line the slow cooker bottom with foil.
2. Combine the chicken with nutmeg and the other ingredients inside.
3. Close the lid and cook chicken for 5.5 hours on High.
4. For the crunchy crust, bake the chicken for 20 minutes at the preheated to the 360F oven.

Nutrition value/serving: calories 347, fat 12.7, fiber 3.2, carbs 2.6, protein 29.4

Chili Chicken
Prep time: 10 minutes
Cooking time: 5 hours
Servings: 4
Ingredients:
- 4 chicken thighs, skinless, boneless
- 1 teaspoon coriander, ground
- 1 teaspoon chili flakes
- ½ teaspoon garlic powder
- ½ teaspoon salt
- 5 oz Pepper Jack cheese, shredded
- 4 tablespoons butter
- ¼ cup of water

Directions:
1. Put chicken thighs in the slow cooker.
2. Add the rest of the ingredients except the cheese.
3. Close the lid and cook chicken on High for 4 hours.
4. Then sprinkle the chicken with shredded Pepper Jack cheese and close the lid.
5. Cook the chicken for 1 hour on High.

Nutrition value/serving: calories 336, fat 23.8, fiber 01, carbs 3.4, protein 32.3

Mozzarella Chicken
Prep time: 15 minutes
Cooking time: 9 hours
Servings: 4
Ingredients:
- 1-pound chicken breast, skinless, boneless and cubed
- 1 cup Mozzarella cheese, shredded
- ½ teaspoon cayenne pepper
- ½ teaspoon coriander, ground
- 1 teaspoon basil, dried
- 3 spring onions, chopped
- 1 cup heavy cream
- Cooking spray

Directions:
1. Spray the slow cooker bottom with cooking spray.
2. Chop the keto tortillas and chicken breast.
3. Combine the chicken with the cheese and the other ingredients, and close the slow cooker lid.
4. Cook the chicken for 9 hours on Low.

Nutrition value/serving: calories 269, fat 17.2, fiber 2.4, carbs 7, protein 30.6

Garlic Chicken
Prep time: 8 minutes
Cooking time: 4.5 hours
Servings: 6
Ingredients:
- 2-pound chicken thighs
- 1 tablespoon chives, chopped
- 1 teaspoon black pepper
- 1 bay leaf
- 2 spring onions, chopped
- 1 teaspoon salt
- 1 ½ cup water
- 1 teaspoon garlic, diced

Directions:
1. Put garlic in the slow cooker.
2. Add chicken and the other ingredients and close the lid.
3. Cook the chicken thighs for 4.5 hours on High.
4. Serve the chicken thighs with hot gravy.

Nutrition value/serving: calories 305, fat 11.3, fiber 5.5, carbs 7.8, protein 44

Chicken and Tomatoes

Prep time: 15 minutes
Cooking time: 5.5 hours
Servings: 4
Ingredients:
- 3 spring onions, chopped
- 1 tablespoon keto tomato sauce
- ¼ cup crushed tomatoes
- 1/3 teaspoon salt
- ½ teaspoon ground black pepper
- 1 ½-pound chicken breast, skinless, boneless
- 1 teaspoon balsamic vinegar
- 1 tablespoon olive oil
- 1 tablespoon basil, chopped
- ½ teaspoon garlic powder
- ½ cup of chicken stock

Directions:
1. Heat up a pan with the oil over medium-high heat, add the chicken, brown for 5 minutes and transfer to the slow cooker.
2. Add the rest of the ingredients and close the lid.
3. Cook cacciatore for 5.5 hours on Low.

Nutrition value/serving: calories 283, fat 8.7, fiber 1.1, carbs 6.4, protein 37

Fennel Chicken Mix

Prep time: 10 minutes
Cooking time: 5 hours
Servings: 7
Ingredients:
- 3-pound chicken drumsticks
- 1 fennel, chopped
- ½ teaspoon fennel seeds
- ½ teaspoon salt
- ½ teaspoon cayenne pepper
- ½ teaspoon garlic powder
- ½ teaspoon coriander, ground
- ½ teaspoon saffron
- ¼ teaspoon ground nutmeg
- ½ teaspoon turmeric
- 2 tablespoons butter
- 1/3 cup almond milk
- ¼ cup fresh cilantro, chopped

Directions:
1. In the slow cooker, mix the chicken with fennel and the other ingredients.
2. Close the lid and cook chicken for 5 hours on High.
3. Divide between plates and serve.

Nutrition value/serving: calories 388, fat 17.2, fiber 0.6, carbs 1.5, protein 53.9

Chicken and Scallions Mix

Prep time: 15 minutes
Cooking time: 4.5 hours
Servings: 4
Ingredients:
- 11 oz chicken breast, skinless, boneless
- 1 teaspoon Italian seasoning
- 1 tablespoon apple cider vinegar
- ¼ cup of olive oil
- 1/2 cup scallions, chopped
- 1/4 cup chicken stock
- ½ teaspoon salt
- ½ teaspoon chili flakes
- ¼ teaspoon cayenne pepper

Directions:
1. Put the chicken in the slow cooker and combine with all the other ingredients.
2. Close the lid and cook on High for 4 hours and 30 minutes.

Nutrition value/serving: calories 304, fat 17.8, fiber 4.8, carbs 6.6, protein 19.7

Basil Chicken

Prep time: 15 minutes
Cooking time: 2 hours
Servings: 2
Ingredients:
- 9 oz chicken breast, skinless, boneless
- ¼ cup fresh basil, chopped
- 1 tomato, chopped
- 1 tablespoon olive oil
- 1 teaspoon coriander, ground
- 1 teaspoon chili powder
- ½ teaspoon cayenne pepper
- ½ teaspoon salt
- ½ teaspoon paprika
- 1 tablespoon olive oil
- ¼ cup of chicken stock

Directions:
1. In the slow cooker, mix the chicken with the basil and the other ingredients, close the lid and cook on High for 2 hours.

Nutrition value/serving: calories 287, fat 18, fiber 4.8, carbs 8.1, protein 28.9

Chicken and Tahini Sauce

Prep time: 10 minutes
Cooking time: 8 hours
Servings: 3

Ingredients:
- 13 oz chicken fillet, sliced
- 1 tablespoon tahini paste
- 1/3 cup coconut milk
- 1 tablespoon sour cream
- 1 teaspoon salt
- ½ teaspoon white pepper
- ½ teaspoon oregano, dried
- ½ teaspoon sweet paprika
- ½ teaspoon turmeric
- 1 teaspoon chili flakes
- 1 tablespoon avocado oil
- 1 green chili, chopped

Directions:
1. In the slow cooker, mix the chicken with the tahini paste and the other ingredients.
2. Close the lid and cook chicken for 8 hours on Low.
3. Divide between plates and serve.

Nutrition value/serving: calories 321, fat 17, fiber 8.2, carbs 4.4, protein 37.4

Paprika Chicken and Sauce

Prep time: 10 minutes
Cooking time: 5.15 hours
Servings: 3
Ingredients:
- 4 chicken thighs, skinless, boneless
- ¼ cup keto tomato sauce
- 1 tablespoon sweet paprika
- 1 teaspoon cayenne pepper
- 1 teaspoon salt

Directions:
1. In the slow cooker, mix the chicken with the sauce and the other ingredients and close the lid.
2. Cook chicken for 6 hours on Low.

Nutrition value/serving: calories 393, fat 15.4, fiber 0.5, carbs 3.5, protein 56.8

Cheddar Chicken

Prep time: 10 minutes
Cooking time: 3 hours
Servings: 4
Ingredients:
- 1-pound chicken breast, skinless, boneless
- 2 oz Cheddar, grated
- 1 teaspoon turmeric powder
- 1 teaspoon oregano, dried
- 1 cup heavy cream
- 1 teaspoon ground black pepper
- 1 teaspoon almond butter

Directions:
1. Put the chicken breast in the slow cooker.
2. Add the rest of the ingredients and close the lid.
3. Cook chicken for 3 hours on High.

Nutrition value/serving: calories 324, fat 19.3, fiber 4.5, carbs 7.4, protein 30.1

Chicken Salad

Prep time: 20 minutes
Cooking time: 2 hours
Servings: 4
Ingredients:
- 7 oz chicken fillet, cut into strips
- 1 teaspoon cayenne pepper
- ½ teaspoon salt
- 1 tablespoon almond butter
- ¼ cup of chicken stock
- 1 cup fresh spinach
- 1 tablespoon olive oil
- ¼ cup cherry tomatoes, halved
- 1 oz Parmesan, grated
- 1 teaspoon dried oregano

Directions:
1. In the slow cooker, mix the chicken with salt, pepper and the other ingredients except the spinach and tomatoes.
2. Close the lid and cook chicken on High for 2 hours.
3. In a bowl, mix the chicken with the remaining ingredients, toss and serve.

Nutrition value/serving: calories 286, fat 13.1, fiber 5.9, carbs 8.4, protein 20.8

Chicken and Eggplant

Prep time: 15 minutes
Cooking time: 7 hours
Servings: 6
Ingredients:
- 2 spring onions, chopped
- 1 big eggplant, cubed
- 2 pounds chicken breast, skinless, boneless and sliced
- 1 tablespoon capers
- 1 teaspoon ground black pepper
- 1 teaspoon salt
- 2 garlic cloves, chopped
- 1 teaspoon chili flakes
- 1 tablespoon keto tomato sauce
- 1 cup of water
- 1 teaspoon avocado oil

Directions:
1. Pour the oil in the skillet and bring it to boil.
2. Place the chicken breast in the skillet and cook it on high heat for 4 minutes from each side.
3. Then transfer the chicken breast in the slow cooker.
4. Add the rest of the ingredients and toss.
5. Close the lid.
6. Cook for 7 hours on Low.

Nutrition value/serving: calories 230, fat 4.9, fiber 1, carbs 3.3, protein 40.6

Chicken and Onions Mix

Prep time: 10 minutes
Cooking time: 2 hours
Servings: 4
Ingredients:
- ¾ cup spring onions, chopped
- 1 teaspoon chili powder
- 1 teaspoon coriander, ground
- 1 cup heavy cream
- 1 bay leaf
- 1 teaspoon chili powder
- ¾ teaspoon ground clove
- 1 teaspoon salt
- 12 oz chicken fillet

Directions:
1. In the slow cooker, mix the chicken with the onion and the other ingredients.
2. Close the lid and cook chicken for 2 hours on High.
3. Divide between plates and serve.

Nutrition value/serving: calories 278, fat 17.6, fiber 4.9, carbs 8.6, protein 25.6

Creamy Chicken

Prep time: 15 minutes
Cooking time: 3 hours
Servings: 2
Ingredients:
- 8 oz chicken fillet, boneless and cut into cubes
- ½ teaspoon salt
- 1 teaspoon turmeric powder
- 1 teaspoon sweet chili pepper, minced
- ½ teaspoon chili powder
- 1 tablespoon butter
- ¾ cup coconut cream

Directions:
1. In the slow cooker, mix the chicken with the salt, turmeric and the other ingredients.
2. Close the lid and cook the chicken for 3 hours on High.

Nutrition value/serving: calories 295, fat 20.6, fiber 5.2, carbs 10.3, protein 19

Turkey and Peppers

Prep time: 15 minutes
Cooking time: 5 hours
Servings: 4
Ingredients:
- 1 green bell pepper, sliced
- 1 red bell pepper, sliced
- 1-pound turkey breast, boneless and sliced
- 1 tablespoon ground paprika
- 1 tablespoon smoked paprika
- 1 tablespoon olive oil
- ¾ cup chicken stock
- 1 teaspoon basil, dried

Directions:
1. In the slow cooker, mix the turkey with the paprika and the other ingredients
2. Cook the chicken for 5 hours on Low.
3. Divide into bowls and serve.

Nutrition value/serving: calories 234, fat 6.6, fiber 6.1, carbs 3.4, protein 24.7

Dill Turkey

Prep time: 5 minutes
Cooking time: 3.5 hours
Servings: 3
Ingredients:
- 2 pounds turkey breast, skinless and sliced
- ¼ cup fresh dill, chopped
- ½ teaspoon turmeric powder
- ½ teaspoon salt
- ½ cup of water
- 1 teaspoon olive oil

Directions:
1. In the slow cooker, mix the turkey with dill and the other ingredients.
2. Close the slow cooker lid and cook for 3.5 hours on High.

Nutrition value/serving: calories 236, fat 5, fiber 4.6, carbs 17.5, protein 25.4

Chicken with Cheese

Prep time: 10 minutes
Cooking time: 2.5 hours
Servings: 4
Ingredients:

- 11 oz chicken fillet, sliced
- 4 oz Cheddar cheese, shaved
- 1 teaspoon salt
- ½ teaspoon cayenne pepper
- 1 teaspoon curry powder
- 1 teaspoon dried marjoram
- 1 teaspoon paprika
- ½ teaspoon dried basil
- ¼ cup almond butter

Directions:
1. In the slow cooker, mix the chicken with cheese and the other ingredients.
2. Close the lid and cook the meal on High for 2 hours.
3. Divide between plates and serve.

Nutrition value/serving: calories 256, fat 14, fiber 4.4, carbs 8.2, protein 30.1

Chicken and Zucchinis

Prep time: 10 minutes
Cooking time: 2.5 hours
Servings: 2
Ingredients:
- 8 oz chicken fillet
- 2 zucchinis, sliced
- 2 tablespoons Dijon mustard
- 1 tablespoon butter
- 1 teaspoon chili flakes
- 1 teaspoon salt
- 1 teaspoon black pepper

Directions:
1. Cut the chicken fillet into 2 servings.
2. Combine the chicken with the zucchinis and the other ingredients in the slow cooker.
3. Cook the meal for 2.5 hours on High.

Nutrition value/serving: calories 277, fat 14.8, fiber 5.5, carbs 10.9, protein 33.3

Ground Chicken Mix

Prep time: 15 minutes
Cooking time: 6 hours
Servings: 4
Ingredients:
- 1 cup baby spinach
- ½ cup, collard greens, chopped
- 1 cup ground chicken meat
- ½ cup of water
- 3 tablespoons olive oil
- 1 teaspoon salt
- 1 teaspoon turmeric
- 1 jalapeno pepper, chopped
- 1 eggplant, chopped

Directions:
1. Pour olive oil in the skillet and heat up over medium heat.
2. Add the meat, brown for 5 minutes and transfer to the slow cooker.
3. Add the rest of the ingredients and toss.
4. Close the lid and cook the stew for 6 hours on Low.

Nutrition value/serving: calories 223, fat 16.3, fiber 4.5, carbs 11.1, protein 9.7

Lime Chicken Drumsticks

Prep time: 10 minutes
Cooking time: 4.5 hours
Servings: 4
Ingredients:
- ½ jalapeno pepper, chopped
- 2 spring onions, chopped
- 1 red bell pepper, chopped
- Juice of 1 lime
- Zest of 1 lime, grated
- 1-pound chicken drumsticks
- 1 cup of water
- 1 teaspoon salt
- ½ teaspoon chili flakes
- 2 tablespoons tahini paste

Directions:
1. In the slow cooker, mix the chicken with lime juice and the other ingredients.
2. Close the lid and cook chicken for 4.5 hours on High.

Nutrition value/serving: calories 301, fat 10.6, fiber 5.6, carbs 6.7, protein 33.1

Chicken with Spinach

Prep time: 15 minutes
Cooking time: 7 hours
Servings: 2
Ingredients:
- 2 chicken thighs, boneless
- 1 ½ cups baby spinach
- 1 teaspoon oregano, dried
- 1 teaspoon minced garlic
- 2 tablespoons butter
- ½ teaspoon salt
- 1 tablespoon fresh parsley, chopped
- ½ cup of chicken stock
- 1 teaspoon ground black pepper

Directions:
1. Toss butter in the skillet and melt it.
2. Add chicken thighs and roast them for 3 minutes from each side.

3. Transfer to the slow cooker, add the rest of the ingredients except the spinach.
4. Close the lid and cook the chicken for 6 hours on Low.
5. Add the spinach, cook on Low for 1 more hour and serve.
Nutrition value/serving: calories 401, fat 22.9, fiber 7.3, carbs 5.3, protein 43.1

Rosemary Turkey

Prep time: 10 minutes
Cooking time: 4 hours
Servings: 5
Ingredients:
- 5 teaspoons butter
- 1 tablespoon rosemary, chopped
- 1 teaspoon sweet paprika
- 1 teaspoon turmeric powder
- 1 tablespoon sour cream
- 2-pound turkey breast, skinless, boneless and sliced
- 1 tablespoon lemon zest, grated
- 1 teaspoon salt
- 1 tablespoon lemon juice

Directions:
1. In the slow cooker, mix the turkey with butter, rosemary and the other ingredients.
2. Close the slow cooker lid and cook chicken thighs for 4 hours on High.
Nutrition value/serving: calories 301, fat 15.3, fiber 4.4, carbs 6.2, protein 22.5

Chicken Breast with Capers

Prep time: 10 minutes
Cooking time: 7 hours
Servings: 4
Ingredients:
- 2 tablespoons capers
- 1-pound chicken breast
- 3 garlic cloves, minced
- 1 tablespoon coriander, ground
- ½ teaspoon salt
- 1 teaspoon smoked paprika
- 1/3 cup olive oil
- ½ teaspoon dried marjoram

Directions:
1. In the slow cooker, mix the chicken with capers and eth other ingredients.
2. Close the lid and cook the chicken for 7 hours on Low.
3. When the chicken is cooked, slice it into the servings.

Nutrition value/serving: calories 305, fat 21.5, fiber 6.4, carbs 6.3, protein 24.3

Duck and Berries

Prep time: 10 minutes
Cooking time: 4 hours
Servings: 4
Ingredients:
- 2 duck breasts, boneless and skin scored
- 2 tablespoons blackberries
- 2 tablespoons blueberries
- 1 teaspoon turmeric powder
- 1 teaspoon liquid stevia
- ¼ teaspoon turmeric
- ½ teaspoon paprika
- 1 teaspoon salt
- 1/3 cup butter

Directions:
1. In the slow cooker, mix the duck with berries and the other ingredients toss and close the lid.
2. Cook the mix for 4 hours on High.
3. Divide between plates and serve.
Nutrition value/serving: calories 272, fat 19.9, fiber 5.4, carbs 10.7, protein 22.1

Chicken and Okra

Prep time: 10 minutes
Cooking time: 4.5 hours
Servings: 2
Ingredients:
- 8 oz chicken breast, skinless, boneless
- 1 tablespoon keto tomato sauce
- 1 cup okra, sliced
- ¼ cup of water
- 1 teaspoon sweet paprika
- ½ teaspoon chili powder
- ½ teaspoon salt
- ½ teaspoon dried oregano

Directions:
1. In the slow cooker, mix the chicken with the tomato sauce and the other ingredients.
2. Close the lid.
3. Cook pulled chicken for 4 hours and 30 minutes.
Nutrition value/serving: calories 213, fat 7.5, fiber 5.2, carbs 8.9, protein 25.9

Chicken and Cucumber

Prep time: 15 minutes
Cooking time: 4.5 hours
Servings: 3

Ingredients:
- 3 cucumbers, roughly cubed
- 9 oz chicken fillet, sliced
- 1 teaspoon oregano, dried
- 1 teaspoon basil, dried
- 2 oz Cheddar cheese, shredded
- 1 teaspoon cayenne pepper
- 1/3 cup heavy cream

Directions:
1. In the slow cooker, mix the chicken with the cucumbers and the other ingredients.
2. Close the lid and cook chicken pepperoni for 4.5 hours on High.

Nutrition value/serving: calories 366, fat 34.3, fiber 0.2, carbs 6.5, protein 38.3

Shredded Chicken

Prep time: 10 minutes
Cooking time: 4.5 hours
Servings: 2
Ingredients:
- 1 teaspoon cumin, ground
- 1 teaspoon sweet paprika
- ½ cup of water
- 1 teaspoon olive oil
- 1 teaspoon cilantro, dried
- 1 teaspoon butter
- 1 teaspoon salt
- 7 oz chicken breast, skinless, boneless

Directions:
1. In the slow cooker, mix the chicken with cumin, paprika and the other ingredients, close the lid and cook it for 4.5 hours on High.
2. After this, with the help of the fork shred the chicken.
3. Divide into bowls and serve with the gravy.

Nutrition value/serving: calories 271, fat 6.7, fiber 7.1, carbs 7.3, protein 21.2

Almond Chicken

Prep time: 10 minutes
Cooking time: 2.5 hours
Servings: 2
Ingredients:
- 4 chicken wings
- ¼ cup keto tomato sauce
- ¼ cup organic almond milk
- ½ cup almonds, chopped
- 1 teaspoon sweet paprika
- 1 teaspoon dried basil

Directions:
1. In the slow cooker, mix the chicken with the sauce, almond milk and the other ingredients and close the lid.
2. Cook the mix for 2.5 hours on High.

Nutrition value/serving: calories 575, fat 22.1, fiber 1 carbs 3, protein 84.6

Chicken and Mushrooms

Prep time: 7 minutes
Cooking time: 8 hours
Servings: 4
Ingredients:
- 1 cup cremini mushrooms, sliced
- 11 oz chicken fillet, sliced
- 1 teaspoon sage, dried
- 1 teaspoon salt
- 1 teaspoon ground black pepper
- ¾ teaspoon chili flakes
- 1 teaspoon butter
- 1 cup heavy cream

Directions:
1. In the slow cooker, mix the chicken with the mushrooms and the other ingredients.
2. After this, close the lid and cook the mix for 8 hours on Low.
3. Mix up the chicken every 3 hours.

Nutrition value/serving: calories 312, fat 18.4, fiber 4.5, carbs 4, protein 24.2

Salsa Chicken

Prep time: 8 minutes
Cooking time: 3.5 hours
Servings: 4
Ingredients:
- 4 chicken drumsticks
- ¼ cup keto salsa
- ¾ cup of water
- ½ teaspoon black pepper
- 1 teaspoon minced garlic
- ½ teaspoon salt
- 1 tablespoon scallions, chopped

Directions:
1. Put chicken drumsticks and the other ingredients in the slow cooker.
2. Close the lid and cook the drumsticks for 3.5 hours on High.

Nutrition value/serving: calories 272, fat 2.6, fiber 6.1, carbs 8.5, protein 12.7

Chicken and Kale

Prep time: 15 minutes
Cooking time: 3.5 hours

Servings: 2
Ingredients:
- 7 oz chicken fillet
- 1/3 cup kale, chopped
- 1 teaspoon butter, softened
- ½ teaspoon salt
- 1 teaspoon saffron powder
- 1 teaspoon coriander, ground
- ½ teaspoon ground black pepper
- ¾ cup sour cream

Directions:
1. In the slow cooker, mix the chicken with kale and the other ingredients and close the lid.
2. Cook the chicken fillet for 3.5 hours on High.
3. Divide into bowls and serve.

Nutrition value/serving: calories 392, fat 27.4, fiber 7.3, carbs 12.2, protein 31.7

Cumin Chicken

Prep time: 10 minutes
Cooking time: 5.5 hours
Servings: 5
Ingredients:
- 1-pound chicken thighs, skinless, boneless
- 1 teaspoon oregano, dried
- ¼ teaspoon basil, chopped
- ½ teaspoon salt
- 1 teaspoon olive oil
- 1/3 cup chicken stock
- ½ teaspoon garlic powder
- ½ teaspoon chili powder
- ½ teaspoon ground cumin

Directions:
1. In the slow cooker, mix the chicken with the oregano and the other ingredients.
2. Close the lid and cook the mix for 5.5 hours on Low.

Nutrition value/serving: calories 394, fat 7.8, fiber 4.3, carbs 7.8, protein 27

Cilantro Chicken

Prep time: 10 minutes
Cooking time: 6 hours
Servings: 4
Ingredients:
- ½ cup cilantro, chopped
- 1 teaspoon garam masala
- 1 teaspoon turmeric powder
- 1/3 cup butter
- 1 teaspoon salt
- 1 teaspoon onion powder
- 1 ½ pound chicken breast, skinless, boneless

Directions:
1. In the slow cooker, mix the chicken with the cilantro, masala and the other ingredients.
2. Close the lid and cook chicken for 6 hours on Low.
3. Transfer to plates and serve.

Nutrition value/serving: calories 334, fat 19.7, fiber 0.3, carbs 1, protein 36.5

Turkey with Tomatoes and Eggplants

Prep time: 10 minutes
Cooking time: 6 hours
Servings: 3
Ingredients:
- 10 oz turkey breast, skinless, boneless
- 1 teaspoon hot paprika
- 1 cup cherry tomatoes, halved
- 1 eggplant, cubed
- ½ teaspoon salt
- ½ teaspoon cayenne pepper
- ¾ cup of coconut milk
- ½ teaspoon dried oregano
- ¼ jalapeno pepper, minced
- 1 teaspoon butter

Directions:
1. In the slow cooker, mix the turkey with paprika, tomatoes and the rest of the ingredients.
2. Close the lid and cook a turkey breast for 6 hours on Low.

Nutrition value/serving: calories 261, fat 17.4, fiber 7.3, carbs 9.9, protein 18.2

Chicken and Sour Cream Sauce

Prep time: 10 minutes
Cooking time: 7 hours
Servings: 4
Ingredients:
- 10 oz chicken fillet
- 1 cup sour cream
- 1 teaspoon turmeric powder
- 1 tablespoon almond flour
- 1 teaspoon paprika
- ½ teaspoon salt
- ½ teaspoon ground black pepper
- 2 tablespoons apple cider vinegar

Directions:
1. In the slow cooker mix the chicken with the cream and the other ingredients and close the lid.
2. Cook the chicken for 7 hours on Low.
Nutrition value/serving: calories 284, fat 11.1, fiber 5.4, carbs 7.1, protein 22.4

Chicken Cubes and Pesto
Prep time: 10 minutes
Cooking time: 3.5 hours
Servings: 4
Ingredients:
- 2 teaspoons hot paprika
- 3 tablespoons basil pesto
- 1-pound chicken breast, skinless, boneless, chopped
- 1 teaspoon salt
- ½ teaspoon minced garlic
- 2 spring onions, chopped
- ½ teaspoon cayenne pepper
- ½ cup chicken stock

Directions:
1. In the slow cooker, mix the chicken with paprika, pesto and the other ingredients, and close the lid.
2. Cook the chicken for 3.5 hours on High.
Nutrition value/serving: calories 320, fat 8.3, fiber 0.9, carbs 3.2, protein 26.3

Chicken and Celery
Prep time: 15 minutes
Cooking time: 3 hours
Servings: 2
Ingredients:
- 1 oz celery root, chopped
- ¼ cup of chicken stock
- ½ cup heavy cream
- ¾ cup tomatoes, cubed
- 8 oz chicken fillet, chopped
- ½ teaspoon salt
- ½ teaspoon ground black pepper
- 1 tablespoon balsamic vinegar
- 1 tablespoon butter

Directions:
1. Put the heavy cream in the slow cooker.
2. Add the celery, chicken and the other ingredients.
3. Close the lid and cook tipsy chicken for 3 hours on High.
Nutrition value/serving: calories 324, fat 28.9, fiber 1.4, carbs 4.9, protein 36.1

Marjoram Chicken
Prep time: 10 minutes
Cooking time: 2.5 hours
Servings: 4
Ingredients:
- 4 chicken thighs, skinless, boneless
- 1 teaspoon hot paprika
- 1 teaspoon curry powder
- 1 teaspoon salt
- 1 tablespoon butter
- 1 teaspoon dried marjoram
- 1/3 cup water

Directions:
1. In the slow cooker, mix the chicken with paprika and the other ingredients.
2. Close the lid and cook the chicken for 2.5 hours on High.
Nutrition value/serving: calories 289, fat 13.8, fiber 3.5, carbs 6.3, protein 42.7

Chicken and Cabbage
Prep time: 10 minutes
Cooking time: 2 hours
Servings: 4
Ingredients:
- 1-pound chicken wings
- 1 tablespoon chili powder
- 1 and ½ cups red cabbage, shredded
- ¼ cup chicken stock
- 1 tablespoon paprika
- ½ teaspoon turmeric
- ½ teaspoon onion powder
- 1 teaspoon olive oil

Directions:
1. In the slow cooker, mix the chicken with cabbage and the other ingredients.
2. Close the lid and cook the chicken wings for 2 hours on High.
Nutrition value/serving: calories 240, fat 10.5, fiber 1, carbs 1.9, protein 33.2

Chicken and Walnuts
Prep time: 10 minutes
Cooking time: 6 hours
Servings: 4
Ingredients:
- ¼ teaspoon mustard seeds
- ½ teaspoon ground ginger
- ¾ teaspoon curry powder
- 1 teaspoon salt
- 1 teaspoon black pepper

- 1 teaspoon garam masala
- 1 tablespoon avocado oil
- ¾ cup of coconut milk
- ½ cup walnuts, chopped
- 10 oz chicken breast, skinless, boneless

Directions:
1. In the slow cooker, mix the chicken with walnuts and the other ingredients.
2. Close the slow cooker lid and cook chicken for 6 hours on Low.

Nutrition value/serving: calories 221, fat 16.1, fiber 7.1, carbs 6.7, protein 16.1

Chicken, Tomatoes and Olives

Prep time: 5 minutes
Cooking time: 7 hours
Servings: 4
Ingredients:
- 1 cup of water
- 14 oz chicken drumsticks
- 1 tablespoon thyme
- 1 cup cherry tomatoes, halved
- 1 cup black olives, pitted and halved
- 1 teaspoon salt
- 1 teaspoon paprika
- 1 tablespoon olive oil
- ½ teaspoon peppercorns

Directions:
1. In the slow cooker, mix the chicken with thyme, tomatoes and the other ingredients.
2. Close the slow cooker lid and cook the mix for 7 hours on Low.

Nutrition value/serving: calories 281, fat 9.2, fiber 0.5, carbs 4.9, protein 27.5

Ground Chicken and Green Beans

Prep time: 10 minutes
Cooking time: 8 hours
Servings: 4
Ingredients:
- 1 cup ground chicken
- 1 teaspoon sweet paprika
- 1 cup green beans, halved
- ½ teaspoon salt
- ½ teaspoon dried oregano
- 1 tablespoon butter
- ½ cup of chicken stock
- 1 teaspoon garlic powder
- 1 tablespoon almonds, chopped
- 2 spring onions, chopped

Directions:
1. In the slow cooker, mix the chicken with the paprika and the other ingredients and close the lid.
2. Cook the sauté for 8 hours on Low or overnight.

Nutrition value/serving: calories 291, fat 6.5, fiber 4.3, carbs 4.5, protein 11.2

Chicken and Tomato Sauce

Prep time: 10 minutes
Cooking time: 3.5 hours
Servings: 1
Ingredients:
- 6 oz chicken fillet
- ¼ cup Cheddar, shredded
- 1 teaspoon coriander, ground
- 1 teaspoon cumin, ground
- ¼ teaspoon salt
- ½ teaspoon turmeric
- 3 tablespoons keto tomato sauce
- 1 teaspoon chives, chopped
- 1 garlic clove, diced
- 1/3 cup water

Directions:
1. In the slow cooker, mix the chicken with the Cheddar and the other ingredients.
2. Close the slow cooker lid and cook the chicken on High for 3.5 hours.
3. Divide into bowls and serve.

Nutrition value/serving: calories 341, fat 18.9, fiber 4.5, carbs 6.5, protein 51.9

Lemon Turkey

Prep time: 10 minutes
Cooking time: 5.5 hours
Servings: 2
Ingredients:
- Juice of 1 lemon
- 1 teaspoon cayenne pepper
- ¼ teaspoon salt
- 1 tablespoon sour cream
- 1 teaspoon turmeric powder
- ½ teaspoon ground black pepper
- 8 oz chicken thighs, skinless, boneless
- 1 tablespoon olive oil

Directions:
1. In the slow cooker, mix the chicken with the turmeric and the other ingredients.
2. Close the lid and cook chicken thighs on Low for 5.5 hours.

Nutrition value/serving: calories 300, fat 17.4, fiber 6.6, carbs 7.8, protein 33.4

Chicken and Coconut Milk

Prep time: 10 minutes
Cooking time: 3.5 hours
Servings: 5
Ingredients:
- 1-pound ground chicken
- 1 teaspoon minced garlic
- ½ teaspoon dried basil
- 1 teaspoon turmeric powder
- 3 oz pepperoni, sliced
- 3 oz Parmesan, grated
- ¼ cup of coconut milk
- ½ teaspoon sage, dried

Directions:
1. In the slow cooker, mix the chicken with the garlic and the other ingredients.
2. Close the slow cooker lid and cook for 3.5 hours on High.

Nutrition value/serving: calories 351, fat 21, fiber 5.9, carbs 6.2, protein 36.3

Chicken and Green Pepper Mix

Prep time: 10 minutes
Cooking time: 10 hours
Servings: 4
Ingredients:
- 9 oz chicken thighs, skinless, boneless
- 1 teaspoon stevia
- ½ teaspoon salt
- ½ teaspoon paprika
- 1 green bell pepper, chopped
- 1 cup of water
- 2 tablespoons keto tomato sauce

Directions:
1. In the slow cooker, mix the chicken with the stevia and the other ingredients.
2. Close the lid and cook goulash for 10 hours on Low.

Nutrition value/serving: calories 245, fat 5.3, fiber 2.9, carbs 5.2, protein 19.3

Chicken Fillets and Mustard Sauce

Prep time: 10 minutes
Cooking time: 7 hours
Servings: 5
Ingredients:
- 5 chicken fillets
- 1 tablespoon butter, softened
- 2 tablespoons mustard
- ½ cup coconut cream
- ½ teaspoon salt
- 1 teaspoon apple cider vinegar
- 4 tablespoons cream cheese

Directions:
1. In the slow cooker, mix the chicken with butter, mustard and the other ingredients and close the lid.
2. Cook chicken or 7 hours on Low. Serve the cooked chicken with sauce.

Nutrition value/serving: calories 326, fat 15.9, fiber 4, carbs 8.2, protein 42.9

Sweet Sticky Chicken Wings

Prep time: 10 minutes
Cooking time: 2.15 hours
Servings: 4
Ingredients:
- 1 tablespoon Erythritol
- 1 teaspoon water
- 1 teaspoon lemon juice
- 4 chicken wings
- 1 tablespoon butter
- 1 teaspoon olive oil
- ½ teaspoon salt
- ½ teaspoon chili flakes
- ¾ cup of water

Directions:
1. Sprinkle chicken wings with salt and chili flakes and transfer in the slow cooker.
2. Add olive oil and lemon juice.
3. Then add a ¾ cup of water and close the lid.
4. Cook the chicken wings for 2 hours on High.
5. Meanwhile, toss the butter in the skillet and melt it.
6. Add water and Erythritol.
7. Melt the mixture and bring it to boil.
8. Sprinkle the mixture over the chicken wings and mix up well.
9. Cook the chicken wings for 15 minutes on High.

Nutrition value/serving: calories 313, fat 14.9, fiber 0, carbs 3.8, protein 42.3

Pozole Blanco

Prep time: 15 minutes
Cooking time: 3.5 hours

Servings: 4
Ingredients:
- 11 oz chicken breast, skinless, boneless, chopped
- 3 tablespoons almond butter
- 2 spring onions, chopped
- ½ teaspoon minced garlic
- ½ jalapeno pepper, chopped
- 1 teaspoon dried oregano
- 1 tablespoon lime juice
- ¾ teaspoon lime zest, grated
- ½ cup of water
- ¼ cup fresh cilantro, chopped

Directions:
1. Put chopped chicken breast and 1 tablespoon of almond butter in the skillet.
2. Roast the poultry for 5 minutes over the medium heat.
3. Then transfer the chicken breast in the slow cooker, add remaining almond butter, diced onion, minced garlic, chopped jalapeno pepper, dried oregano, lime juice, and lime zest.
4. Mix up the ingredients and pour water.
5. Close the lid and cook the meal for 3.5 hours on High.
6. When Pozole Blanco is cooked, transfer it in the serving plates and garnish with chopped fresh cilantro.

Nutrition value/serving: calories 176, fat 8.8, fiber 2.1, carbs 5.4, protein 19.5

Chicken with Nuts

Prep time: 15 minutes
Cooking time: 4.5 hours
Servings: 4
Ingredients:
- 1-pound chicken fillet
- 1 cup coconut cream
- 1 tablespoon butter, softened
- 1 tablespoon walnuts, chopped
- 1 tablespoon pecans, chopped
- 1 tablespoon almonds, chopped
- 1 teaspoon salt
- ¼ cup heavy cream
- 1 teaspoon oregano, dried

Directions:
1. In the slow cooker, mix the chicken with the cream and the other ingredients and close the lid.
2. Cook the chicken for 4.5 hours on High.
3. Divide between plates and serve.

Nutrition value/serving: calories 281, fat 15.3, fiber 4.3, carbs 7.8, protein 33.7

Chicken and Hot Sauce

Prep time: 6 minutes
Cooking time: 3 hours
Servings: 6
Ingredients:
- 9 oz chicken breast, cooked, shredded
- 1/3 cup sour cream
- 3 tablespoons hot sauce
- 1 tablespoon scallions, chopped
- ¾ teaspoon cayenne pepper
- 1 tablespoon fresh dill, chopped

Directions:
1. Put the chicken and the other ingredients in the slow cooker.
2. Close the slow cooker lid and cook dip on Low for 3 hours.
3. Divide into bowls and serve

Nutrition value/serving: calories 218, fat 6.7, fiber 4.2, carbs 1.4, protein 12.5

Cheesy Turkey and Sauce

Prep time: 10 minutes
Cooking time: 9 hours
Servings: 4
Ingredients:
- 3 oz Monterey Jack cheese, shredded
- 1-pound turkey breast, skinless, boneless
- 1/3 cup keto salsa
- 1 teaspoon almond butter
- 1 teaspoon salt
- 1 teaspoon black pepper
- 1 teaspoon curry powder

Directions:
1. Put almond butter in the slow cooker.
2. Then place the chicken breast and the other ingredients inside.
3. Close the lid.
4. Cook the chicken on Low for 9 hours.

Nutrition value/serving: calories 239, fat 11.6, fiber 5.8, carbs 7.3, protein 30.4

Coconut Milk Turkey Breast

Prep time: 10 minutes
Cooking time: 4.5 hours
Servings: 5
Ingredients:
- 1 cup of coconut milk
- 1 teaspoon onion powder
- ¾ teaspoon garlic powder

- 1 teaspoon butter
- 9 oz turkey breast, boneless
- ½ teaspoon dried oregano
- 3 oz leek, chopped

Directions:
1. Pour coconut milk in the slow cooker and add onion powder, garlic powder, dried oregano, and leek.
2. Then add butter.
3. Chop the turkey breast roughly and transfer it in the slow cooker.
4. Close the lid and cook the meal for 4.5 hours on High.
5. Serve the turkey breast with coconut milk-leek gravy.

Nutrition value/serving: calories 184, fat 13.1, fiber 1.8, carbs 8, protein 10.2

Chicken and Spring Onions

Prep time: 10 minutes
Cooking time: 3 hours
Servings: 6
Ingredients:
- 2 tablespoons sweet paprika
- 1 tablespoon olive oil
- ½ teaspoon minced garlic
- 1 cup spring onions, chopped
- 1 teaspoon paprika
- ½ teaspoon salt
- 1 tablespoon olive oil
- 2-pound chicken fillet

Directions:
1. In the slow cooker mix the chicken and the other ingredients and close the lid.
2. Cook it on High for 3 hours.

Nutrition value/serving: calories 286, fat 16.9, fiber 6.7, carbs 6.6, protein 24.7

Chicken Breast with Avocados

Prep time: 10 minutes
Cooking time: 6 hours
Servings: 6
Ingredients:
- 16 oz chicken breast, skinless, boneless
- 2 avocados, peeled, pitted and cubed
- ½ teaspoon salt
- ½ teaspoon minced garlic
- ½ cup butter
- 1 tablespoon cream cheese

Directions:
1. In the slow cooker, mix the chicken with the avocado and the other ingredients.
2. Close the lid and cook the meal for 6 hours on Low.
3. Divide between plates and serve.

Nutrition value/serving: calories 305, fat 23.7, fiber 4.4 carbs 8.4., protein 21.6

Chives Chicken Teriyaki

Prep time: 20 minutes
Cooking time: 4.5 hours
Servings: 3
Ingredients:
- 1 teaspoon apple cider vinegar
- 1 teaspoon soy sauce
- 1 teaspoon turmeric powder
- 1 teaspoon oregano, dried
- 2 tablespoons chives, chopped
- 1 teaspoon olive oil
- 1 tablespoon Erythritol
- ½ teaspoon salt
- ½ teaspoon ground ginger
- 8 oz chicken fillet, chopped
- 1 tablespoon almond butter

Directions:
1. Put the chicken fillet in the slow cooker.
2. Add the rest of the ingredients and toss.
3. Close the lid and cook chicken for 4.5 hours on Low.
4. Divide between plates and serve.

Nutrition value/serving: calories 201, fat 10.8, fiber 1, carbs 7.1, protein 23.4

Chicken and Creamy Onions and Peppers

Prep time: 8 minutes
Cooking time: 9 hours
Servings: 5
Ingredients:
- 1 tablespoon olive oil
- 1 teaspoon salt
- 1 teaspoon black pepper
- 15 oz chicken fillet, chopped
- 1 teaspoon curry powder
- ½ cup of coconut milk
- ¼ cup heavy cream
- 2 spring onions, chopped
- 1 red bell pepper, sliced
- 1 green bell pepper, sliced
- ½ cup of water
- ½ teaspoon minced ginger

- 1 teaspoon apple cider vinegar

Directions:
1. In the slow cooker, mix the chicken with the oil, salt, pepper and the other ingredients..
2. Close the slow cooker lid and cook the mix overnight (for 9 hours).
3. Divide into bowls and serve.

Nutrition value/serving: calories 314, fat 15.9, fiber 5.5, carbs 6.1, protein 26.6

Oregano Chicken and Chilies

Prep time: 10 minutes
Cooking time: 7.5 hours
Servings: 2
Ingredients:
- ¼ cup green chilies, chopped
- 1 tablespoon keto tomato sauce
- 1 tablespoon oregano, chopped
- ¾ teaspoon chili powder
- 1 teaspoon hot paprika
- 1 tablespoon olive oil
- 2 spring onions, chopped
- ¾ cup organic coconut milk
- 7 oz chicken breast, skinless, boneless, chopped

Directions:
1. In the slow cooker, mix the chilies with chicken, oregano and the other ingredients.
2. Close the lid and cook chicken for 7.5 hours on Low.

Nutrition value/serving: calories 292, fat 14.3, fiber 4.8, carbs 6.8, protein 26.2.

Butter Turkey and Olives

Prep time: 20 minutes
Cooking time: 5.5 hours
Servings: 3
Ingredients:
- 1-pound turkey breast, skinless, boneless and cut into strips
- 1 cup kalamata olives, pitted and halved
- 3 spring onions, chopped
- ½ teaspoon salt
- ½ teaspoon cayenne pepper
- ½ teaspoon ground black pepper
- ½ tablespoon apple cider vinegar
- 2 tablespoons butter

Directions:
1. Grease the slow cooker with the butter, add the turkey and the other ingredients inside and toss.
2. Close the lid and cook for 5.5 hours on Low.

Nutrition value/serving: calories 364, fat 10.1, fiber 3.2, carbs 5.7, protein 49.4

Meat

Pork and Rutabaga
Prep time: 15 minutes
Cooking time: 5 hours
Servings: 4
Ingredients:
- 1-pound pork sirloin, chopped
- 1 teaspoon sage, dried
- 1 teaspoon sweet paprika
- 1 teaspoon curry powder
- ½ teaspoon salt
- 1 teaspoon ground black pepper
- ½ teaspoon turmeric
- 1 teaspoon keto tomato sauce
- 1 tablespoon olive oil
- 7 oz rutabaga, chopped
- 1 cup of water

Directions:
1. Pour olive oil in the skillet and preheat it.
2. Add the pork, sage, paprika and curry, brown for 5 minutes and transfer to the slow cooker.
3. Add the rest of the ingredients except the rutabaga
4. Close the slow cooker lid and cook beef for 4 hours on High.
5. Then open the lid, mix up the beef well and add rutabaga.
6. Close the lid and cook the stew for 1 hour on High.

Nutrition value/serving: calories 283, fat 12.8, fiber 3.7, carbs 5, protein 35.2

Turmeric Beef
Prep time: 15 minutes
Cooking time: 4.5 hours
Servings: 4
Ingredients:
- 10 oz beef steak
- 1 tablespoon avocado oil
- 1 teaspoon sweet paprika
- 1 teaspoon cumin, ground
- 1 teaspoon coriander, ground
- 1 tablespoon lemon juice
- ½ teaspoon salt
- 1 teaspoon paprika
- ½ teaspoon turmeric
- ¼ cup fresh cilantro, chopped

Directions:
1. In the slow cooker, mix the beef with oil, paprika and the other ingredients.
2. Cook the mix for 4.5 hours on High, divide between plates and serve with a side salad.

Nutrition value/serving: calories 283, fat 11.3, fiber 3.8, carbs 5.1, protein 28.2

Adobo Beef
Prep time: 15 minutes
Cooking time: 10 hours
Servings: 5
Ingredients:
- 1-pound beef chuck roast
- 1 tablespoon olive oil
- 1 teaspoon garlic powder
- 1 teaspoon chili powder
- 1 teaspoon minced garlic
- 1 teaspoon chipotle in Adobo sauce
- ½ teaspoon green chilies
- 1 oz spring onions, chopped
- 3 tablespoons lime juice
- ¼ teaspoon ground cumin
- 1 teaspoon dried oregano
- ½ teaspoon salt
- ½ cup of water

Directions:
1. Place chuck roast in the skillet. Add the oil and roast the chuck roast for 3 minutes from each side on high heat.
2. Then transfer beef chuck roast in the slow cooker.
3. Add the rest of the ingredients and toss.
4. Close the lid and cook meat for 10 hours on Low.
5. Divide between plates and serve.

Nutrition value/serving: calories 455, fat 37.1, fiber 3.3, carbs 5.4, protein 25.1

Cilantro Beef Tenderloin
Prep time: 15 minutes
Cooking time: 6 hours
Servings: 2
Ingredients:
- 10 oz beef tenderloin
- 3 spring onions, chopped
- 1 teaspoon oregano, dried
- 1 teaspoon basil dried
- 1 tablespoon fresh cilantro, chopped
- 1 teaspoon butter, softened
- ½ teaspoon salt

- ½ teaspoon black pepper
- 1/3 cup chicken stock

Directions:
1. In the slow cooker, mix the beef with onion, spring onions and the other ingredients.
2. Close the lid and cook beef tenderloin for 6 hours on High.
3. Divide between plates and serve.

Nutrition value/serving: calories 366, fat 14.7, fiber 4.5, carbs 7.2, protein 29.7

Beef Brisket

Prep time: 10 minutes
Cooking time: 8 hours
Servings: 4
Ingredients:
- 1-pound beef brisket
- 1 teaspoon olive oil
- ½ teaspoon salt
- ½ teaspoon ground black pepper
- 1 teaspoon keto tomato sauce
- 1 teaspoon paprika
- 1 teaspoon chili flakes
- 1 teaspoon cumin, ground
- 1 teaspoon oregano, dried
- 1 teaspoon dried oregano

Directions:
1. In the slow cooker, mix the beef with the oil and the other ingredients.
2. Close the lid and cook beef for 8 hours on Low.

Nutrition value/serving: calories 349, fat 19.2, fiber 3.5, carbs 5.3, protein 45.1

Marinara Beef and Chives

Prep time: 10 minutes
Cooking time: 8 hours
Servings: 2
Ingredients:
- 1 cup spring onions, chopped
- ¼ cup chicken stock
- 1 tablespoon balsamic vinegar
- 10 oz beef chuck, boneless, chopped
- 1/4 cup keto marinara sauce
- ½ teaspoon chili powder
- 1 teaspoon Italian seasoning
- ½ cup of water
- 1 teaspoon salt
- 2 tablespoons chives, chopped
- 1 teaspoon keto tomato sauce
- ½ teaspoon thyme

Directions:
1. In the slow cooker, mix the beef with spring onions, stock and the other ingredients.
2. Stir the ingredients gently with the help of a spatula and close the lid.
3. Cook the beef burgundy for 8 hours on Low.

Nutrition value/serving: calories 407, fat 15.1, fiber 4.2, carbs 5.1, protein 39.4

Thyme and Coriander Brisket

Prep time: 25 minutes
Cooking time: 12 hours
Servings: 6
Ingredients:
- 1 cup water
- ½ cup chicken stock
- 1 teaspoon ground coriander
- 1 teaspoon ground thyme
- ½ teaspoon salt
- 1 teaspoon cumin, ground
- ½ teaspoon ground black pepper
- ½ teaspoon basil, dried
- ½ teaspoon chili powder
- ½ teaspoon paprika
- 1 tablespoon olive oil
- 1 tablespoon balsamic vinegar
- 2-pound beef brisket

Directions:
1. In a bowl, mix the beef with coriander, thyme and the other ingredients except the water and stock and leave aside for 20 minutes.
2. Transfer the mix to the slow cooker, add the remaining ingredients and toss.
3. Close the lid and cook the meat for 12 hours on Low.

Nutrition value/serving: calories 376, fat 12, fiber 4.4, carbs 4.8, protein 46

Lemon Beef

Prep time: 10 minutes
Cooking time: 5 hours
Servings: 4
Ingredients:
- 1-pound beef sirloin, chopped
- 3 tablespoons lemon juice
- 1 teaspoon curry powder
- 1 teaspoon chili flakes
- 1 teaspoon lemon zest, grated
- ½ teaspoon salt

- 1 tablespoon keto tomato sauce
- 1 teaspoon butter
- ½ cup of water
- ½ teaspoon cayenne pepper

Directions:
1. In the slow cooker, mix the beef with lemon juice and zest and the other ingredients and toss.
2. Close the lid and cook beef sirloin for 5 hours on High.
3. Divide between plates and serve.

Nutrition value/serving: calories 229, fat 8.7, fiber 0.2, carbs 1.2, protein 34.5

Smoked Pork

Prep time: 15 minutes
Cooking time: 9 hours
Servings: 4
Ingredients:
- 11 oz pork shoulder
- 1 teaspoon salt
- ½ teaspoon smoked paprika
- 1 teaspoon chili powder
- 1 red chili pepper, minced
- Juice of 1 lime
- 1 teaspoon liquid smoke
- 1 tablespoon butter
- ¾ cup of water

Directions:
1. In the slow cooker, mix the pork with paprika, chili and the other ingredients.
2. Close the lid and cook pork for 9 hours on low.
3. After this, shred the pork.
4. Divide into bowls and serve.

Nutrition value/serving: calories 301, fat 19.7, fiber 4.5, carbs 5.6, protein 18.8

Steak and Dill Sauce

Prep time: 20 minutes
Cooking time: 5 hours
Servings: 4
Ingredients:
- 14 oz flank steak
- 1 teaspoon minced garlic
- ½ cup of coconut milk
- 2 tablespoons fresh dill, chopped
- ½ teaspoon turmeric powder
- 1 teaspoon curry powder
- 1 teaspoon oregano, dried
- ½ teaspoon salt
- 1 teaspoon almond butter
- 1 teaspoon chili powder

Directions:
1. In the cockpit, mix the steaks with the garlic and the other ingredients.
2. Close the lid, and cook on High for 5 hours.
3. Serve the flank steak hot.

Nutrition value/serving: calories 405, fat 21.6, fiber 5.1, carbs 4.7, protein 31.3

Ribs and Celery

Prep time: 15 minutes
Cooking time: 4.5 hours
Servings: 4
Ingredients:
- 1 ½ pound beef short ribs
- 1 teaspoon sage, dried
- 1 teaspoon cumin, ground
- 1 teaspoon coriander, ground
- ½ teaspoon salt
- 1 tablespoon lemon juice
- ½ teaspoon garlic powder
- ½ teaspoon ground black pepper
- 2 spring onions, chopped
- ½ oz celery root, peeled, chopped
- 1 cup of water

Directions:
1. In a bowl, mix the ribs with the sage and the other ingredients except the water and leave aside for 10 minutes.
2. Then transfer them in the slow cooker.
3. Add the water and close the lid.
4. Cook the short ribs for 4.5 hours on High.

Nutrition value/serving: calories 350, fat 7.4, fiber 0.6, carbs 2.4, protein 49.5

Ground Pork and Veggies

Prep time: 15 minutes
Cooking time: 8 hours
Servings: 5
Ingredients:
- 2 cups ground pork
- 1 tablespoon minced garlic
- 1 green bell pepper, chopped
- 1 red bell pepper, chopped
- 1 zucchini, chopped
- 1 eggplant, chopped
- ½ cup cherry tomatoes, halved
- ½ cup keto tomato sauce
- 2 spring onions, chopped
- 1 teaspoon cayenne pepper

- ½ teaspoon salt
- ½ teaspoon ground coriander
- 1 tablespoon butter, softened

Directions:
1. In the slow cooker, mix the pork with garlic, pepper and the other ingredients, toss, close the lid and cook for 8 hours on Low.
2. Divide into bowls and serve.

Nutrition value/serving: calories 349, fat 16.3, fiber 2.3, carbs 5.5, protein 13.8

Sausages and Cabbage

Prep time: 10 minutes
Cooking time: 8 hours
Servings: 7
Ingredients:
- 1-pound sausages, sliced
- 3 tablespoons keto tomato sauce
- ¾ cup crushed tomatoes
- 1 teaspoon oregano, dried
- 1 teaspoon chili powder
- 1 teaspoon butter
- 1 teaspoon ground black pepper
- ½ cup of water
- 1 teaspoon salt
- 1 ½ cup white cabbage, shredded

Directions:
1. In the slow cooker, mix the sausages with sauce, tomatoes and the other ingredients.
2. Close the lid and cook the meal on Low for 8 hours.

Nutrition value/serving: calories 300, fat 17.2, fiber 5.6, carbs 7.5, protein 9.5

Caraway Ribs

Prep time: 20 minutes
Cooking time: 4.5 hours
Servings: 4
Ingredients:
- 15 oz pork spare ribs
- 1 ½ teaspoons caraway seeds
- ½ teaspoon cumin, ground
- ½ teaspoon sweet paprika
- ½ teaspoon garam masala
- ½ teaspoon dried oregano
- ½ teaspoon dried basil
- 1 tablespoon olive oil
- 1/3 cup water

Directions:
1. In your slow cooker, mix the ribs with caraway seeds and the other ingredients. Close the lid.
2. Cook the spare ribs for 4.5 hours on High.

Nutrition value/serving: calories 311 fat 15, fiber 3.2, carbs 7.3, protein 20.1

Mint Lamb Roast

Prep time: 10 minutes
Cooking time: 3.5 hours
Servings: 4
Ingredients:
- 1-pound rack of lamb, chopped
- 1 tablespoon minced garlic
- ½ teaspoon salt
- ½ teaspoon black pepper
- 1 teaspoon mint, dried
- ½ cup sour cream
- 1 tablespoon balsamic vinegar
- 2 tablespoons olive oil
- ½ teaspoon fresh rosemary, chopped

Directions:
1. In the slow cooker, mix the lamb with garlic, salt, pepper and the other ingredients,
2. Close the lid and cook lamb for 3.5 hours on High.

Nutrition value/serving: calories 370, fat 26.6, fiber 4.1, carbs 6.3, protein 29.5

Pork and Green Peas

Prep time: 10 minutes
Cooking time: 4.5 hours
Servings: 6
Ingredients:
- 1 ½ pound pork loin, chopped
- 1 cup green peas
- 1 teaspoon minced garlic
- 2 spring onions, chopped
- 1 teaspoon oregano, dried
- 1 teaspoon ground coriander
- 1 teaspoon salt
- 1 teaspoon paprika
- ½ teaspoon black pepper
- 1 cup chicken stock
- 1/3 cup keto tomato sauce

Directions:
1. In your slow cooker, mix the pork with peas, garlic and the other ingredients.
2. Then close the lid and cook Pork Pozole for 4.5 hours on High.

Nutrition value/serving: calories 342, fat 12.4, fiber 4.2, carbs 5.7, protein 34.5

Coconut Pork Ribs

Prep time: 10 minutes
Cooking time: 3.5 hours
Servings: 5
Ingredients:
- 1-pound pork ribs, chopped
- ½ teaspoon paprika
- ¾ teaspoon turmeric powder
- 1 teaspoon garam masala
- ½ cup coconut cream
- ¼ cup of coconut oil

Directions:
1. Put the coconut oil in the slow cooker.
2. Add the pork ribs, coconut cream and the other ingredients.
3. Cook the pork ribs for 3.5 hours on High.

Nutrition value/serving: calories 368, fat 27.2, fiber 4.2, carbs 7.7, protein 24.5

Garlic Pork Chops

Prep time: 10 minutes
Cooking time: 7.5 hours
Servings: 4
Ingredients:
- ¼ cup crushed tomatoes
- 1 teaspoon smoked paprika
- ½ teaspoon garlic powder
- 1 teaspoon coriander, ground
- ½ teaspoon onion powder
- 1 tablespoon minced garlic
- 1 tablespoon butter
- ¼ cup of water
- 4 pork chops
- ½ teaspoon salt

Directions:
1. Mix up together the pork chops with garlic, paprika and the other ingredients.
2. Close the lid and cook the pork chops for 7.5 hours on Low.

Nutrition value/serving: calories 310, fat 15.8, fiber 4.6, carbs 1.8, protein 18.5

Thyme Pork and Beans

Prep time: 15 minutes
Cooking time: 5 hours
Servings: 4
Ingredients:
- 11 oz pork sirloin, cubed
- ½ cup green beans, trimmed and halved
- 2 celery stalks, chopped
- 2 spring onions, chopped
- 2 shallots, chopped
- 1 garlic clove, peeled
- 1 teaspoon salt
- 1 cup of water
- 1 tablespoon thyme, chopped

Directions:
1. In the slow cooker, mix the pork with green beans, onions and the other ingredients.
2. Close the lid and cook the mix for 5 hours on High.

Nutrition value/serving: calories 239, fat 9.8, fiber 4.3, carbs 3.9, protein 10.9

Ginger Ham

Prep time: 15 minutes
Cooking time: 9 hours
Servings: 4
Ingredients:
- 1 tablespoon Dijon mustard
- 2 teaspoons ginger, minced
- ½ teaspoon salt
- ½ teaspoon black pepper
- ½ teaspoon garam masala
- 1 teaspoon turmeric powder
- 2 tablespoons butter, melted
- ¼ cup chicken stock
- 1 teaspoon paprika
- 1-pound ham, sliced

Directions:
1. In the slow cooker, mix the ham with the ginger, salt, pepper and the other ingredients, toss and close the lid.
2. Cook the ham for 9 hours on Low.
3. Divide between plates and serve.

Nutrition value/serving: calories 311, fat 15.8, fiber 4.8, carbs 6.3, protein 19.2

Sausage and Zucchini Stew

Prep time: 15 minutes
Cooking time: 6 hours
Servings: 8
Ingredients:
- 1-pound sausage links, chopped
- 1 red chili pepper, chopped
- 2 zucchinis, chopped
- 2 spring onions, chopped
- 1 tomato, chopped
- 1 garlic clove, peeled, crushed
- 1 cup of water
- 1 tablespoon keto tomato sauce

- ½ teaspoon salt
- 1 teaspoon smoked paprika
- 1 tablespoon butter

Directions:
1. Put butter in the skillet and melt it.
2. Add chopped eggplant and cook it for 4 minutes on the medium heat.
3. Place the chopped sausages in the slow cooker.
4. Add the rest of the ingredients and toss.
5. Close the lid.
6. Cook the stew for 6 hours on Low.
7. Mix up the stew carefully before serving.

Nutrition value/serving: calories 306, fat 18.2, fiber 4.8, carbs 7.2, protein 7.8

Beef and Cauliflower

Prep time: 15 minutes
Cooking time: 5 hours
Servings: 4
Ingredients:
- 2 cups cauliflower florets
- 1-pound beef stew meat, cubed
- ½ cup chicken stock
- 1 tablespoon chives, chopped
- ½ teaspoon salt
- 1 teaspoon black pepper

Directions:
1. In the slow cooker, mix the cauliflower with the beef and the other ingredients.
2. Close the lid and cook on High for 5 hours.

Nutrition value/serving: calories 216, fat 12.2, fiber 4.3, carbs 4.2, protein 10.9

Beef and Broccoli

Prep time: 10 minutes
Cooking time: 4 hours
Servings: 4
Ingredients:
- 1 cup broccoli florets
- 1-pound beef sirloin, sliced
- 1 teaspoon ground coriander
- 1 teaspoon cumin, ground
- 1 teaspoon sweet paprika
- ½ teaspoon salt
- 1 teaspoon olive oil
- 3 spring onions, chopped
- ½ teaspoon ground black pepper
- 1 tablespoon butter
- 1/3 cup water
- 1 tablespoon chives, chopped

Directions:
1. In the slow cooker, mix the broccoli with the beef and the other ingredients.
2. Close the lid and cook on High for 4 hours.
3. Divide into bowls and serve.

Nutrition value/serving: calories 308, fat 8.3, fiber 4.1, carbs 3.8, protein 7.5

Pork and Bok Choy

Prep time: 15 minutes
Cooking time: 4.5 hours
Servings: 4
Ingredients:
- 1-pound pork stew meat, roughly cubed
- 1 sweet red pepper, chopped
- 1 green bell pepper, chopped
- 7 oz bok choy, chopped
- 2 shallots, chopped
- ½ teaspoon salt
- ½ teaspoon black pepper
- 2 tablespoons olive oil
- ¾ cup of water

Directions:
1. Heat up a pan with the oil over medium-high heat, add the meat, brown for 5 minutes and transfer to the slow cooker.
2. Add the rest of the ingredients and toss.
3. Close the lid and cook the meal for 4.5 hours on Low.

Nutrition value/serving: calories 309, fat 24.8, fiber 4.2, carbs 6.5, protein 11.9

Sumac Beef

Prep time: 10 minutes
Cooking time: 9 hours
Servings: 6
Ingredients:
- 3-pound beef tenderloin
- ½ teaspoon paprika
- 1 teaspoon black pepper
- 1 teaspoon sumac
- ½ teaspoon salt
- ½ teaspoon basil, dried
- 1 teaspoon Italian seasoning
- 2 tablespoons keto tomato sauce
- 3 teaspoons olive oil
- 1 teaspoon minced garlic
- ¼ cup of water

Directions:
1. In the slow cooker, mix the beef with paprika, sumac and the other ingredients.

2. Close the lid and beef tenderloin for 9 hours on Low.
3. Then slice the meat and sprinkle it with "meat juice" from the slow cooker.
Nutrition value/serving: calories 446, fat 17.2, fiber 5.5, carbs 5.9, protein 66.1

Lamb in Grape Leaves
Prep time: 15 minutes
Cooking time: 6.5 hours
Servings: 4
Ingredients:
- 1 cup ground lamb
- ½ teaspoon salt
- ½ teaspoon ground black pepper
- 1 teaspoon garlic powder
- 1 teaspoon hot paprika
- 1 teaspoon garam masala
- 1 teaspoon chili powder
- ¼ cup of water
- ¾ cup keto tomato sauce
- 1 tablespoon avocado oil
- 4 oz grape leaves

Directions:
1. In the mixing bowl, mix up together ground meat with salt, pepper, garlic powder and the other ingredients except the leaves, water, tomato sauce and oil and stir.
2. Fill the grape leaves with the mix and roll.
3. Arrange the rolled grape leaves in the slow cooker.
4. Add tomato sauce, water, and the oil.
5. Close the slow cooker lid and cook the meal for 6.5 hours on Low.
Nutrition value/serving: calories 313, fat 7.2, fiber 3.1, carbs 8, protein 13.4

Butter and Lemon Lamb
Prep time: 10 minutes
Cooking time: 4.5 hours
Servings: 7
Ingredients:
- 1-pound lamb chops
- 2 tablespoons stevia
- 3 tablespoons butter
- 4 tablespoons lemon juice
- 2 tablespoons lemon zest, grated
- 1 teaspoon turmeric powder
- 1 teaspoon coriander, ground

Directions:
1. In the slow cooker, mix the lamb with stevia, butter and the other ingredients.
2. Close the lid and cook on High for 4.5 hours.
Nutrition value/serving: calories 234, fat 11.8, fiber 4.1, carbs 7.5, protein 13.2

Beef and Asparagus
Prep time: 15 minutes
Cooking time: 11 hours
Servings: 5
Ingredients:
- 1-pound beef steak
- 1 cup asparagus, trimmed and halved
- 3 scallions, chopped
- 1 teaspoon sweet paprika
- 1 teaspoon coriander, ground
- 1 teaspoon butter
- ½ teaspoon dried dill
- 1/3 cup water

Directions:
1. In the slow cooker, mix the beef with scallions and the other ingredients except the asparagus and close the lid.
2. Cook the beef roll for 10 hours on Low.
3. Add the asparagus, close the lid, cook on Low for 1 more hour and serve.
Nutrition value/serving: calories 301, fat 11.2, fiber 3.2, carbs 6.1, protein 32.1

Curry Pork Mix
Prep time: 15 minutes
Cooking time: 6.5 hours
Servings: 6
Ingredients:
- 1 tablespoon olive oil
- 2 tablespoons red curry paste
- 1 teaspoon curry powder
- 1 teaspoon oregano, dried
- 1 teaspoon basil, dried
- 1 teaspoon Kosher salt
- ¼ teaspoon chili powder
- 1 ½-pound pork shoulder
- 1 teaspoon thyme
- 1 teaspoon minced garlic
- 4 tablespoons lime juice
- 2 tablespoons water

Directions:
1. In the slow cooker, mix the pork with the oil curry paste and the other ingredients.
2. Close the lid and cook Cuban pork for 6.5 hours on High.

Nutrition value/serving: calories 322, fat 14.6, fiber 0.3, carbs 5.7, protein 16.5

Crushed Tomatoes, Lamb and Chives

Prep time: 15 minutes
Cooking time: 4 hours
Servings: 6
Ingredients:
- 1-pound lamb chops
- ¼ cup spring onions, chopped
- 1 cup crushed tomatoes
- 1 teaspoon ground black pepper
- ½ teaspoon garam masala
- 1 teaspoon keto tomato sauce
- 1/3 cup water
- 1 teaspoon dried basil
- ½ teaspoon paprika
- 1 tablespoon chives, chopped
- 1 tablespoon butter

Directions:
1. Toss the butter in the skillet and melt.
2. Add the lamb, brown for 5 minutes and transfer to the slow cooker.
3. Add the rest of the ingredients and toss.
4. Close the lid and cook for 4 hours on High.

Nutrition value/serving: calories 288, fat 10.2, fiber 4.8, carbs 7.4, protein 13.6

Stevia Pork Mix

Prep time: 10 minutes
Cooking time: 3 hours
Servings: 2
Ingredients:
- 10 oz pork tenderloins
- 1 tablespoon avocado oil
- 1 and ½ teaspoon stevia
- 1 teaspoon cayenne pepper
- ½ teaspoon salt
- ½ teaspoon apple cider vinegar
- ¾ teaspoon ground nutmeg

Directions:
1. In the slow cooker, mix the pork with the oil, stevia and the other ingredients.
2. Close the lid and cook meat on High for 3 hours.

Nutrition value/serving: calories 322, fat 18.8, fiber 3.5, carbs 5.1, protein 42.5

Chili Lamb Skewers

Prep time: 15 minutes
Cooking time: 3.5 hours
Servings: 2
Ingredients:
- 7 oz lamb stew meat, cubed
- ½ cup cremini mushroom caps
- 1 tablespoon avocado oil
- 1 teaspoon curry powder
- 1 teaspoon cumin, ground
- ½ teaspoon salt
- 1 teaspoon chili powder
- 1 tablespoon apple cider vinegar

Directions:
1. In a bowl, mix the lamb with mushroom and the other ingredients and toss.
2. Then string the lamb and mushroom caps one-by-one on the skewers.
3. Place the skewers in the slow cooker and close the lid.
4. Cook the meal for 3.5 hours on High.

Nutrition value/serving: calories 326, fat 36.2, fiber 0.4, carbs 5.1, protein 14.8

Almond Beef

Prep time: 10 minutes
Cooking time: 8 hours
Servings: 4
Ingredients:
- 1-pound beef rib eye steak, cubed
- 1 tablespoon almond butter
- 1 teaspoon almonds, chopped
- ½ cup organic almond milk
- 1 teaspoon turmeric powder
- ½ teaspoon cayenne pepper
- ½ teaspoon garam masala
- 1 teaspoon salt
- ¾ tablespoon chives, chopped

Directions:
1. In the slow cooker, mix the beef with the almond butter, almonds and the other ingredients.
2. Close the lid and cook the meat for 8 hours on Low.
3. Serve the meat with almond gravy hot.

Nutrition value/serving: calories 301, fat 14, fiber 3.2, carbs 4.1, protein 3.6

Cajun Lamb

Prep time: 10 minutes
Cooking time: 5.5 hours
Servings: 4
Ingredients:

- 13 oz lamb chops
- 1 tablespoon Cajun seasonings
- 1 teaspoon curry powder
- 1 teaspoon coriander, ground
- 1 teaspoon oregano, dried
- 1 tablespoon butter
- ½ teaspoon dried rosemary
- 1 teaspoon salt
- 1/3 cup heavy cream

Directions:
1. In the slow cooker, mix the lamb with Cajun seasoning and the other ingredients. Close the lid.
2. Cook meat for 5.5 hours on High.

Nutrition value/serving: calories 312, fat 12.3, fiber 4.1, carbs 4.4, protein 28.2

Tomato Beef and Spices

Prep time: 10 minutes
Cooking time: 7 hours
Servings: 1
Ingredients:
- 6 oz beef loin, cubed
- 1/2 cup crushed tomatoes
- 1 teaspoon nutmeg, ground
- 1 teaspoon cinnamon powder
- 1 teaspoon cumin, ground
- 1 teaspoon coriander, ground
- 1 teaspoon sweet paprika
- 1 teaspoon garam masala
- 1 teaspoon keto tomato sauce
- 3 spring onions, chopped
- 1 teaspoon olive oil
- ½ teaspoon salt
- 1/3 cup water

Directions:
1. In the slow cooker, mix the beef with crushed tomatoes, spices and the other ingredients and close the lid.
2. Cook the beef cubes for 7 hours on Low.

Nutrition value/serving: calories 367, fat 18.9, fiber 4.3, carbs 5.6, protein 46

Simple Beef Steaks

Prep time: 10 minutes
Cooking time: 8 hours
Servings: 4
Ingredients:
- 12 oz beef steak
- 1 teaspoon basil, dried
- 1 teaspoon oregano, dried
- 1 teaspoon chili flakes
- 1 teaspoon salt
- ½ teaspoon ground black pepper
- ½ teaspoon ground paprika
- ¾ cup of chicken stock

Directions:
1. In the slow cooker, mix the steaks with basil, oregano and the other ingredients.
2. Close the lid and cook the meat for 8 hours on Low.

Nutrition value/serving: calories 110, fat 4.6, fiber 3.7, carbs 4.3, protein 17.5

Coffee Lamb

Prep time: 10 minutes
Cooking time: 11 hours
Servings: 6
Ingredients:
- 2-pound lamb chops
- 1/3 cup brewed coffee
- 1 teaspoon ground paprika
- 1 teaspoon cinnamon powder
- 1 cup of water
- ½ teaspoon salt
- 1 teaspoon garam masala
- 1 garlic clove, peeled, crushed

Directions:
1. In the slow cooker, mix the lamb with coffee and the other ingredients.
2. Close the lid and cook for 11 hours on Low.

Nutrition value/serving: calories 389, fat 22.1, fiber 0.6, carbs 2.2, protein 19.8

Turmeric Chops

Prep time: 15 minutes
Cooking time: 4.5 hours
Servings: 3
Ingredients:
- 1-pound pork chops
- 1 tablespoon basil, chopped
- 2 tablespoons chives, chopped
- 1 teaspoon salt
- 1 teaspoon turmeric
- 1 teaspoon avocado oil
- 1 teaspoon keto tomato sauce
- ½ teaspoon garlic powder
- ½ cup of water

Directions:
1. In the slow cooker, mix the pork chops with turmeric, basil and the other ingredients.
2. Close the lid and cook for 4.5 hours on High.

3. Serve with a side salad.
Nutrition value/serving: calories 327, fat 11.7, fiber 3.8, carbs 4.1, protein 28.8

Mustard Beef
Prep time: 25 minutes
Cooking time: 8 hours
Servings: 4
Ingredients:
- 1 teaspoon garam masala
- ½ cup of water
- 1-pound beef chuck roast
- 1 tablespoon mustard
- ½ teaspoon salt
- 1 tablespoon olive oil
- ¼ teaspoon cayenne pepper
- ½ teaspoon mayonnaise

Directions:
1. In the slow cooker, mix the beef with mustard, masala and the other ingredients.
2. Close the lid.
3. Cook harissa braised beef for 8 hours on Low.

Nutrition value/serving: calorie 327, fat 22.6, fiber 4.3, carbs 4.1, protein 30

Lamb and Leeks
Prep time: 15 minutes
Cooking time: 6 hours
Servings: 4
Ingredients:
- 3 oz leeks, roughly chopped
- 1-pound lamb chops
- 1 teaspoon dried basil
- 1 teaspoon Italian seasoning
- ½ teaspoon salt
- ½ teaspoon black pepper
- 1 teaspoon ground paprika
- 1 garlic clove, diced
- 2 spring onions, chopped
- ½ teaspoon chili pepper
- ¼ cup heavy cream
- 1 teaspoon olive oil

Directions:
1. In the slow cooker, mix the lamb with leeks, basil, seasoning and the other ingredients.
2. Close the lid.
3. Cook the pot roast for 6 hours on High.

Nutrition value/serving: calories 296, fat 14.3, fiber 4.2, carbs 6.6, protein 17.8

Pork Shoulder and Zucchinis
Prep time: 10 minutes
Cooking time: 11 hours
Servings: 7
Ingredients:
- 2.5-pound pork shoulder, boneless
- 1 teaspoon salt
- 1 teaspoon black pepper
- 1 cup zucchinis, cubed
- 1 teaspoon sweet paprika
- 1 teaspoon chili flakes
- 1 tablespoon olive oil
- 1 ½ cup water

Directions:
1. In the slow cooker, mix the pork with salt, pepper and the other ingredients.
2. Close the lid and cook the meat for 11 hours.

Nutrition value/serving: calories 368, fat 26.3, fiber 0.1, carbs 7.2, protein 17.8

Beef and Scallions
Prep time: 10 minutes
Cooking time: 5 hours
Servings: 4
Ingredients:
- 10 oz beef tenderloin, cubed
- 1/2 cup scallions, chopped
- 1 tablespoon olive oil
- 1/2 teaspoon black pepper
- 1 teaspoon salt
- 1 tablespoon keto tomato sauce
- 3 garlic cloves, peeled, crushed
- 1 cup of water
- 1 teaspoon coriander, ground

Directions:
1. In the slow cooker, mix the beef with the scallions, oil and the other ingredients.
2. Close the lid and cook the meat for 5 hours on High.

Nutrition value/serving: calories 329, fat 6.1, fiber 3.4, carbs 5.6, protein 14.2

Dill Pork Stew
Prep time: 10 minutes
Cooking time: 4.5 hours
Servings: 5
Ingredients:
- ¼ cup fresh dill, chopped
- 1 teaspoon sweet paprika
- 1 tablespoon chives, chopped

- 1 zucchini, chopped
- 1 cup of water
- ½ cup of coconut milk
- ½ teaspoon chili powder
- ½ teaspoon ground coriander
- 1 teaspoon salt
- 1 teaspoon olive oil
- 1 teaspoon basil, dried
- ½ teaspoon cayenne pepper
- 1-pound pork chops, chopped

Directions:
1. In the slow cooker, mix the pork with paprika, chives and the other ingredients.
2. Mix up the ingredients gently and cook for 4.5 hours on High.
3. Divide into bowls and serve.

Nutrition value/serving: calories 267, fat 19.4, fiber 3.5, carbs 4.1, protein 11.9

Lamb and Spinach

Prep time: 15 minutes
Cooking time: 8 hours
Servings: 4
Ingredients:
- 1 teaspoon cumin, ground
- 1 tablespoon olive oil
- ¼ teaspoon chili powder
- ½ teaspoon black pepper
- ½ teaspoon salt
- 1-pound lamb chops
- ½ cup fresh spinach
- ¼ cup of water

Directions:
1. In the slow cooker, mix the lamb with cumin, oil and the other ingredients except the spinach.
2. Close the lid.
3. Cook the rack of lamb for 7 hours on Low.
4. Add the spinach, cook on Low for 1 hour, divide into bowls and serve.

Nutrition value/serving: calories 328, fat 14.9, fiber 4.2, carbs 4.2, protein 23.3

Shredded Beef

Prep time: 10 minutes
Cooking time: 6.5 hours
Servings: 4
Ingredients:
- 12 oz beef shoulder, boneless
- 1 cup of chicken stock
- ½ teaspoon mustard
- ½ teaspoon salt
- ½ teaspoon black pepper
- ½ teaspoon basil, dried
- 1 teaspoon chili flakes
- 1 teaspoon butter
- 1 tablespoon coconut cream

Directions:
1. In the slow cooker, mix the beef with stock and the other ingredients.
2. Close the lid and cook lamb for 6.5 hours on High.
3. Shred the meat, divide into bowls and serve.

Nutrition value/serving: calories 212, fat 8.7, fiber 4.1, carbs 7.3, protein 14.1

Beef Curry

Prep time: 10 minutes
Cooking time: 3.5 hours
Servings: 2
Ingredients:
- 8 oz beef stew meat, cubed
- 1 tablespoon butter, soft
- ½ teaspoon salt
- 1 tablespoon oregano, chopped
- 1 teaspoon curry paste
- 1 tablespoon water
- ¾ cup organic coconut milk
- ½ teaspoon turmeric

Directions:
1. In the slow cooker, mix the beef with soft butter and the other ingredients.
2. Close the lid and cook the curry for 3.5 hours on High. Divide into bowls and serve.

Nutrition value/serving: calories 332, fat 20.9, fiber 4.1, carbs 4.1, protein 20.7

Lamb Shanks and Olives

Prep time: 15 minutes
Cooking time: 7.hours
Servings: 2
Ingredients:
- 8 oz lamb shank, boneless
- 1 tablespoon thyme
- ½ cup black olives, pitted and halved
- 1 teaspoon curry powder
- 1/3 teaspoon ground black pepper
- ½ teaspoon salt
- 1 cup of coconut milk

Directions:
1. Pour coconut milk in the slow cooker.

2. Add the lamb, curry powder and the other ingredients, close the lid and cook for 7 hours on Low.
Nutrition value/serving: calories 392, fat 22.7, fiber 4.2, carbs 7.7, protein 34.8

Beef with Bok Choy
Prep time: 10 minutes
Cooking time: 5.5 hours
Servings: 2
Ingredients:
- 7 oz beef loin, cubed
- 3 spring onions, chopped
- 1 cup bok choy, chopped
- 1 teaspoon salt
- 1 teaspoon coconut oil
- ¼ teaspoon sweet paprika
- 1 cup of water

Directions:
1. Place coconut oil in the skillet and melt it.
2. Add the meat, brown for 5 minutes and transfer to the slow cooker.
3. Add the rest of the ingredients and toss. Close the lid.
4. Cook the mix for 5.5 hours on High.
Nutrition value/serving: calories 362, fat 12.5, fiber 3.1, carbs 8.4, protein 27.8

Lamb and Brussels Sprouts
Prep time: 10 minutes
Cooking time: 10 hours
Servings: 2
Ingredients:
- 1 cup Brussels sprouts, halved
- 1-pound lamb shoulder, cubed
- 1 teaspoon salt
- 1 teaspoon black pepper
- 1 teaspoon keto tomato sauce
- 1 tablespoon chives, chopped
- 1 teaspoon liquid stevia
- ¾ teaspoon cumin, ground
- 1 green bell pepper, chopped
- 1 bay leaf
- ½ cup of water

Directions:
1. In your slow cooker, mix the sprouts with the lamb and the other ingredients, toss and close the lid.
2. Cook the mix for 10 hours on Low.
Nutrition value/serving: calories 328, fat 7.6, fiber 5.4, carbs 7.7, protein 23.4

Basil Lamb and Apples
Prep time: 10 minutes
Cooking time: 4 hours
Servings: 4
Ingredients:
- 1-pound lamb chops
- 2 apples, cored and cut into wedges
- 1 tablespoon olive oil
- 1 teaspoon dried basil
- ½ teaspoon salt
- 1 teaspoon cinnamon powder
- 1 teaspoon coriander, ground

Directions:
1. In the slow cooker, mix the lamb with apples, oil and the other ingredients and put the lid on.
2. Cook the mix for 4 hours on High.
Nutrition value/serving: calories 259, fat 16.3, fiber 3, carbs 7.4, protein 17

Lamb and Berries Mix
Prep time: 10 minutes
Cooking time: 8 hours
Servings: 4
Ingredients:
- 11 oz lamb shoulder, boneless
- 1 cup blackberries
- 1/2 teaspoon sweet paprika
- ½ cup chicken stock
- ½ teaspoon peppercorns
- ½ teaspoon dried rosemary

Directions:
1. In the slow cooker, mix the lamb with the berries and the other ingredients.
2. Close the lid and cook lamb one pot for 8 hours on Low.
Nutrition value/serving: calories 284, fat 5.9, fiber 4.2, carbs 4.2, protein 22.5

Lamb, Celery and Tomatoes
Prep time: 15 minutes
Cooking time: 5 hours
Servings: 4
Ingredients:
- 1 cup cherry tomatoes, halved
- 1 garlic clove, diced
- 3 oz celery stalk, chopped
- ½ teaspoon salt
- ½ teaspoon black pepper
- 1 tablespoon olive oil
- 1-pound lamb shank

- 1 cup chicken stock
- ½ teaspoon ground black pepper
- 1 teaspoon chili powder
- ½ teaspoon dried cilantro

Directions:
1. In the slow cooker, mix the lamb with tomatoes and the other ingredients and toss.
2. Close the lid and cook the meat for 5 hours on High.

Nutrition value/serving: calories 307, fat 14.6, fiber 4.3, carbs 4.9, protein 22.4

Lamb Meatballs

Prep time: 10 minutes
Cooking time: 3.5 hours
Servings: 4
Ingredients:
- 1 ½ cup ground lamb
- 1 tablespoon almond flour
- 1 teaspoon garlic powder
- 1 teaspoon sweet paprika
- 1 teaspoon mint, dried
- ¼ teaspoon ground nutmeg
- ½ teaspoon dried dill
- 3 tablespoons olive oil
- 1 egg, beaten

Directions:
1. In the mixing bowl, mix up together the lamb with flour and the other ingredients except the oil, stir and shape medium meatballs.
2. Arrange the meatballs in the slow cooker and add the oil.
3. Close the lid and cook the meatballs for 3.5 hours on High.

Nutrition value/serving: calories 261, fat 12.9, fiber 3.3, carbs 4.4, protein 11.4

Lamb Chops with Dill Butter

Prep time: 15 minutes
Cooking time: 6 hours
Servings: 3
Ingredients:
- 1-pound lamb chops
- 3 tablespoons butter, softened
- 1/3 cup fresh dill, chopped
- ¼ teaspoon turmeric powder
- ½ teaspoon garam masala
- ½ teaspoon salt
- ½ teaspoon ground black pepper
- 1 teaspoon olive oil

Directions:
1. In the slow cooker, mix the lamb with the butter, dill and the other ingredients and close the lid.
2. Cook the mix for 6 hours on Low. Divide between plates and serve.

Nutrition value/serving: calories 375, fat 6.5, fiber 3.8, carbs 3.4, protein 22.2

Pork Meatloaf

Prep time: 15 minutes
Cooking time: 4.5 hours
Servings: 4
Ingredients:
- 1 teaspoon ground turmeric
- 1 teaspoon ground paprika
- 1 teaspoon garlic powder
- ½ teaspoon salt
- 1 teaspoon turmeric powder
- 2 cups ground pork
- 2 eggs, beaten
- Cooking spray

Directions:
1. Spray the loaf mold with cooking spray.
2. In a bowl, mix the pork with the turmeric and the other ingredients, stir and transfer it in the prepared loaf mold.
3. Arrange the mold in the slow cooker and close the lid.
4. Cook the meatloaf for 4.5 hours on High.
5. Slice and serve.

Nutrition value/serving: calories 323, fat 18.8, fiber 5.6, carbs 5.7, protein 23.1

Chipotle Beef

Prep time: 10 minutes
Cooking time: 3 hours
Servings: 2
Ingredients:
- 1 cup beef stock
- 1 red chipotle pepper, chopped
- 1 teaspoon sweet paprika
- 1-pound beef stew meat, cubed
- ¼ cup fresh cilantro, chopped
- ½ teaspoon salt
- ½ zucchini, chopped
- 2 tablespoons heavy cream

Directions:
1. In the slow cooker, mix the beef with the stock, pepper and the other ingredients.
2. Close the lid and cook soup for 3 hours on High.
3. Divide into bowls and serve.

Nutrition value/serving: calories 229, fat 8.1, fiber 4.7, carbs 2.3, protein 20.8

Creamy Ground Beef with Kale

Prep time: 10 minutes
Cooking time: 3 hours
Servings: 4
Ingredients:
- 1 ½ cup kale, chopped
- 8 oz ground beef
- 1 teaspoon white pepper
- ¾ teaspoon ground coriander
- ½ teaspoon salt
- 1 tablespoon butter
- ¾ cup of coconut milk
- 1 oz Parmesan, grated

Directions:
1. Put the ground beef in the slow cooker.
2. Add white pepper, ground coriander, salt, butter, and coconut milk.
3. Mix the meat mixture well and close the lid.
4. Cook it for 2 hours on High.
5. Then open the lid and add chopped kale. Mix up the meal well.
6. Close the lid and cook it for 1 hour more.
7. Add grated Parmesan and mix up.
8. The cooked meal should be mushy.

Nutrition value/serving: calories 271, fat 18.7, fiber 1.5, carbs 5.7, protein 21.4

Beef Stuffed Mushrooms

Prep time: 15 minutes
Cooking time: 3 hours
Servings: 4
Ingredients:
- 1 cup cremini mushroom caps
- ½ cup ground beef
- 1 tablespoon butter, soft
- 1 teaspoon coriander, ground
- 1 teaspoon sweet paprika
- 1 teaspoon dried dill
- 1 oz Parmesan, grated
- ¾ cup of water

Directions:
1. In a bowl, mix ground beef, butter, coriander, dill and paprika.
2. Fill every mushroom cap with the meat mixture and arrange them in the slow cooker.
3. Add water.
4. Top every mushroom cap with Parmesan and close the lid.
5. Cook the mushroom caps for 3 hours on High.

Nutrition value/serving: calories 260, fat 5.8, fiber 4.4, carbs 8.6, protein 7.4

Pork Tenderloin and Kale

Prep time: 10 minutes
Cooking time: 8 hours
Servings: 4
Ingredients:
- 1 tablespoon chives, chopped
- 1 cup kale, chopped
- 10 oz pork tenderloin, sliced
- 1 cup heavy cream
- 1 teaspoon curry powder
- ½ teaspoon salt
- ½ teaspoon black pepper
- 1 teaspoon lemongrass, crushed
- ½ teaspoon garlic powder

Directions:
1. In the slow cooker, mix the pork with kale, chives and the other ingredients,
2. Close the lid and cook for 8 hours on Low.
3. Divide between plate sand serve.

Nutrition value/serving: calories 262, fat 13.7, fiber 4.3, carbs 6.8, protein 19.3

Chili Lamb

Prep time: 15 minutes
Cooking time: 10 hours
Servings: 4
Ingredients:
- 1 teaspoon stevia
- ½ teaspoon cayenne pepper
- 1 teaspoon cumin, ground
- 1 teaspoon green chili, minced
- 1 teaspoon minced garlic
- 1 tablespoon mustard
- 1 teaspoon keto tomato sauce
- 1-pound lamb shoulder, boneless
- ½ cup of water
- 1 tablespoon olive oil
- ½ teaspoon chili powder
- ¾ teaspoon garam masala

Directions:
1. In your slow cooker, mix the lamb with the stevia, cayenne and the other ingredients.
2. Close the lid and cook the pork for 10 hours on Low.

3. Divide between plates and serve.
Nutrition value/serving: calories 309, fat 18.6, fiber 3.8, carbs 8.4, protein 27.3

Vegetable Meals

Butter Green Peas
Prep time: 10 minutes
Cooking time: 3 hours
Servings: 4
Ingredients:
- 1 cup green peas
- 1 teaspoon minced garlic
- 1 tablespoon butter, softened
- ½ teaspoon cayenne pepper
- 1 tablespoon olive oil
- ¾ teaspoon salt
- 1 teaspoon paprika
- 1 teaspoon garam masala
- ½ cup chicken stock

Directions:
1. In the slow cooker, mix the peas with butter, garlic and the other ingredients,
2. Close the lid and cook for 3 hours on High.

Nutrition value/serving: calories 121, fat 6.5, fiber 3, carbs 3.4, protein 0.6

Lemon Asparagus
Prep time: 8 minutes
Cooking time: 5 hours
Servings: 2
Ingredients:
- 8 oz asparagus
- ½ cup butter
- juice of 1 lemon
- Zest of 1 lemon, grated
- ½ teaspoon turmeric
- 1 teaspoon rosemary, dried

Directions:
1. In your slow cooker, mix the asparagus with butter, lemon juice and the other ingredients and close the lid.
2. Cook the vegetables on Low for 5 hours. Divide between plates and serve.

Nutrition value/serving: calories 139, fat 4.6., fiber 2.5, carbs 3.3, protein 3.5

Lime Green Beans
Prep time: 10 minutes
Cooking time: 2.5 hours
Servings: 5
Ingredients:
- 1-pound green beans, trimmed and halved
- 2 spring onions, chopped
- 2 tablespoons lime juice
- ½ teaspoon lime zest, grated
- 2 tablespoons olive oil
- ¼ teaspoon ground black pepper
- ¾ teaspoon salt
- ¾ cup of water

Directions:
1. In the slow cooker, mix the green beans with the spring onions and the other ingredients and close the lid.
2. Cook for 2.5 hours on High.

Nutrition value/serving: calories 67, fat 5.6, fiber 2, carbs 4, protein 2.1

Cheese Asparagus
Prep time: 10 minutes
Cooking time: 3 hours
Servings: 4
Ingredients:
- 10 oz asparagus, trimmed
- 4 oz Cheddar cheese, sliced
- 1/3 cup butter, soft
- 1 teaspoon turmeric powder
- ½ teaspoon salt
- ¼ teaspoon white pepper

Directions:
1. In the slow cooker, mix the asparagus with butter and the other ingredients, put the lid on and cook for 3 hours on High.

Nutrition value/serving: calories 214, fat 6.2, fiber 1.7, carbs 3.6, protein 4.2

Creamy Broccoli
Prep time: 15 minutes
Cooking time: 1 hour
Servings: 4
Ingredients:
- ½ cup coconut cream
- 2 cups broccoli florets
- 1 teaspoon mint, dried
- 1 teaspoon garam masala
- 1 teaspoon salt
- 1 tablespoon almonds flakes
- ½ teaspoon turmeric

Directions:
1. In the slow cooker, mix the broccoli with the mint and the other ingredients.
2. Close the lid and cook vegetables for 1 hour on High.
3. Divide between plates and serve.

Nutrition value/serving: calories 102, fat 9, fiber 1.9, carbs 4.3, protein 2.5

Curry Cauliflower

Prep time: 15 minutes
Cooking time: 2.5 hours
Servings: 4
Ingredients:
- 1 ½ cup cauliflower, trimmed and florets separated
- 1 tablespoon curry paste
- ½ cup coconut cream
- 1 teaspoon butter
- ½ teaspoon garam masala
- ¾ cup chives, chopped
- 1 tablespoon rosemary, chopped
- 2 tablespoons Parmesan, grated

Directions:
1. In the slow cooker, mix the cauliflower with the curry paste and the other ingredients.
2. Cook the cauliflower for 2.5 hours on High.

Nutrition value/serving: calories 146, fat 4.3, fiber 1.9, carbs 5.7, protein 5.3

Garlic Eggplant

Prep time: 15 minutes
Cooking time: 2 hours
Servings: 4
Ingredients:
- 1-pound eggplant, trimmed and roughly cubed
- 1 tablespoon balsamic vinegar
- 1 garlic clove, diced
- 1 teaspoon tarragon
- 1 teaspoon salt
- 1 tablespoon olive oil
- ½ teaspoon ground paprika
- ¼ cup of water

Directions:
1. In the slow cooker, mix the eggplant with the vinegar, garlic and the other ingredients, close the lid and cook on High for 2 hours.
2. Divide into bowls and serve.

Nutrition value/serving: calories 132, fat 2.8, fiber 4.7, carbs 8.5, protein 1.6

Coconut Brussels Sprouts

Prep time: 10 minutes
Cooking time: 4 hours
Servings: 6
Ingredients:
- 2 cups Brussels sprouts, halved
- ½ cup of coconut milk
- 1 teaspoon garlic powder
- 1 teaspoon salt
- ½ teaspoon coriander, ground
- 1 teaspoon dried oregano
- 1 tablespoon balsamic vinegar
- 1 teaspoon butter

Directions:
1. Place Brussels sprouts in the slow cooker.
2. Add the rest of the ingredients, toss, close the lid and cook the Brussels sprouts for 4 hours on Low.
3. Divide between plates and serve.

Nutrition value/serving: calories 128, fat 5.6, fiber 1.7, carbs 4.4, protein 3.6

Cauliflower Pilaf with Hazelnuts

Prep time: 15 minutes
Cooking time: 2 hours
Servings: 6
Ingredients:
- 3 cups cauliflower, chopped
- 1 cup chicken stock
- 1 teaspoon ground black pepper
- ½ teaspoon turmeric
- ½ teaspoon ground paprika
- 1 teaspoon salt
- 1 tablespoon dried dill
- 1 tablespoon butter
- 2 tablespoons hazelnuts, chopped

Directions:
1. Put cauliflower in the blender and blend until you get cauliflower rice.
2. Then transfer the cauliflower rice in the slow cooker.
3. Add ground black pepper, turmeric, ground paprika, salt, dried dill, and butter.
4. Mix up the cauliflower rice. Add chicken stock and close the lid.
5. Cook the pilaf for 2 hours on High.
6. Then add chopped hazelnuts and mix u the pilaf well.

Nutrition value/serving: calories 48, fat 3.1, fiber 1.9, carbs 4.8, protein 1.6

Cauliflower and Turmeric Mash

Prep time: 10 minutes
Cooking time: 3 hours
Servings: 3
Ingredients:
- 1 cup cauliflower florets
- 1 teaspoon turmeric powder
- 1 cup of water
- 1 teaspoon salt
- 1 tablespoon butter
- 1 tablespoon coconut cream
- 1 teaspoon coriander, ground

Directions:
1. In the slow cooker, mix the cauliflower with water and salt.
2. Close the lid and cook for 3 hours on High.
3. Then drain water and transfer the cauliflower to a blender.
4. Add the rest of the ingredients, blend and serve.

Nutrition value/serving: calories 58, fat 5.2, fiber 1.2, carbs 2.7, protein 1.1

Spinach and Olives Mix

Prep time: 15 minutes
Cooking time: 3.5 hours
Servings: 6
Ingredients:
- 2 cups spinach
- 2 tablespoons chives, chopped
- 5 oz Cheddar cheese, shredded
- ½ cup heavy cream
- 1 teaspoon ground black pepper
- ½ teaspoon salt
- 1 cup black olives, pitted and halved
- 1 teaspoon sage
- 1 teaspoon sweet paprika

Directions:
1. In the slow cooker, mix the spinach with the chives and the other ingredients, toss and close the lid.
2. Cook for 3.5 hours on Low and serve.

Nutrition value/serving: calories 189, fat 6.2, fiber 0.6, carbs 3, protein 3.4

Red Cabbage and Walnuts

Prep time: 15 minutes
Cooking time: 6 hours
Servings: 4
Ingredients:
- 2 cups red cabbage, shredded
- 3 spring onions, chopped
- ½ cup chicken stock
- 1 tablespoon olive oil
- 1 teaspoon salt
- 1 teaspoon cumin, ground
- 1 teaspoon hot paprika
- 1 tablespoon keto tomato sauce
- 1 oz walnuts
- 1/3 cup fresh parsley, chopped

Directions:
1. In the slow cooker, mix the cabbage with the spring onions and the other ingredients.
2. Close the lid and cook cabbage for 6 hours on Low.
3. Divide into bowls and serve.

Nutrition value/serving: calories 112, fat 5.1, fiber 2, carbs 5.8, protein 3.5

Paprika Bok Choy

Prep time: 15 minutes
Cooking time: 2.5 hours
Servings: 6
Ingredients:
- 1-pound bok choy, torn
- ½ cup of coconut milk
- 1 tablespoon almond butter, softened
- 1 teaspoon ground paprika
- 1 teaspoon turmeric
- ½ teaspoon cayenne pepper

Directions:
1. In the slow cooker, mix the bok choy with the coconut milk and the other ingredients, toss and close the lid.
2. Cook the meal for 2.5 hours on High.

Nutrition value/serving: calories 128, fat 3.2, fiber 3.9, carbs 4.9, protein 4.1

Zucchini Mix

Prep time: 10 minutes
Cooking time: 3 hours
Servings: 6
Ingredients:
- 1-pound zucchinis, roughly cubed
- 2 spring onions, chopped
- 1 teaspoon curry paste
- 1 teaspoon basil, dried
- 1 teaspoon salt
- 1 teaspoon ground black pepper
- 1 bay leaf
- ½ cup beef stock

Directions:
1. In the slow cooker, mix the zucchinis with the onion and the other ingredients.

2. Close the lid and cook on Low for 3 hours.
Nutrition value/serving: calories 34, fat 1.3, fiber 3.6, carbs 4.7, protein 3.6

Zucchini and Spring Onions
Prep time: 20 minutes
Cooking time: 2 hours
Servings: 8
Ingredients:
- 1-pound zucchinis, sliced
- 1 teaspoon avocado oil
- 1 teaspoon salt
- 1 teaspoon white pepper
- 2 spring onions, chopped
- 1/3 cup organic almond milk
- 2 tablespoons butter
- ½ teaspoon turmeric powder

Directions:
1. In the slow cooker, mix the zucchinis with the spring onions, oil and the other ingredients.
2. Close the lid and cook for 2 hours on High.

Nutrition value/serving: calories 82, fat 5.6, fiber 2.8, carbs 5.6, protein 3.2

Creamy Portobello Mix
Prep time: 15 minutes
Cooking time: 7 hours
Servings: 4
Ingredients:
- 4 Portobello mushrooms
- ½ cup Monterey Jack cheese, grated
- ½ cup heavy cream
- 1 teaspoon curry powder
- 1 teaspoon basil, dried
- ½ teaspoon salt
- 1 teaspoon olive oil

Directions:
1. In the slow cooker, mix the mushrooms with the cheese and the other ingredients.
2. Close the lid and cook the meal for 7 hours on Low.

Nutrition value/serving: calories 126, fat 5.1, fiber 1.6, carbs 5.9, protein 4.4

Eggplant Mash
Prep time: 10 minutes
Cooking time: 2.5 hours
Servings: 2
Ingredients:
- 7 oz eggplant, trimmed
- 1 tablespoon butter
- 1 teaspoon basil, dried
- 1 teaspoon chili powder
- ½ teaspoon garlic powder
- 1/3 cup water
- ½ teaspoon salt

Directions:
1. Peel the eggplant and rub with salt.
2. Then put it in the slow cooker and water.
3. Close the lid and cook the eggplant for 2.5 hours on High.
4. Then drain water and mash the eggplant.
5. Add the rest of the ingredients, whisk and serve.

Nutrition value/serving: calories 206, fat 6.2, fiber 3.6, carbs 7.9, protein 8.6

Cheddar Artichoke
Prep time: 15 minutes
Cooking time: 3 hours
Servings: 6
Ingredients:
- 1 teaspoon garlic, diced
- 1 tablespoon olive oil
- 1-pound artichoke hearts, chopped
- 3 oz Cheddar cheese, shredded
- 1 teaspoon curry powder
- 1 cup chicken stock
- 1 teaspoon butter
- 1 teaspoon garam masala

Directions:
1. In the slow cooker, mix the artichokes with garlic, oil and the other ingredients.
2. Cook the artichoke hearts for 3 hours on High.
3. Divide between plates and serve.

Nutrition value/serving: calories 135, fat 3.9, fiber 4.3, carbs 4.9, protein 4.3

Squash and Zucchinis
Prep time: 15 minutes
Cooking time: 4 hours
Servings: 6
Ingredients:
- 4 cups spaghetti squash, cubed
- 2 zucchinis, cubed
- ½ cup coconut milk
- ½ teaspoon ground cinnamon
- ¾ teaspoon ground ginger
- 3 tablespoons oregano
- 1 teaspoon butter

Directions:
1. In the slow cooker, mix the squash with the zucchinis, milk and the other ingredients.
2. Close the lid and cook the vegetables on Low for 4 hours.
Nutrition value/serving: calories 40, fat 2.2, fiber 1.8, carbs 4.3, protein 1.1

Dill Leeks
Prep time: 10 minutes
Cooking time: 3 hours
Servings: 3
Ingredients:
- 2 cups leeks, sliced
- 1 cup chicken stock
- 2 tablespoons fresh dill, chopped
- ½ teaspoon turmeric powder
- 1 teaspoon sweet paprika
- 1 tablespoon coconut cream
- 1 teaspoon butter

Directions:
1. In the slow cooker, mix the beets with the stock, dill and the other ingredients.
2. Cook on Low for 3 hours and serve.
Nutrition value/serving: calories 123, fat 2.9, fiber 2.2, carbs 7.5, protein 4.3.

Vegetable Lasagna
Prep time: 20 minutes
Cooking time: 6 hours
Servings: 4
Ingredients:
- 1 eggplant, sliced
- 1 cup kale, chopped
- 3 eggs, beaten
- 2 tablespoons keto tomato sauce
- ½ teaspoon ground black pepper
- 1 cup Cheddar, grated
- ½ teaspoon chili flakes
- 1 tablespoon tomato sauce
- 1 teaspoon coconut oil
- ½ teaspoon butter

Directions:
1. Place coconut oil in the skillet and melt it.
2. Then add sliced eggplants and roast them for 1 minute from each side.
3. After this, transfer them in the bowl.
4. Toss butter in the skillet.
5. Place 1 beaten egg in the skillet and stir it to get the shape of a pancake.
6. Roast the egg pancake for 1 minute from each side.
7. Repeat the steps with remaining eggs.
8. Separate the eggplants into 2 parts.
9. Place 1 part of eggplants in the slow cooker. You should make the eggplant layer.
10. Then add ½ cup chopped parsley and 1 egg pancake.
11. Sprinkle the egg pancakes with 1/3 cup of Parmesan.
12. Then add remaining eggplants and second egg pancake.
13. Sprinkle it with ½ part of remaining Parmesan and top with the last egg pancake.
14. Then spread it with tomato sauce, kale and sprinkle with chili flakes and ground black pepper.
15. Add tomato sauce and top lasagna with remaining cheese.
16. Close the lid and cook lasagna for 6 hours on Low.
Nutrition value/serving: calories 257, fat 15.9, fiber 4.5, carbs 10.5, protein 21.5

Cauliflower Rice Mix
Prep time: 15 minutes
Cooking time: 2 hours
Servings: 2
Ingredients:
- 1 cup cauliflower rice
- 1 tablespoon coconut butter
- ¼ teaspoon salt
- ¾ teaspoon turmeric
- 1 teaspoon cayenne pepper
- 1 teaspoon curry powder
- 2 oz Provolone cheese
- 1 ½ cups chicken stock

Directions:
1. In the slow cooker, mix the cauliflower with the butter and the other ingredients except the cheese, close the lid and cook on High for 1 hour.
2. Add the cheese, cook on High for 1 more hour, divide between plates and serve.
Nutrition value/serving: calories 131, fat 4.5, fiber 2.1, carbs 6.2, protein 4.5

Vegetable Cream
Prep time: 15 minutes
Cooking time: 3 hours
Servings: 4
Ingredients:

- 1 cup heavy cream
- 2 cups broccoli, chopped
- 2 spring onions, chopped
- 1 teaspoon olive oil
- 1 teaspoon salt
- 1 teaspoon ground paprika
- 1 oz celery stalk, chopped
- 1 cup chicken stock
- 1 tablespoon fresh chives, chopped
- ½ cup mushrooms

Directions:
1. In the slow cooker, mix the broccoli with the onion and the other ingredients, close the lid and cook on High for 3 hours.
2. Blend using an immersion blender and serve.

Nutrition value/serving: calories 218, fat 5.6, fiber 1.9, carbs 5.6, protein 4.4

Coconut Okra

Prep time: 15 minutes
Cooking time: 3 hours
Servings: 6
Ingredients:
- 1-pound okra, trimmed
- 1/3 cup coconut cream
- 1/3 cup butter
- ½ teaspoon salt
- ½ teaspoon turmeric powder
- ¾ teaspoon ground nutmeg

Directions:
1. In the slow cooker, mix the okra with cream, butter and the other ingredients.
2. Cook okra for 3 hours on High.

Nutrition value/serving: calories 203, fat 6.7, fiber 2.5, carbs 6.2, protein 3.3

Pecan Kale Mix

Prep time: 15 minutes
Cooking time: 4 hours
Servings: 6
Ingredients:
- 1 cup pecans, chopped
- 2 tablespoons butter, softened
- 1-pound kale, torn
- ¼ teaspoon salt
- 2 tablespoons cilantro, chopped
- 1 teaspoon turmeric
- ½ teaspoon onion powder
- 1/2 cup chicken stock

Directions:
1. In the slow cooker, mix the kale with cilantro, pecans and the other ingredients and close the lid.
2. Cook the mix on Low for 4 hours and serve.

Nutrition value/serving: calories 126, fat 4.8, fiber 4.6, carbs 6, protein 1.1

Mushroom Soup

Prep time: 6 minutes
Cooking time: 7 hours
Servings: 4
Ingredients:
- 1 cup cremini mushrooms, chopped
- 2 spring onions, chopped
- 1 garlic clove, diced
- 1 tablespoon oregano, chopped
- 1 teaspoon olive oil
- ¾ teaspoon ground black pepper
- 2 cups of water
- 1 cup of coconut milk

Directions:
1. In your slow cooker, mix the mushrooms with spring onions and the other ingredients and close the lid.
2. Cook the soup for 7 hours on Low.
3. When the soup is cooked, blend with an immersion blender and serve.

Nutrition value/serving: calories 214, fat 12..5, fiber 2.2, carbs 6.7, protein 2.3

Artichoke and Asparagus Mix

Prep time: 15 minutes
Cooking time: 2 hours
Servings: 4
Ingredients:
- 2 artichokes, trimmed and halved
- 1-pound asparagus, trimmed and roughly chopped
- 2 spring onions, chopped
- 1 tablespoon almond butter
- ½ cup coconut cream
- ½ teaspoon salt
- 1 teaspoon chili pepper
- ¼ jalapeno pepper, minced
- ½ cup chicken stock

Directions:
1. In the slow cooker, mix the artichokes with the asparagus, onion and the other ingredients, close the lid and cook on Low for 2 hours.

Nutrition value/serving: calories 122, fat 5.9, fiber 4.5, carbs 5.2, protein 8.4

Butter Green Beans

Prep time: 5 minutes
Cooking time: 4.5 hours
Servings: 6
Ingredients:
- 2 cups green beans, trimmed and halved
- ½ cup butter
- 1 teaspoon salt

Directions:
1. Mix up together snap peas with salt and transfer them in the slow cooker.
2. Add butter and close the lid.
3. Cook the vegetables on Low for 4.5 hours.

Nutrition value/serving: calories 175, fat 15.5, fiber 2.5, carbs 7, protein 2.8

Hot Eggplant Mix

Prep time: 15 minutes
Cooking time: 2 hours
Servings: 4
Ingredients:
- 1 teaspoon coconut oil, melted
- 3 eggplants, sliced
- 1 teaspoon minced garlic
- 1 red chili pepper, minced
- 1 teaspoon keto tomato sauce
- 1 tablespoon butter
- 1 teaspoon hot paprika
- 1 teaspoon chives, chopped

Directions:
1. In the slow cooker, mix the eggplants with the coconut oil and the other ingredients and close the lid.
2. Cook the eggplant mix for 2 hours on Low.

Nutrition value/serving: calories 202, fat 5.2, fiber 6.5, carbs 4.5, protein 5.1

Zucchini Balls

Prep time: 20 minutes
Cooking time: 30 minutes
Servings: 4
Ingredients:
- 1 cup zucchini, grated
- ½ cup almond flour
- ¼ cup Parmesan, grated
- 1 egg, whisked
- 1 tablespoon avocado oil
- ¾ cup of coconut milk
- ½ teaspoon salt

Directions:
1. In the mixing bowl zucchinis with flour and the other ingredients except the coconut milk and the oil and shape medium balls.
2. Preheat avocado oil in the skillet and add zucchini balls.
3. Roast them for 2 minutes from each side.
4. After this, transfer the zucchini balls in the slow cooker. Add coconut milk and close the lid.
5. Cook the meal for 30 minutes on High.

Nutrition value/serving: calories 207, fat 5.5, fiber 1.8, carbs 4.5, protein 3.6

Broccoli Sauté

Prep time: 15 minutes
Cooking time: 5 hours
Servings: 4
Ingredients:
- 2 cups broccoli florets
- 1 teaspoon salt
- 1 teaspoon ground nutmeg
- 1 teaspoon coriander, ground
- 1 tablespoon olive oil
- 1 teaspoon cumin, ground
- ½ cup chicken stock
- 1 oz Cheddar cheese, shredded

Directions:
1. In the slow cooker, mix the broccoli with the coriander, salt and the other ingredients.
2. Close the lid and cook on Low for 5 hours.

Nutrition value/serving: calories 143, fat 4.1, fiber 2.3, carbs 5.2, protein 5.2

Spinach and Sauce

Prep time: 10 minutes
Cooking time: 1 hour
Servings: 2
Ingredients:
- 2 cups fresh spinach, chopped
- 1/2 cup keto tomato sauce
- ½ teaspoon Italian seasoning
- 2 tablespoons butter
- 2 tablespoons water

Directions:
1. In the slow cooker, mix the spinach with the tomato sauce and the other ingredients.
2. Close the lid and cook it on High for 1 hour.

3. Transfer the cooked meal in the serving plate.
Nutrition value/serving: calories 143, fat 4.1, fiber 1.1, carbs 3.4, protein 1.3

Sesame Zucchini
Prep time: 15 minutes
Cooking time: 2.5 hours
Servings: 4
Ingredients:
- 1-pound zucchinis, cubed
- 1 tablespoon chives, chopped
- 1 teaspoon sesame seeds
- 1 teaspoon salt
- 1 teaspoon coriander, ground
- 1 teaspoon turmeric powder
- 4 tablespoons olive oil
- ¾ cup of veggie stock

Directions:
1. In the slow cooker, mix the zucchinis with chives, sesame seeds and the other ingredients, close the lid and cook on High for 2.5 hours.
2. Divide between plates and serve.
Nutrition value/serving: calories 132, fat 8.3, fiber 2, carbs 4.2, protein 1.8

Creamy Avocado
Prep time: 8 minutes
Cooking time: 1.2 hours
Servings: 4
Ingredients:
- 3 avocados, peeled, pitted and roughly cubed
- 1 oz chives, chopped
- 1 tablespoon butter
- ¾ cup coconut cream
- ¼ teaspoon ground ginger

Directions:
1. In the slow cooker, mix the avocados with chives and the other ingredients.
2. Close the lid and cook for 1.5 hours on Low.
3. Divide between plates and serve.
Nutrition value/serving: calories 67, fat 2.5, fiber 1.6, carbs 3.7, protein 2.7

Cauliflower Cream Soup
Prep time: 10 minutes
Cooking time: 3.5 hours
Servings: 2
Ingredients:
- 1 cup cauliflower florets
- 1 teaspoon coriander, ground
- 1 cup heavy cream
- 2 cups water
- 1 teaspoon butter
- 1 tablespoon chives
- ¼ teaspoon salt
- ¼ teaspoon basil, dried
- 1 oz Cheddar cheese, shredded

Directions:
1. In the slow cooker, mix the cauliflower with coriander and the other ingredients except the cheese and cream, close the lid and cook for 3.5 hour on High.
2. Add the remaining ingredients and stir.
3. Then blend the soup with the help of the hand blender.
4. Ladle the cooked cream soup in the bowls.
Nutrition value/serving: calories 229, fat 8.9, fiber 3.7, carbs 3.4, protein 5.4

Radish Soup
Prep time: 15 minutes
Cooking time: 2 hours
Servings: 4
Ingredients:
- 2 cups radishes, halved
- ½ teaspoon coriander, ground
- 1 cup coconut cream
- 1 and ½ cups water
- 1 tablespoon butter, soft
- 1 teaspoon black pepper
- 1 teaspoon salt

Directions:
1. In the slow cooker, mix the radishes with the coriander and the other ingredients except the cream, close the lid and cook for 2 hours on High.
2. Add the cream, blend the soup and serve.
Nutrition value/serving: calories 143, fat 7.5, fiber 1.5, carbs 5.4, protein 3.1

Zucchini Dip
Prep time: 15 minutes
Cooking time: 2 hours
Servings: 6
Ingredients:
- 1-pound zucchinis, chopped
- 1 tablespoon butter
- ¼ cup cream cheese
- 1 teaspoon minced garlic

- ½ cup of coconut milk
- 1 teaspoon turmeric powder
- 1 teaspoon cumin, ground
- 1 tablespoon fresh parsley, chopped
- ¼ teaspoon ground coriander
- ¾ teaspoon sweet paprika

Directions:
1. In the slow cooker, mix the zucchinis with the butter and the other ingredients.
2. Close the lid and cook it on Low for 2 hours.
3. Blend using an immersion blender, divide into bowls and serve.

Nutrition value/serving: calories 209, fat 4.5, fiber 1.3, carbs 6.4, protein 4.3

Celery Dip

Prep time: 5 minutes
Cooking time: 7 hours
Servings: 8
Ingredients:
- 2 teaspoons turmeric powder
- 1 cup Cheddar cheese, shredded
- ½ cup coconut cream
- 3 oz celery stalk, chopped
- 1 teaspoon butter
- 1 tablespoon chives, chopped

Directions:
1. In the slow cooker, mix the celery with the turmeric and the other ingredients.
2. Close the lid and cook dip for 7 hours on Low.
3. Blend using an immersion blender and serve.

Nutrition value/serving: calories 107, fat 4.3, fiber 0.7, carbs 1.7, protein 3.8

Bell Peppers and Spinach

Prep time: 10 minutes
Cooking time: 4 hours
Servings: 4
Ingredients:
- 1 cup fresh spinach, chopped
- 2 green bell pepper, chopped
- 2 red bell peppers, chopped
- 2 orange bell peppers, chopped
- 3 tablespoons butter
- ½ teaspoon salt
- 3 spring onions, chopped
- ¾ cup of chicken stock

Directions:
1. In the slow cooker, mix the spinach with peppers and the other ingredients.
2. Cook the sauté for 4 hours on Low.
3. Divide between plates and serve.

Nutrition value/serving: calories 93, fat 3.7, fiber 0.9, carbs 3.7, protein 0.8

Green Beans, Leeks and Artichokes

Prep time: 15 minutes
Cooking time: 5 hours
Servings: 5
Ingredients:
- 1-pound green beans, trimmed and halved
- 2 artichokes, trimmed and halved
- 2 leeks, sliced
- 1 cup Cheddar cheese, shredded
- ½ cup of coconut milk
- 1 teaspoon salt
- 1 teaspoon curry powder
- 1 teaspoon butter, softened

Directions:
1. In the slow cooker, mix the green beans with the artichokes and the other ingredients, toss and close the slow cooker lid.
2. Cook the mix for 5 hours on Low.

Nutrition value/serving: calories 162, fat 5.5, fiber 2.2, carbs 7.6, protein 7.1

Brussel Sprouts Saute

Prep time: 15 minutes
Cooking time: 3 hours
Servings: 5
Ingredients:
- 11 oz Brussels sprouts, trimmed and halved
- ½ teaspoon coriander, ground
- ½ teaspoon turmeric powder
- ¾ teaspoon cayenne pepper
- ½ teaspoon salt
- ¾ teaspoon sage
- ¼ teaspoon caraway seeds
- 1 teaspoon almond butter
- 1 cup chicken stock

Directions:
1. Put Brussels sprouts in the slow cooker.
2. Add the rest of the ingredients and toss.
3. Close the lid and cook vegetables for 3 hours on High.
4. Divide between plates and serve.

Nutrition value/serving: calories 130, fat 2.3, fiber 3.4, carbs 4.9, protein 3.3

Coriander Broccoli

Prep time: 15 minutes
Cooking time: 1 hour
Servings: 3
Ingredients:
- 2 cups broccoli florets
- 1 tablespoon butter
- 1 teaspoon turmeric powder
- ¾ cup organic almond milk
- 1 teaspoon coriander, ground

Directions:
1. In the slow cooker, combine the broccoli with the butter and the other ingredients and close the lid.
2. Cook broccoli mix for 1 hour on High.
3. Divide between plates and serve.

Nutrition value/serving: calories 132, fat 7.1, fiber 3.5, carbs 2.9, protein 3.4

Balsamic Cauliflower

Prep time: 7 minutes
Cooking time: 3 hours
Servings: 1
Ingredients:
- 1 cup cauliflower florets
- ¼ cup butter
- ½ teaspoon salt
- ¼ teaspoon cayenne pepper
- 1 teaspoon curry powder
- 1 tablespoon balsamic vinegar
- 1 teaspoon liquid stevia

Directions:
1. In the slow cooker, mix the cauliflower with the butter, salt and the other ingredients.
2. Close the lid and cook onions for 3 hours on High.
3. Divide between plates and serve.

Nutrition value/serving: calories 220, fat 6.1, fiber 0.4, carbs 2.5, protein 3.8

Eggplant Loaf

Prep time: 15 minutes
Cooking time: 7 hours
Servings: 6
Ingredients:
- 3 tablespoons flaxseed meal
- 2 eggplants, chopped
- 1 cup bok choy, chopped
- 1 teaspoon salt
- ½ teaspoon ground black pepper
- 1 tablespoon Ketogenic tomato sauce
- 1/3 cup coconut flour
- Cooking spray

Directions:
1. In a blender, mix the eggplants, bok choy and the other ingredients except the cooking spray and pulse.
2. Spray the loaf mold with cooking spray and transfer the eggplant mix inside.
3. Flatten it well and cover with foil. Secure the edges.
4. Transfer the loaf in the slow cooker and close the lid.
5. Cook the loaf for 7 hours on Low.

Nutrition value/serving: calories 181, fat 3.4, fiber 2.7, carbs 6.4, protein 2.4

Kale Chowder

Prep time: 10 minutes
Cooking time: 2.5 hours
Servings: 3
Ingredients:
- 1 cup organic coconut milk
- 7 oz kale, chopped
- 1 teaspoon ground black pepper
- 1 tablespoon coconut cream
- ½ teaspoon curry powder
- ¼ cup spring onions, chopped
- 1 tablespoon chives, chopped
- ½ cup chicken stock
- 1 teaspoon salt

Directions:
1. In the slow cooker, mix the kale with coconut milk, cream and the other ingredients, close the lid and cook on High for 2.5 hours.
2. Blend using an immersion blender, divide into bowls and serve.

Nutrition value/serving: calories 158, fat 4.8, fiber 1.4, carbs 7.2, protein 4.1

Sprouts and Zucchinis

Prep time: 10 minutes
Cooking time: 30 minutes
Servings: 2
Ingredients:
- 1 cup Brussels sprouts, quartered
- 2 zucchinis, cubed
- ¼ teaspoon turmeric powder
- ½ teaspoon salt
- ¾ teaspoon oregano, dried

- ¼ teaspoon cumin powder
- 1 cup chicken stock
- 1 cup of water
- 1 teaspoon almond butter
- 1 tablespoon sour cream

Directions:
1. In the slow cooker, mix the sprouts with the zucchinis and the other ingredients.
2. Close the lid and cook the meal for 30 minutes on High.
3. Then stir the meal very well and transfer in the serving plates.

Nutrition value/serving: calories 151, fat 6.3, fiber 4.9, carbs 6, protein 3.4

Sautéed Cabbage

Prep time: 5 minutes
Cooking time: 2.5 hours
Servings: 4
Ingredients:
- 11 oz white cabbage, shredded
- 1/3 cup butter
- ½ teaspoon black pepper
- ½ cup veggie stock
- 1 teaspoon coriander, ground
- ½ teaspoon salt

Directions:
1. In the slow cooker, mix the cabbage with the butter and the other ingredients.
2. Cook the meal for 2.5 hours on High.

Nutrition value/serving: calories 249, fat 15.5, fiber 4.3, carbs 2.5, protein 4.7

Garlic Kale and Mushrooms

Prep time: 15 minutes
Cooking time: 5 hours
Servings: 4
Ingredients:
- 2 cups white mushrooms, sliced
- 1 cup kale, chopped
- 1 teaspoon minced garlic
- ½ teaspoon sweet paprika
- ½ teaspoon salt
- 1 tablespoon butter
- 1 tablespoon dried oregano
- ½ teaspoon chili powder
- 1 teaspoon olive oil

Directions:
1. In the slow cooker, mix the mushrooms with the kale, garlic and the other ingredients.
2. Cook the mix for 5 hours on Low.

Nutrition value/serving: calories 163, fat 4.6, fiber 4.3, carbs 5.6, protein 1.5

Kale Stew

Prep time: 10 minutes
Cooking time: 3 hours
Servings: 4
Ingredients:
- 2 cups kale, torn
- 1 cup cherry tomatoes, halved
- 1 red chili pepper, chopped
- 1 garlic clove, diced
- 1 teaspoon coriander, ground
- 1 teaspoon ground paprika
- ½ cup of coconut milk
- 2/3 cup cauliflower, chopped
- 1 tablespoon butter, soft
- ½ teaspoon salt
- ½ teaspoon turmeric
- 1 teaspoon chives, chopped

Directions:
1. In the slow cooker, mix the kale with the tomatoes and the other ingredients, toss and close the lid.
2. Cook the stew for 3 hours on High.
3. Divide into bowls and serve.

Nutrition value/serving: calories 120, fat 5.6, fiber 3, carbs 5.4, protein 3.3

Okra Sauté

Prep time: 8 minutes
Cooking time: 4 hours
Servings: 5
Ingredients:
- 1-pound okra, chopped
- 1 chili pepper, minced
- 1 teaspoon coriander, ground
- 1 teaspoon turmeric powder
- 1 tablespoon curry paste
- 2 tablespoons sour cream
- ½ cup heavy cream

Directions:
1. In the slow cooker, mix the okra with the chili pepper and the other ingredients.
2. Close the lid and cook for 4 hours on Low.

Nutrition value/serving: calories 133, fat 4.4, fiber 3.3, carbs 4.9, protein 2.5

Desserts

Cocoa Cake

Prep time: 10 minutes
Cooking time: 3.5 hours
Servings: 4
Ingredients:
- 1/3 cup stevia
- ¼ cup coconut flour
- 1 ½ tablespoon cocoa powder
- ¾ teaspoon salt
- ¼ teaspoon baking soda
- ½ teaspoon lime juice
- 3 tablespoons butter
- 2 eggs, beaten
- ¼ cup of water
- 1 teaspoon almond extract
- Cooking spray

Directions:
1. In a bowl mix the stevia with the flour, cocoa and the other ingredients except the cooking spray and blend the mixture with the help of the hand mixer.
2. Spray the slow cooker bottom with the cooking spray.
3. Pour the cake mixture in the slow cooker and flatten it with the help of the spatula.
4. Close the lid and cook the dessert for 3.5 hours on Low.
5. Chill the cake well before serving.

Nutrition value/serving: calories 216, fat 6.2, fiber 3.8, carbs 2.1, protein 3.6

Zucchini Cake

Prep time: 15 minutes
Cooking time: 4 hours
Servings: 8
Ingredients:
- 1 cup almond flour
- 3 tablespoons coconut flour
- 1 teaspoon baking soda
- ½ teaspoon apple cider vinegar
- 1 teaspoon cocoa powder
- 2 zucchinis, grated
- 2 tablespoons pecans, chopped
- 1/3 cup organic coconut milk
- 2 eggs, beaten
- 1/3 cup stevia
- 1 teaspoon coconut oil
- 2 tablespoons cream cheese

Directions:
1. In the mixing bowl mix up together the flour with the baking soda and the other ingredients and whisk.
2. Line the slow cooker with baking paper and transfer the cake mixture inside.
3. Flatten it gently.
4. Cook the cake for 4 hours on Low.
5. Cut the cake into the servings.

Nutrition value/serving: calories 215, fat 6.2, fiber 4.3, carbs 4.7, protein 5.4

Lemon Cake

Prep time: 15 minutes
Cooking time: 4 hours
Servings: 8
Ingredients:
- 3 eggs
- 1/3 cup stevia
- 1 ½ cup coconut flour
- ½ cup coconut cream
- ½ teaspoon baking soda
- 1 teaspoon lemon zest, grated
- 1 tablespoon lemon juice
- 1 teaspoon vanilla extract

Directions:
1. In a bowl mix the eggs with stevia, flour and the other ingredients and whisk really well.
2. Line the slow cooker with baking paper.
3. Put the cake mixture in the slow cooker, flatten it gently and close the lid.
4. Cook the cake for 4 hours on Low.

Nutrition value/serving: calories 237, fat 8.2, fiber 4.3, carbs 4.2, protein 6.8

Pumpkin Cake

Prep time: 10 minutes
Cooking time: 5 hours
Servings: 4
Ingredients:
- 2 tablespoons coconut butter, soft
- 1 teaspoon almond extract
- 1 teaspoon baking powder
- 1/3 cup Swerve
- 1 teaspoon lime juice
- 1 cup almond flour
- ¼ cup organic almond milk
- 1 teaspoon avocado oil
- 1/4 cup pumpkin puree

Directions:
1. In a bowl, mix the pumpkin puree with coconut butter, almond extract and the other ingredients and stir.
2. Line the slow cooker with parchment paper, pour the cake mix and close the lid.
3. Cook the cake for 5 hours on Low.
4. Cool down and serve.

Nutrition value/serving: calories 329, fat 3.4, fiber 1.8, carbs 4.4, protein 6.3

Mascarpone Fudge

Prep time: 20 minutes
Cooking time: 40 minutes
Servings: 8
Ingredients:
- 2 tablespoons coconut cream
- 2 tablespoons Mascarpone cheese, soft
- 1 teaspoon almond extract
- 1 teaspoon Erythritol
- 1/3 cup sugar-free chocolate chips
- 1 teaspoon coconut butter

Directions:
1. In the slow cooker, mix the mascarpone with the cream and eth other ingredients and close the lid.
2. Cook it for 40 minutes on High.
3. Meanwhile, line the baking tray with baking paper.
4. Transfer in the baking tray.
5. Cover it with the second sheet of baking paper.
6. With the help of the rolling pin, roll up the fudge into the square.
7. Cool it in the fridge for 10 minutes.
8. Then discard the baking paper and cut fudge into the serving squares.
9. Store dessert in the cool place.

Nutrition value/serving: calories 56, fat 3.5, fiber 0.1, carbs 7, protein 0.9

Walnut Cake

Prep time: 20 minutes
Cooking time: 4.5 hours
Servings: 8
Ingredients:
- 1 cup almond flour
- 4 tablespoons butter, softened
- 1 teaspoon almond extract
- ½ cup stevia
- 3 tablespoons Ricotta cheese
- 2 tablespoons walnuts, chopped
- 3 eggs, beaten
- 1/3 cup coconut milk
- 2 egg yolks
- 1 teaspoon peanut butter

Directions:
1. In a bowl, mix the coconut milk with the flour and the other ingredients and whisk well.
2. Line the slow cooker with baking paper, pour the cake mix inside and close the lid.
3. Cook the mix for 4.5 hours on Low.
4. Cool down and serve.

Nutrition value/serving: calories 214, fat 4.3, fiber 0.6, carbs 2.3, protein 6.8

Vanilla Cake

Prep time: 15 minutes
Cooking time: 5 hours
Servings: 6
Ingredients:
- 4 tablespoons chocolate chips, softened
- 1 cup organic coconut milk
- 1 cup almond flour
- 1 teaspoon baking powder
- 1 teaspoon apple cider vinegar
- 2 tablespoons Erythritol
- 2 teaspoons vanilla extract
- 3 eggs, beaten

Directions:
1. In the big bowl combine together the coconut milk with the flour and the other ingredients and whisk.
2. Line the slow cooker with the baking paper.
3. Pour the batter in the slow cooker. Flatten it with the help of the spatula if needed.
4. Cook the cake for 5 hours on Low.
5. Then chill the cake well and remove it from the slow cooker.
6. Discard the baking paper and cut the cake into the servings.

Nutrition value/serving: calories 239, fat 14.6, fiber 4.5, carbs 10.4, protein 5.4

Chocolate Pudding

Prep time: 10 minutes
Cooking time: 15 minutes
Servings: 3
Ingredients:
- ½ cup heavy cream
- 1 oz dark chocolate

- 1 tablespoon Truvia
- ½ teaspoon vanilla extract

Directions:
1. Put dark chocolate and vanilla extract in the slow cooker.
2. Close the lid and cook the chocolate for 15 minutes on High.
3. Meanwhile, whip the heavy cream.
4. Add Truvia and stir it well.
5. Gradually start to add the melted dark chocolate. Stir it until smooth.
6. Transfer the cooked pudding in the serving cups.

Nutrition value/serving: calories 124, fat 10.7., fiber 0.7, carbs 7.5, protein 0.8

Lime Vanilla Bites

Prep time: 10 minutes
Cooking time: 2 hours
Servings: 4
Ingredients:
- ¾ cup butter, softened
- ½ teaspoon vanilla extract
- 1 tablespoon stevia
- 1 teaspoon lime zest, grated
- 2 tablespoons lime juice
- ½ teaspoon baking soda
- 5 tablespoons coconut flour
- 1 egg, beaten

Directions:
1. Mix up together the butter with vanilla, stevia and the other ingredients until smooth.
2. Then put the mixture into 4 ramekins and flatten gently.
3. Transfer the ramekins in the slow cooker.
4. Cook the lemon bites for 2 hours on High.

Nutrition value/serving: calories 242, fat 7.4, fiber 0.4, carbs 5.2, protein 2.5

Cinnamon Cake

Prep time: 10 minutes
Cooking time: 2.5 hours
Servings: 6
Ingredients:
- 1 cup coconut flour
- 2 eggs, beaten
- 2 teaspoons ground cinnamon
- ¾ cup almond butter, melted
- 2 tablespoons Swerve
- 1 teaspoon baking soda
- 1 tablespoon lime juice
- ½ teaspoon almond extract

Directions:
1. In the mixing bowl combine the coconut flour with the eggs and the other ingredients and whisk.
2. Mix up the mixture well and transfer it in the slow cooker.
3. Make the swirls with the help of the fork and close the lid.
4. Cook the cake for 2.5 hours on High.
5. Chill the cooked cake well and cut into the servings.
6. After this, remove the cake from the slow cooker.

Nutrition value/serving: calories 234, fat 5.3, fiber 1.3, carbs 2.8, protein 3.4

Berry Brownies

Prep time: 10 minutes
Cooking time: 2.5 hours
Servings: 6
Ingredients:
- 1 cup coconut flour
- ½ cup blackberries
- 1 teaspoon baking soda
- 4 tablespoons cocoa powder
- 1/3 cup butter, softened
- 2 tablespoons stevia
- ½ teaspoon cinnamon powder

Directions:
1. Line the slow cooker with baking paper.
2. Blend together the flour with berries and the other ingredients and pour into the slow cooker.
3. Flatten gently, close the lid and cook brownie for 2.5 hours on High.
4. Then chill the cooked brownie well and remove it from the slow cooker.
5. Cut it into the square serving pieces.

Nutrition value/serving: calories 213, fat 5,4, fiber 9.1, carbs 7.5, protein 4.8

Cream Cheese Cookies

Prep time: 15 minutes
Cooking time: 4.5 hours
Servings: 4
Ingredients:
- 1 teaspoon baking soda
- 1 tablespoon apple cider vinegar
- 3 tablespoons sugar-free chocolate chips
- ¼ cup stevia

- 1/3 cup avocado oil
- 1 cup almond flour
- 1 egg, beaten
- 1 teaspoon cream cheese
- 1 teaspoon almond extract

Directions:
1. In a bowl, mix the egg with flour, cream cheese and the other ingredients and whisk.
2. Transfer the cookies mixture in the slow cooker.
3. Flatten the surface of the cookie dough with the help of the spatula.
4. Cook the chip cookies for 4.5 hours on Low.

Nutrition value/serving: calories 245, fat 14.3, fiber 0.8, carbs 6.4, protein 3.2

Chocolate Pecan Cake

Prep time: 10 minutes
Cooking time: 5 hours
Servings: 4
Ingredients:
- 1 cup coconut flour
- 1/3 cup almond butter, melted
- ¼ cup of water
- 1 teaspoon almond extract
- 2 tablespoons Stevia
- 1 teaspoon baking powder
- ½ oz dark chocolate, chopped
- 3 eggs, beaten
- 2 pecans, chopped
- Cooking spray

Directions:
1. In a bowl mix the coconut flour with almond butter water and the other ingredients except the cooking spray.
2. Spray the slow cooker with cooking spray from inside and pour cake mixture.
3. Flatten the surface of the cake mixture well and close the lid.
4. Cook the spoon cake for 5 hours on Low.

Nutrition value/serving: calories 180, fat 4.6, fiber 2, carbs 7.2, protein 4.3

Lemon Scones

Prep time: 15 minutes
Cooking time: 2.5 hours
Servings: 6
Ingredients:
- 2 cups almond flour
- ½ cup of coconut oil
- 2 tablespoons lemon juice
- 1 teaspoon cinnamon powder
- 1 teaspoon baking powder
- 1 egg, beaten
- 4 tablespoons Swerve

Directions:
1. In the mixing bowl, combine the flour with the coconut oil and the other ingredients and stir well.
2. Line the slow cooker with baking paper.
3. Make the ball from the dough and place it in the slow cooker.
4. Cut the dough into 6 scones and close the lid.
5. Cook the scones for 2.5 hours on High.
6. Then chill the cooked dessert well and cut the dough into scones again.

Nutrition value/serving: calories 221, fat 14.4, fiber 1, carbs 6.6, protein 3.1

Strawberries Cake

Prep time: 15 minutes
Cooking time: 4.5 hours
Servings: 4
Ingredients:
- 1/3 cup strawberries, chopped
- 1 cup coconut flour
- ¼ cup butter, softened
- ¾ cup stevia
- 1 teaspoon vanilla extract
- ¾ teaspoon cinnamon powder
- 1 teaspoon coconut oil

Directions:
1. Spread the slow cooker bottom with coconut oil.
2. Place the chopped strawberries in the slow cooker and flatten them to get the layer shape.
3. In a bowl mix the rest of the ingredients, stir and knead the dough a bit.
4. Then place the dough over the strawberries. Flatten it well and close the lid.
5. Cook the cake for 4.5 hours on Low.
6. When the cake is cooked, transfer it in the serving plates and eat hot.

Nutrition value/serving: calories 160, fat 16.2, fiber 1.1, carbs 3.2, protein 1.7

Almond Roll

Prep time: 15 minutes
Cooking time: 3.5 hours
Servings: 6
Ingredients:

- 1 teaspoon baking powder
- 1 cup almond flour
- 1 tablespoon ground cinnamon
- 2 tablespoons stevia
- 1/3 cup coconut oil
- 1 teaspoon almond extract
- 1 egg, beaten
- ¾ cup Mascarpone cream

Directions:
1. In a bowl mix the flour with coconut oil and the other ingredients except the cinnamon and stevia.
2. Mix up together ground cinnamon with stevia
3. Roll up the dough with the help of the rolling pin.
4. Spread the surface of the dough with ground cinnamon mixture and roll it into the log.
5. Cut the log into 6 buns and secure the edges of every bun.
6. Line the crockpot with baking paper.
7. Place the buns in the crockpot and close the lid.
8. Cook the cinnamon roll for 3.5 hours on High.
9. Check if the rolls are cooked with the help of the toothpick – if it is dry, the buns are cooked.
10. Chill the dessert well and then remove from the crockpot in the serving plate.

Nutrition value/serving: calories 208, fat 15.3, fiber 1.1, carbs 8.2, protein 4.2

Keto Flan

Prep time: 10 minutes
Cooking time: 10 hours
Servings: 3
Ingredients:
- 1 cup heavy cream
- 3 eggs, beaten
- ½ teaspoon vanilla extract
- ¼ cup Swerve
- ½ teaspoon butter
- ½ cup water, for cooking

Directions:
1. Put butter in the skillet and melt it.
2. Add Swerve and simmer the liquid over the medium heat for 3 minutes.
3. Then pour the butter sweet mixture into the ramekins.
4. Mix up together beaten eggs, vanilla extract, and heavy cream.
5. When the liquid is smooth, pour it over the sweet butter mixture in the ramekins.
6. Pour water in the crockpot.
7. Place the ramekins with flan in the water and close the lid.
8. Cook flan for 10 hours on Low.
9. Chill the flan little and turn the ramekins over in the plates to get flan.

Nutrition value/serving: calories 209, fat 19.8, fiber 0, carbs 1.7, protein 6.4

Peanut Pie

Prep time: 10 minutes
Cooking time: 6 hours
Servings: 10
Ingredients:
- 1 cup peanut butter
- ¼ cup hazelnuts
- 1 tablespoon chocolate chips
- 1 teaspoon avocado oil
- 1 teaspoon vanilla extract
- ¾ cup organic coconut milk
- 2 cups coconut flour
- 1/3 cup Monk fruit
- ¼ cup almond, chopped

Directions:
1. In the big mixing bowl mix up together the peanut butter with hazelnuts and the other ingredients.
2. Line the crockpot with baking paper and place pie dough on it.
3. Flatten the dough with the help of the wet fingertips and close the lid.
4. Cook the nut pie for 6 hours on Low.
5. Chill the cooked pie well and cut into the servings.

Nutrition value/serving: calories 248, fat 11.3, fiber 10.8, carbs 17.9, protein 8.6

Rutabaga Cake

Prep time: 20 minutes
Cooking time: 4.5 hours
Servings: 6
Ingredients:
- 1 cup coconut flour
- ¾ cup butter, softened
- 1 tablespoon stevia
- 1 teaspoon almond extract
- ½ teaspoon vanilla extract
- 1 cup rutabaga, chopped

- 1 tablespoon coconut oil
- Cooking spray

Directions:
1. For the pie crust: mix up together coconut flour, butter, and knead the soft dough.
2. Then cut the dough into 2 parts.
3. Spray the crockpot bottom with cooking spray from inside.
4. Roll up first dough part with the help of the rolling pin and place it in the crockpot.
5. Then mix up together rutabaga with the other ingredients and arrange this over the crust.
6. Then roll up the second dough part and cover the rutabaga.
7. Close the crockpot lid and cook the cake for 4.5 hours on Low.
8. When the pie is cooked, chill it well and only them cut into the pieces.

Nutrition value/serving: calories 260, fat 27.7, fiber 1.3, carbs 5.8, protein 1.5

Coffee Cream

Prep time: 10 minutes
Cooking time: 2 hours
Servings: 4
Ingredients:
- 1 cup of water
- 1 cup heavy cream
- 1 oz brewed coffee
- 1 tablespoon cinnamon powder
- 1 tablespoon coconut oil
- 2 teaspoons stevia

Directions:
1. In the crockpot, mix the water with cream and the other ingredients.
2. Close the lid and cook hot chocolate for 2 hours on High.
3. Then pour the cooked hot mix in the serving glasses.

Nutrition value/serving: calories 136, fat 5.2, fiber 0.9, carbs 5.1, protein 1.1

Cashew Cream Mix

Prep time: 10 minutes
Cooking time: 7.5 hours
Servings: 4
Ingredients:
- 1 cup cashew milk
- ¾ cup cashew butter
- ½ cup coconut cream
- 2 tablespoons allulose
- ¾ teaspoon baking soda
- ½ teaspoon vanilla extract

Directions:
1. In the crockpot, mix the cashew with cashew butter and the other ingredients and close the lid.
2. Cook on Low for 7.5 hours.
3. Stir the cooked meal well and pour in the glass jar.

Nutrition value/serving: calories 125, fat 5.8, fiber 3.4, carbs 1, protein 0.5

Strawberry Cobbler

Prep time: 10 minutes
Cooking time: 4 hours
Servings: 2
Ingredients:
- ¼ cup strawberries
- ¾ teaspoon almond extract
- 1 teaspoon vanilla extract
- 1 tablespoon Monk fruit
- 1 cup almond flour
- 3 tablespoons coconut butter
- 1 teaspoon liquid stevia
- 1 egg, beaten
- Cooking spray

Directions:
1. Mix up together strawberries almond extract and vanilla extract. Mash the mixture gently.
2. Then spray the crockpot bottom with cooking spray.
3. Place the berry mixture inside the crockpot and flatten it gently.
4. After this, mix up together Monk fruit with the remaining ingredients.
5. Stir the mixture until homogenous.
6. Then transfer the prepared almond flour mixture over the berry mixture and flatten gently.
7. Cook the cobbler for 4 hours on High.

Nutrition value/serving: calories 241, fat 6.7, fiber 3.1, carbs 4.6, protein 5.3

Chocolate Walnut Pie

Prep time: 10 minutes
Cooking time: 2.5 hours
Servings:
Ingredients:
- 1 cup of coconut milk
- 1 ½ cup almond flour

- 1 teaspoon almond extract
- 3 tablespoons walnuts chopped
- 1 tablespoon chocolate chips, melted
- 1/3 cup peanut butter
- 1 tablespoon Erythritol
- ½ cup coconut flakes

Directions:
1. Mix up together coconut milk with the flour and the other ingredients and stir.
2. When the mixture is homogenous, pour it in the crockpot.
3. Add butter and close the lid.
4. Cook the mix for 2.5 hours.

Nutrition value/serving: calories 202, fat 12.5, fiber 3.1, carbs 10.1, protein 6.2

Almond Blondies

Prep time: 10 minutes
Cooking time: 3.5 hours
Servings: 14
Ingredients:
- ½ cup almond butter, softened
- 1 cup stevia
- 1 egg, beaten
- 1 teaspoon almond extract
- 1 cup almond flour
- 1 oz white chocolate, melted

Directions:
1. In the mixing bowl combine the butter with the stevia and the other ingredients and whisk.
2. Line the crockpot with baking paper and pour blondies mixture inside.
3. Flatten it and cook for 3.5 hours.
4. Then remove the blondies from the crockpot and cut into the servings.

Nutrition value/serving: calories 145, fat 2.5, fiber 3.1, carbs 5.2, protein 1.7

Green Tea Cupcakes

Prep time: 10 minutes
Cooking time: 3.5 hours
Servings: 4
Ingredients:
- 1 teaspoon green tea powder
- 4 eggs, beaten
- 1 cup coconut flour
- 1 teaspoon baking soda
- 1 teaspoon lemon juice
- 1 tablespoon stevia
- ½ teaspoon almond extract
- 1 tablespoon peanut butter, softened

Directions:
1. In the mixing bowl whisk together the green tea powder with the eggs and the other ingredients and whisk.
2. Fill ½ part of every cupcake mold with matcha batter and transfer in the crockpot.
3. Close the lid and cook cupcakes for 3.5 hours on High.

Nutrition value/serving: calories 233, fat 11.9, fiber 3.3, carbs 8.2, protein 4.1

Blueberry Crisp

Prep time: 10 minutes
Cooking time: 5 hours
Servings: 2
Ingredients:
- 1/2 cup blueberries
- ¼ cup coconut flakes
- 2 tablespoons almond butter, softened
- 1 teaspoon almond extract
- ¾ teaspoon ground nutmeg
- 1 tablespoon Erythritol
- 1 egg, beaten

Directions:
1. In the mixing bowl, combine the berries with the flakes and the other ingredients and whisk.
2. Put the homogenous berries mixture in the crockpot and flatten well.
3. Flatten the crisp gently.
4. Close the lid.
5. Cook the crisp 5 hours on Low.

Nutrition value/serving: calories 202, fat 7.5, fiber 2.8, carbs 5.3, protein 4.5

Biscuits

Prep time: 15 minutes
Cooking time: 2 hours
Servings: 6
Ingredients:
- 1 cup coconut flour
- ¼ cup coconut flakes
- 1/3 cup almond butter, softened
- 1 teaspoon almond extract
- 1 teaspoon baking powder
- 1 teaspoon lemon juice
- 2 tablespoons Erythritol
- Cooking spray

Directions:
1. Knead the dough: mix up together flour with the coconut flakes and the other ingredients except the cooking spray.

2. The dough should be very soft but non-sticky.
3. After this, roll the dough into a log and cut into pieces.
4. Roll up the dough pieces into the round biscuits with the help of the rolling pin.
5. Line the crockpot bottom with baking paper and spray with cooking spray.
6. Carefully place the almond biscuits in the crockpot and cook them for 2 hours on High.
7. Chill the biscuits well before serving.
Nutrition value/serving: calories 203, fat 14.6, fiber 1, carbs 5.4, protein 2

Mint Cake

Prep time: 10 minutes
Cooking time: 3 hours
Servings: 6
Ingredients:
- 1 teaspoon dried mint
- 1 teaspoon mint extract
- 1 teaspoon almond extract
- 1 cup almond flour
- ½ cup of coconut milk
- 1 teaspoon butter, melted
- 1 teaspoon baking soda
- 1 cup almond flour
- ½ cup Monk fruit

Directions:
1. Line the crockpot with baking paper.
2. In the big mixing bowl mix up together all ingredients.
3. When you get a smooth batter, pour it in the crockpot.
4. Flatten it gently and close the lid.
5. Cook the mint cake on High for 3 hours.
6. When the cake is cooked, chill it well and only then remove from the crockpot.
7. Slice it into the servings.

Nutrition value/serving: calories 215, fat 11.1, fiber 5.4, carbs 4.6, protein 5.5

Pecan Pie

Prep time: 15 minutes
Cooking time: 3.5 hours
Servings: 8
Ingredients:
- 1 tablespoon chocolate chips
- 4 tablespoons peanut butter
- 4 pecans, chopped
- 1 teaspoon baking powder
- 1 tablespoon lemon juice
- 2 cups almond flour
- 3 tablespoons Erythritol
- 1 teaspoon vanilla extract

Directions:
1. Make the dough: in the mixing bowl, mix up together chocolate chips, peanut butter, chopped pecans, baking powder, lemon juice, almond flour, Erythritol, and vanilla extract.
2. Knead the smooth and non-sticky dough.
3. Then line the crockpot with baking paper.
4. Make the shape of bun from the dough and put it in the crockpot.
5. Flatten it well with the help of the fingertips.
6. Close the lid and cook pecan pie for 3.5 hours on High.
7. Chill the cooked pie well and then remove from the crockpot.
8. Slice it into the servings.

Nutrition value/serving: calories 145, fat 12.9, fiber 2, carbs 7.2, protein 4.4

Cinnamon and Blackberry Pie

Prep time: 15 minutes
Cooking time: 7.5 hours
Servings: 12
Ingredients:
- 1 tablespoon cinnamon powder
- 1 teaspoon baking soda
- 1 teaspoon apple cider vinegar
- 1 cup almond flour
- ½ cup coconut flour
- 3 tablespoons coconut shred
- ½ cup blackberries, mashed
- 1/3 cup Erythritol
- 5 eggs, beaten
- 1 teaspoon avocado oil

Directions:
1. Mix up together the flour with the cinnamon and the other ingredients except the oil.
2. Then brush the crockpot with the oil from inside.
3. Pour the batter in the crockpot and flatten it gently.
4. Close the lid and cook per for 7.5 hours on Low.

Nutrition value/serving: calories 130, fat 4.7, fiber 4.1, carbs 8.8, protein 2.9

Zucchini Muffins

Prep time: 10 minutes
Cooking time: 2.5 hours
Servings: 4
Ingredients:
- 4 teaspoons butter, softened
- 1 teaspoon baking powder
- 1 cup almond flour
- 1 teaspoon almond extract
- ¼ cup heavy cream
- 4 teaspoons stevia
- 1/2 cup zucchinis, grated

Directions:
1. In the crockpot, mix the butter with the zucchinis and the other ingredients.
2. Stir it until smooth.
3. Pour the muffin mixture in the muffin molds and transfer molds in the crockpot.
4. Close the lid and cook muffins for 2.5 hours on High.

Nutrition value/serving: calories 215, fat 10.1, fiber 4.8, carbs 7.8, protein 3.7

Vanilla Bars

Prep time: 10 minutes
Cooking time: 5 hours
Servings: 6
Ingredients:
- 1 cup almond flour
- ¼ cup coconut butter, softened
- 4 eggs, beaten
- ½ cup coconut cream
- 1 tablespoon stevia
- 1 teaspoon vanilla extract
- Cooking spray

Directions:
1. In the bowl, combine together eggs with almond flour and the other ingredients and stir.
2. Transfer this to the lined and sprayed crockpot, and cook on Low for 5 hours.
3. Cool down, cut into bars and serve.

Nutrition value/serving: calories 207, fat 7.7, fiber 0.5, carbs 4.5, protein 6.2

Vanilla Pudding

Prep time: 6 minutes
Cooking time: 4 hours
Servings: 2
Ingredients:
- 1 cup organic coconut milk
- 1 teaspoon vanilla extract
- 4 tablespoons coconut flakes
- 2 tablespoons stevia

Directions:
1. In the crockpot, mix the coconut milk and vanilla and the other ingredients.
2. Close the lid.
3. Cook the pudding for 4 hours on Low.

Nutrition value/serving: calories 149, fat 5.8, fiber 7.8, carbs 6.2, protein 4

Zucchini and Pumpkin Pie

Prep time: 15 minutes
Cooking time: 4 hours
Servings: 8
Ingredients:
- 1 tablespoon pumpkin spices
- 1 tablespoon pumpkin puree
- ½ cup of coconut milk
- ½ cup zucchini, grated
- 2 tablespoons stevia
- 1 teaspoon almond extract
- 2 tablespoons butter, softened
- 2 cups almond flour
- ½ teaspoon lemon zest, grated
- 1 teaspoon baking soda
- 1 teaspoon apple cider vinegar

Directions:
1. In a bowl mix the pumpkin puree with zucchini and the other ingredients and stir.
2. When the mixture is smooth, pour it un the crockpot. Flatten it with the help of the spatula if needed.
3. Close the lid.
4. Cook the zucchini for 4 hours on High.
5. Chill the cooked pie well and slice it.

Nutrition value/serving: calories 225, fat 10.1, fiber 3.3, carbs 7.1, protein 1.9

Chocolate Muffins

Prep time: 15 minutes
Cooking time: 2.5 hours
Servings: 4
Ingredients:
- 1 tablespoon chocolate chips, softened
- ½ cup butter, softened
- 1 teaspoon baking soda
- ½ teaspoon ground cinnamon
- 1 cup almond flour
- 4 teaspoons stevia
- 1 egg, beaten

Directions:

1. Make the muffin batter: in a bowl, mix the chocolate with the butter and the other ingredients and whisk.
2. Pour it in the muffin molds (fill ½ part of every mold) and transfer in the crockpot.
3. Cook the muffins for 2.5 hours on High.
Nutrition value/serving: calories 225, fat 17.7, fiber 1.3, carbs 8.3, protein 3.3

Strawberry Jam
Prep time: 10 minutes
Cooking time: 15 hours
Servings: 4
Ingredients:
- 1 cup strawberries
- ¼ teaspoon ground nutmeg
- ½ cup Monk fruit

Directions:
1. Put berries in the bowl and mash until smooth with the help of the spoon.
2. Then add ground nutmeg and Monk fruit.
3. Mix up the mixture well and transfer in the crockpot.
4. Cook the jam for 5 hours on Low.
5. Then transfer the cooked jam in the glass jar and store it in the fridge.
Nutrition value/serving: calories 30, fat 0.2, fiber 2, carbs 2.6, protein 0.5

Espresso Cookie
Prep time: 15 minutes
Cooking time: 3 hours
Servings: 6
Ingredients:
- 4 eggs, beaten
- 2 cups almond flour
- 1 teaspoon vanilla extract
- 1 teaspoon ground ginger
- 2 tablespoons espresso powder
- ½ teaspoon fresh ginger, minced
- 2 tablespoons stevia
- 2 tablespoons butter
- 1 teaspoon of cocoa powder
- 1 teaspoon baking soda

Directions:
1. Whisk together eggs, flour and the other ingredients and knead until you obtain a dough.
2. Line the crockpot with baking paper.
3. Put the dough in the crockpot and flatten it well.
4. Cook the cookie for 3 hours on High.
Nutrition value/serving: calories 173, fat 5.5, fiber 1.1, carbs 6.3, protein 4.8

Blackberry Pancake
Prep time: 10 minutes
Cooking time: 1 hour
Servings: 6
Ingredients:
- 1 cup almond flour
- ½ cup coconut flour
- 1 teaspoon vanilla extract
- ¼ teaspoon ground nutmeg, ground
- ½ cup blackberries, pureed
- 3 eggs, beaten
- 1 tablespoon stevia
- 1 teaspoon butter
- ¼ cup coconut cream
- Cooking spray

Directions:
1. In the mixing bowl, combine the flour with vanilla, nutmeg and the other ingredients except the cooking spray and whisk.
2. Spray the crockpot bottom with the cooking spray.
3. Pour pancake batter in the crockpot and flatten it gently.
4. Cook the pancake for 50 minutes on High.
5. Then open the lid and add butter.
6. Let the pancake rest for 10 minutes.
Nutrition value/serving: calories 131, fat 4.7, fiber 4.7, carbs 4.8, protein 5.9

Almond Spread
Prep time: 15 minutes
Cooking time: 40 minutes
Servings: 10
Ingredients:
- 1 cup almond butter
- 1/3 cup almonds, chopped
- 2 tablespoons cocoa powder
- ½ teaspoon almond extract
- ¼ cup stevia

Directions:
1. In the crockpot, mix the almonds with almond butter and the other ingredients and whisk
2. Close the lid and the mixture for 40 minutes in High.

3. Then whisk the mixture with the help of the hand mixer/blender.
4. Divide into bowls and serve.
Nutrition value/serving: calories 100, fat 2.6, fiber 0.7, carbs 4.3, protein 0.9

Walnut Squares
Prep time: 20 minutes
Cooking time: 3 hours
Servings:6
Ingredients:
- 1 cup walnuts, chopped
- 2 tablespoons stevia
- 1 teaspoon vanilla extract
- 2 eggs, beaten
- 1 cup
- ½ cup coconut flour
- 1 teaspoon baking soda
- 1 tablespoon butter, softened
- Cooking spray

Directions:
1. Spray the crockpot with cooking spray from inside.
2. In the mixing bowl, combine the walnuts with stevia and the other ingredients and stir until you obtain a dough.
3. Transfer the dough in the crockpot and flatten it well with the help of the spatula.
4. Close the lid and cook the dough for 3 hours on High. The time of cooking depends on the dough thicknesses.
5. When the dough is cooked, carefully transfer it on the chopping board and let chill to the room temperature.
6. Cut it into the squares.
Nutrition value/serving: calories 230, fat 11.4, fiber 4.5, carbs 11.9, protein 7.9

Avocado Mousse
Prep time: 10 minutes
Cooking time: 2 hours
Servings:2
Ingredients:
- 2 avocados, peeled, pitted and mashed
- ¼ cup heavy cream
- ½ teaspoon almond extract
- 3 egg yolks
- 2 tablespoons monk fruit
- ¼ cup organic almond milk

Directions:
1. In the crockpot, mix the avocados with the cream and the other ingredients, whisk and close the lid.
2. Cook the mixture for 2 hours in Low.
3. Divide into cups and serve cold.
Nutrition value/serving: calories 217, fat 14.7, fiber 3.4, carbs 5.8, protein 5

Almond Coffee Cream
Prep time: 20 minutes
Cooking time: 40 minutes
Servings:5
Ingredients:
- 2 tablespoons almonds, chopped
- 2 oz dark chocolate, melted
- 1 cup brewed coffee
- ½ cup coconut cream
- 1 tablespoon coconut oil

Directions:
1. In your crockpot, mix the chocolate with coffee and the other ingredients, close the lid and cook on High for 40 minutes.
2. Divide into bowls and serve cold.
Nutrition value/serving: calories 141, fat 7.9, fiber 4.1, carbs 4.9, protein 3.9

Avocado and Walnuts Balls
Prep time: 30 minutes
Cooking time: 2.5 hours
Servings:6
Ingredients:
- 1 avocado, pitted, peeled
- 1 oz dark chocolate
- 3 tablespoons almond butter
- 1 tablespoon stevia
- 2 tablespoons walnuts, chopped
- ½ teaspoon vanilla extract

Directions:
1. In the crockpot, mix the chocolate with almond butter and the other ingredients except the avocado.
2. Close the lid and cook on Low for 2.5 hours.
3. Meanwhile, place the avocado in the blender and blend until fluffy.
4. When the time is over, open the crockpot lid and transfer the walnuts mix in the mixing bowl.
5. Add blended avocado and stir until homogenous. Chill the mixture in the fridge for 15-20 minutes.

6. Make the small balls from the mixture, arrange on a platter and keep in the fridge until serving.
Nutrition value/serving: calories 212, fat 11.4, fiber 3.7, carbs 7.8, protein 2.5

Chia Bites
Prep time: 15 minutes
Cooking time: 1 hour
Servings: 6
Ingredients:
- 1 tablespoon chocolate chips
- 3 tablespoons almond butter, softened
- 1 cup almond flour
- ½ teaspoon almond extract
- 1 tablespoon chia seeds
- 1 tablespoon liquid stevia

Directions:
1. Churn together butter with flour with chocolate chips, almond butter and the other ingredients and stir.
2. Then line the crockpot with baking paper.
3. Scoop the dough and place it in the crockpot. You should get small bites. Press the scooped bites gently.
4. Cook the dough bites for 1 hour on High.
Nutrition value/serving: calories 132, fat 4.6, fiber 5.3, carbs 7.7, protein 4.2

Red Berry Gummies
Prep time: 15 minutes
Cooking time: 1 hour
Servings: 5
Ingredients:
- 1 tablespoon gelatin
- 1 cup of water
- 1 teaspoon red food coloring
- 2 tablespoons blueberries puree
- 1 tablespoon stevia

Directions:
1. Mix up together the gelatin and 5 tablespoons of water. Stir the mixture and leave it for 10 minutes.
2. Meanwhile, pour the remaining water in the crockpot.
3. Add stevia, berries puree and food coloring. Stir the liquid and cook it for 1 hour on High.
4. Then switch off the crockpot and add gelatin mixture.
5. Stir it well until homogenous.

6. Pour the liquid in the gummy bear's molds and chill until solid.
7. Discard the gummy bears from the molds and store them in the cool place.
Nutrition value/serving: calories 5, fat 0, fiber 0, carbs 3, protein 1

Creamy Mousse
Prep time: 2 hours
Cooking time: 2.5 hours
Servings: 4
Ingredients:
- 1 cup heavy cream
- ¾ cup coconut cream
- 2 tablespoons Ricotta cheese
- 1 tablespoon stevia
- 2 eggs, beaten
- ½ teaspoon almond extract

Directions:
1. In the mixing bowl whisk together cream with Ricotta and the other ingredients and whisk well.
2. When the liquid is smooth, pour it in the crockpot and cook for 2.5 hours on Low.
3. When the time is over, pour the liquid in the blender and blend until it is fluffy.
4. Then pour the mousse in the serving cups and chill for 2-3 hours in the fridge or 1 hour in the freezer. Stir the mousse every 30 minutes.
Nutrition value/serving: calories 208, fat 13.9, fiber 2.1, carbs 3.5, protein 4.3

Cayenne Mousse
Prep time: 15 minutes
Cooking time: 1 hour
Servings: 4
Ingredients:
- 3 tablespoons butter, softened
- 2 oz dark chocolate, soft
- 1 cup heavy cream
- ¾ teaspoon cayenne pepper
- 3 tablespoons organic almond milk
- 1 teaspoon liquid stevia

Directions:
1. In the crockpot, mix the chocolate with the cream and the other ingredients and whisk well.
2. Close the lid and cook the mixture on High for 1 hour.
3. After this, open the crockpot divide the mousse into bowls and serve.

Nutrition value/serving: calories 186, fat 9.6, fiber 2.6, carbs 3.7, protein 3.2

Vanilla Avocado Cookies
Prep time: 15 minutes
Cooking time: 1 hour
Servings: 3
Ingredients:
- ½ cup almond flour
- 1 avocado, peeled, pitted and mashed
- ½ teaspoon vanilla extract
- 1 tablespoon stevia
- 1 tablespoon butter
- ½ teaspoon avocado oil
- Cooking spray

Directions:
1. In the mixing bowl, mix up together flour with avocado and the other ingredients except the cooking spray and stir until you obtain a dough
2. Knead the soft but non-sticky dough.
3. Brush the crockpot bowl with cooking spray from inside.
4. Make the small balls from the dough and press them gently with the help of the fork.
5. Put the cookies in the crockpot and cook for 1 hour on High.

Nutrition value/serving: calories 124, fat 6.3, fiber 2.5, carbs 6.1, protein 2.1

Peanut Butter Bars
Prep time: 15 minutes
Cooking time: 4 hours
Servings: 7
Ingredients:
- 4 tablespoons peanut butter
- ½ teaspoon almond extract
- 2 tablespoons almonds, chopped
- 1 tablespoon coconut shred
- 1 teaspoon ground ginger
- 1 teaspoon nutmeg, ground
- 1 teaspoon cinnamon powder
- 2 tablespoons stevia
- ¾ cup heavy cream
- Cooking spray

Directions:
1. In the crockpot, mix the peanut butter with almond extract and the other ingredients except the cooking spray and close the lid
2. Cook the mixture on Low for 4 hours.
3. Then stir it carefully.
4. Grease a baking sheet with cooking spray and spread the peanut butter mix inside.
5. Spread well, freeze for 1.5 hours, cut into bars and serve.

Nutrition value/serving: calories 128, fat 8.1, fiber 3.8, carbs 7.3, protein 3.1

Ricotta and Pecan Cupcakes
Prep time: 25 minutes
Cooking time: 3 hours
Servings: 4
Ingredients:
- 1 cup almond flour
- 1 teaspoon almond extract
- 1 teaspoon ground nutmeg
- 4 tablespoons butter, frozen
- 1 teaspoon Ricotta cheese
- 2 tablespoons pecans, chopped
- 1 tablespoon stevia

Directions:
1. Mix up together the flour with almond extract and the other ingredients and stir until you obtain a dough
2. After this, transfer the dough in the freezer for 20 minutes.
3. Remove the dough from the freezer and grated it.
4. Divide the dough into muffin molds.
5. After this, arrange the cupcakes in the crockpot.
6. Close the lid and cook them on High for 3 hours.

Nutrition value/serving: calories 209, fat 15.1, fiber 5.1, carbs 6.1, protein 3.8

Appendix : Recipes Index

A

Adobo Beef 87
Almond Avocado Mix 13
Almond Bars 53
Almond Beef 94
Almond Blondies 119
Almond Buns 16
Almond Chicken 79
Almond Coffee Cream 123
Almond Granola 49
Almond Roll 116
Almond Spread 122
Artichoke and Asparagus Mix 107
Artichoke and Asparagus Mix 20
Artichoke and Broccoli Mix 37
Asparagus and Onion Mix 40
Avocado and Shrimp 68
Avocado and Walnuts Balls 123
Avocado and Zucchini Bake 13
Avocado Mousse 123

B

Bacon and Zucchinis 32
Bacon Dip 52
Balsamic Beef 34
Balsamic Beef Meatballs 54
Balsamic Cauliflower 111
Balsamic Leeks 36
Balsamic Mussels 63
Balsamic Salmon 61
Balsamic Scallops 68
Basil Chicken 74
Basil Lamb and Apples 98
Basil Sprouts and Eggs 19
Beef and Asparagus 93
Beef and Broccoli 92
Beef and Cauliflower 92
Beef and Mushrooms 23
Beef and Scallions 96
Beef and Zucchini Wraps 48
Beef Brisket 88
Beef Casserole 13
Beef Curry 97
Beef Meatloaf 21
Beef Stuffed Mushrooms 100
Beef with Bok Choy 98
Bell Peppers and Spinach 110
Berry Brownies 115
Berry Pudding 20

Biscuits 119
Blackberry Pancake 122
Blueberry Crisp 119
Bok Choy and Radishes 44
Broccoli and Cauliflower Bake 42
Broccoli Sauté 108
Broccoli Soup 23
Brussel Sprouts Saute 110
Butter and Lemon Lamb 93
Butter Green Beans 108
Butter Green Peas 102
Butter Mushrooms 36
Butter Pork Ribs 51
Butter Salmon and Avocado 67
Butter Turkey and Olives 86
Butter Zucchini 35

C

Cabbage and Tomatoes 39
Cabbage Stew 27
Cajun Lamb 94
Cajun Shrimp 61
Calamari Rings and Broccoli 66
Calamari Stew 26
Caraway Cod 70
Caraway Ribs 90
Cashew Cream Mix 118
Cauliflower and Turmeric Mash 103
Cauliflower Bites 48
Cauliflower Bowls 23
Cauliflower Cream Soup 109
Cauliflower Frittata 8
Cauliflower Pilaf with Hazelnuts 103
Cauliflower Popcorn 56
Cauliflower Rice and Tomatoes 31
Cauliflower Rice and Turkey Casserole 12
Cauliflower Rice Mix 106
Cayenne Chorizo 56
Cayenne Mousse 124
Cayenne Shrimps 57
Cayenne Sprouts Hash 21
Celery Dip 110
Celery Puree 41
Chard and Radishes 44
Cheddar Artichoke 105
Cheddar Beef and Sprouts Casserole 19
Cheddar Chicken 75
Cheddar Dip 55

Cheese Asparagus 102
Cheese Sticks 49
Cheesy Bacon Casserole 12
Cheesy Egg and Bacon 8
Cheesy Tuna 65
Cheesy Turkey and Sauce 84
Cherry Tomatoes Sauté 45
Chia Bites 124
Chia Bowls 20
Chia Chicken Bites 51
Chicken and Cabbage 81
Chicken and Celery 81
Chicken and Coconut Milk 83
Chicken and Creamy Onions and Peppers 85
Chicken and Cucumber 78
Chicken and Eggplant 75
Chicken and Green Pepper Mix 83
Chicken and Hot Sauce 84
Chicken and Kale 79
Chicken and Mushrooms 79
Chicken and Okra 78
Chicken and Okra Stew 26
Chicken and Olives Stew 25
Chicken and Onions Mix 76
Chicken and Scallions Mix 74
Chicken and Sour Cream Sauce 80
Chicken and Spring Onions 85
Chicken and Tahini Sauce 74
Chicken and Tomato Sauce 82
Chicken and Tomatoes 74
Chicken and Walnuts 81
Chicken and Zucchinis 77
Chicken Bites 48
Chicken Breast with Avocados 85
Chicken Breast with Capers 78
Chicken Cubes and Pesto 81
Chicken Dip 51
Chicken Fillets and Mustard Sauce 83
Chicken Meatballs 16
Chicken Salad 75
Chicken Soup 23
Chicken Stew 24
Chicken with Cheese 76
Chicken with Nuts 84
Chicken with Spinach 77
Chicken, Tomatoes and Olives 82
Chili Bake 11
Chili Chicken 73
Chili Dip 52
Chili Eggplant Eggs 14

Chili Frittata 19
Chili Lamb 100
Chili Lamb Skewers 94
Chili Shrimp and Okra 70
Chili Soup 24
Chili Squid 66
Chili Tomatoes Bowls 15
Chili Walnuts 49
Chipotle Beef 99
Chives and Sprouts Casserole 17
Chives Chicken Teriyaki 85
Chives Wings 55
Chocolate Muffins 121
Chocolate Pecan Cake 116
Chocolate Pudding 114
Chocolate Walnut Pie 118
Cilantro Beef Tenderloin 87
Cilantro Chicken 80
Cilantro Pork Meatballs 19
Cinnamon and Blackberry Pie 120
Cinnamon Beef 31
Cinnamon Cake 115
Cinnamon Eggs 11
Cinnamon Mackerel 64
Cocktail Shrimp 51
Cocoa Cake 113
Coconut Avocado and Chicken Mix 10
Coconut Brussels Sprouts 103
Coconut Catfish 69
Coconut Celery 41
Coconut Halibut 30
Coconut Milk Turkey Breast 84
Coconut Muffins 14
Coconut Mushroom Mix 28
Coconut Mushrooms Caps 51
Coconut Okra 107
Coconut Pork Ribs 91
Coconut Porridge 20
Coconut Radish Mix 42
Coconut Sausage Mix 8
Coconut Sausages 17
Cod Patties 68
Cod Soup 69
Coffee Cream 118
Coffee Lamb 95
Collard Greens and Mushrooms 37
Coriander Broccoli 111
Crab Dip 62
Cream Cheese Cookies 115
Creamy Asparagus Bake 12
Creamy Avocado 109

Creamy Beef Mix 23
Creamy Broccoli 102
Creamy Chicken 76
Creamy Dip 56
Creamy Eggs 12
Creamy Eggs and Broccoli 15
Creamy Green Beans 37
Creamy Green Tea 17
Creamy Ground Beef with Kale 100
Creamy Mousse 124
Creamy Portobello Mix 105
Creamy Sea Bass 62
Creamy Tuna 61
Crushed Tomatoes, Lamb and Chives 94
Cumin Chicken 80
Curry Cauliflower 103
Curry Mushrooms 41
Curry Pork Mix 93

D

Dill and Avocado Frittata 11
Dill Broccoli 35
Dill Leeks 106
Dill Pork Stew 96
Dill Turkey 76
Duck and Berries 78

E

Eggplant Bread 49
Eggplant Loaf 111
Eggplant Mash 105
Eggplant Stew 29
Eggplants and Olives 43
Espresso Cookie 122

F

Fennel Chicken Mix 74
Feta Eggs 17
Fish and Salsa Bowl 71
Fish Bites 56
French Onion Soup 27

G

Garlic Chicken 73
Garlic Chicken Mix 33
Garlic Eggplant 103
Garlic Eggplant Mix 46
Garlic Green Beans 40
Garlic Kale and Mushrooms 112
Garlic Pork Chops 91
Garlic Pork Slices 58
Ginger and Broccoli Soup 29
Ginger Ham 91
Ginger Lamb 33
Ginger Mackerel 62

Ginger Peppers 45
Glazed Leeks 43
Green Beans and Radishes 43
Green Beans and Tomato Casserole 38
Green Beans Casserole 18
Green Beans Stew 26
Green Beans, Leeks and Artichokes 110
Green Tea Cupcakes 119
Ground Beef and Leeks 30
Ground Beef Soup 28
Ground Chicken and Green Beans 82
Ground Chicken Mix 77
Ground Pork and Veggies 89

H

Ham and Kale Bake 11
Ham and Tomato Bake 21
Herbed Mushrooms 44
Herbed Shrimp 71
Hot Eggplant Mix 108
Hot Green Beans 35
Hot Ham 55
Hot Tomatoes 45

I

Italian Shrimp Tortillas 60

K

Kale and Shrimp 32
Kale Chowder 111
Kale Muffins 16
Kale Stew 112
Keto Flan 117

L

Lamb and Berries Mix 98
Lamb and Brussels Sprouts 98
Lamb and Coconut Stew 26
Lamb and Leeks 96
Lamb and Spinach 97
Lamb Chops with Dill Butter 99
Lamb in Grape Leaves 93
Lamb Meatballs 99
Lamb Shanks and Olives 97
Lamb, Celery and Tomatoes 98
Leeks and Cauliflower Mash 44
Leeks Soup 31
Lemon Asparagus 102
Lemon Beef 88
Lemon Cake 113
Lemon Cod 64
Lemon Crab Legs 68
Lemon Lamb and Cauliflower 25
Lemon Pancake 10
Lemon Pork Stew 26

Lemon Scones 116
Lemon Turkey 82
Lemongrass Short Ribs 31
Lime Cauliflower 40
Lime Chicken Drumsticks 77
Lime Cod and Shrimps 70
Lime Green Beans 102
Lime Nutmeg Roll 14
Lime Vanilla Bites 115
Lime Zucchini Noodles 38

M

Marinara Beef and Chives 88
Marinara Shrimp 67
Marjoram Chicken 81
Masala Broccoli 41
Masala Green Beans Bowl 57
Masala Hazelnuts 54
Mascarpone Fudge 114
Milky Chicken Sticks 56
Mint Cake 120
Mint Lamb Roast 90
Mint Peppers 39
Mixed Nuts 48
Mixed Veggies Burrito 18
Mozzarella Broccoli Bites 52
Mozzarella Chicken 73
Mozzarella Fish 67
Mozzarella Zucchinis and Leeks 45
Mushroom and Kale 37
Mushroom Eggs 9
Mushroom Soup 107
Mushroom Stew 44
Mustard Beef 96
Mustard Shrimp 67

N

Nutmeg Artichokes 42
Nutmeg Chicken 73
Nutmeg Halibut 70

O

Okra and Artichokes 42
Okra Sauté 112
Okra Stew 25
Oregano Beans and Cucumber 43
Oregano Chicken and Chilies 86
Oregano Crab 62
Oregano Dip 57
Oregano Green Beans 40
Oregano Salmon 62

P

Paprika Almonds 48
Paprika and Shallots Omelet 22
Paprika Bok Choy 104
Paprika Chicken and Sauce 75
Paprika Dip 53
Paprika Green Beans 36
Paprika Peppers 38
Paprika Spaghetti Squash 46
Parmesan Eggs 9
Parmesan Salmon 63
Parsley and Tomato Green Beans 38
Parsley Eggs 9
Parsley Salmon 64
Peanut Butter Bars 125
Peanut Pie 117
Pecan Kale Mix 107
Pecan Pie 120
Pecans Bowls 50
Peppers and Eggs Mix 9
Pizza Dip 54
Poached Trout 59
Pork and Bok Choy 92
Pork and Green Peas 90
Pork and Rutabaga 87
Pork Bites 50
Pork Casserole 9
Pork Meatloaf 99
Pork Shoulder and Zucchinis 96
Pork Stew 31
Pork Tenderloin and Kale 100
Pozole Blanco 83
Pumpkin Cake 113

R

Radish and Tomato Salad 46
Radish Soup 109
Red Berry Gummies 124
Red Cabbage and Walnuts 104
Red Cabbage Sauté 42
Rhubarb and Zucchini Mix 47
Ribs and Celery 89
Ricotta and Pecan Cupcakes 125
Ricotta Eggs 10
Roast and Peppers 32
Rosemary Bok Choy 41
Rosemary Cauliflower 36
Rosemary Turkey 78
Rutabaga Cake 117

S

Saffron Tilapia 69
Sage Halibut 71
Salmon and Asparagus 67
Salmon and Cauliflower Chowder 69
Salmon and Radish Soup 61

Salmon and Spinach Bake 66
Salmon Skewers 29
Salmon Soup 59
Salmon Spread 54
Salmon Stew 28
Salsa Chicken 79
Sausage and Spinach 12
Sausage and Zucchini Stew 91
Sausage Bites and Sauce 55
Sausage Dip 50
Sausage Soup 24
Sausage Stew 32
Sausages and Cabbage 90
Sausages and Peppers Hash 18
Sautéed Cabbage 112
Sea Bass and Celery 71
Seafood Bowls 59
Seafood Stew 65
Sesame Zucchini 109
Shredded Beef 97
Shredded Chicken 79
Shrimp and Fennel Soup 60
Shrimp and Green Beans 65
Shrimp and Salmon Skewers 60
Shrimp and Tomatoes 33
Shrimp and Zucchini 64
Shrimp Bake 59
Shrimp Casserole 14
Shrimp Curry 71
Shrimp Meatballs 57
Shrimp Omelet 20
Shrimp Salad 60
Shrimp Skewers 55
Shrimp Soup 24
Shrimp Tortillas 52
Simple Beef Steaks 95
Smashed Cauliflower 46
Smoked Hazelnuts 52
Smoked Pork 89
Spiced Chicken 33
Spiced Shrimp 65
Spicy Chicken Soup 27
Spicy Kale 37
Spicy Tuna 63
Spinach and Olives Mix 104
Spinach and Sauce 108
Spinach and Tomato Soup 27
Spinach Casserole 10
Spinach Mix 35
Sprouts and Zucchinis 111
Squash and Zucchinis 105

Steak and Dill Sauce 89
Steak and Tomato Salad 25
Stevia Pork Mix 94
Stevia Salmon 72
Strawberries Cake 116
Strawberry Cobbler 118
Strawberry Jam 122
Stuffed Peppers 15
Sugar Snap Peas Soup 33
Sumac Beef 92
Sweet Sticky Chicken Wings 83
Swiss Chard Mix 38
Swiss Chard Saute 43

T

Thyme and Coriander Brisket 88
Thyme Mushrooms 39
Thyme Pork and Beans 91
Thyme Sea bass 64
Tilapia and Radish Bites 68
Tilapia and Tomatoes 66
Tofu and Green Beans 40
Tofu Bites 56
Tomato and Eggplant Salad 46
Tomato and Radish 36
Tomato and Spaghetti Squash 35
Tomato Beef and Spices 95
Tomato Chicken Wings 53
Tomato Chili 29
Tomato Frittata 8
Tomato Salmon Meatballs 50
Tomato Shrimps 61
Tuna and Cabbage Mix 66
Turkey and Peppers 76
Turkey Bites and Sauce 53
Turkey Meatballs 50
Turkey Soup 28
Turkey with Tomatoes and Eggplants 80
Turmeric Beef 87
Turmeric Calamari 63
Turmeric Chops 95

V

Vanilla Avocado Cookies 125
Vanilla Bars 121
Vanilla Cake 114
Vanilla Pudding 121
Vegetable Cream 106
Vegetable Lasagna 106
Veggie Casserole 15

W

Walnut Beef Mix 29
Walnut Cake 114

Walnut Squares 123
Walnuts Yogurt 21
Worcestershire Chicken 53

Z

Zucchini and Cabbage 39
Zucchini and Pumpkin Pie 121
Zucchini and Radish Mix 39
Zucchini and Shrimp 30
Zucchini and Spring Onions 105
Zucchini Balls 108

Zucchini Bites 58
Zucchini Bread 17
Zucchini Cake 113
Zucchini Casserole 13
Zucchini Dip 109
Zucchini Mix 104
Zucchini Muffins 121
Zucchini Quiche 18
Zucchini Stew 30

Milton Keynes UK
Ingram Content Group UK Ltd.
UKHW020152250324
439991UK00011B/1358

9 781649 844224